Complete Study Edition

Hamlet

Commentary | Complete Text | Glossary

edited by

SIDNEY LAMB

Associate Professor of English,
Sir George Williams University, Montreal

INCORPORATED

LINCOLN, NEBRASKA   68501

Hamlet

SHAKESPEARE WAS NEVER MORE MEANINGFUL—

. . . than when read in Cliff's "Complete Study Edition." The introductory sections give you all of the background information about the author and his work necessary for reading with understanding and appreciation. A descriptive bibliography provides guidance in the selection of works for further study. The inviting three-column arrangement of the complete text offers the maximum in convenience to the reader. Adjacent to the text there is a running commentary that provides clear supplementary discussion of the play as it develops. Obscure words and obsolete usages used by Shakespeare are explained in the glosses directly opposite to the line in which they occur. The numerous allusions are also clarified.

SIDNEY LAMB—

. . . the editor of this Shakespeare "Complete Study Edition," attended Andover Academy and Columbia University, receiving the Prince of Wales Medal for Philosophy and the Moyes Travelling Fellowship. Following graduate studies in Elizabethan literature at King's College, Cambridge, from 1949 to 1952, he became a member of the English Faculty of the University of London's University of the Gold Coast in West Africa. Professor Lamb joined the faculty of Sir George Williams University, Montreal, in 1956.

Hamlet

Contents

hath bene fundry times publiquely ;
right Honourable the Lord Cham
his Seruants.

THE MOST EX-
cellent and lamentable
Tragedie, of Romeo and *Iuliet.*

an introductior

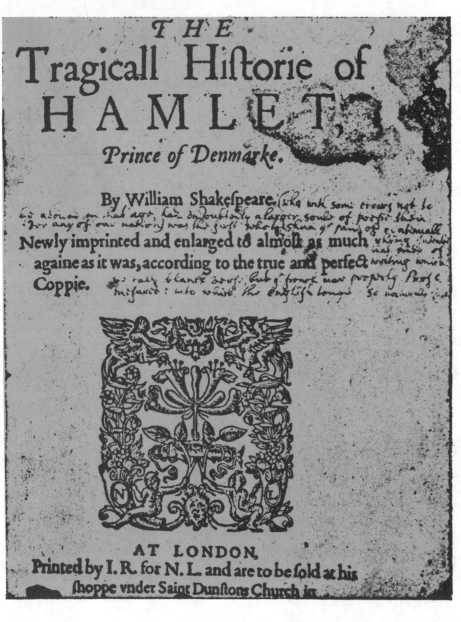

THE
Tragicall Historie of
HAMLET,
Prince of Denmarke.

By William Shakefpeare.

Newly imprinted and enlarged to almoft as much
againe as it was, according to the true and perfect
Coppie.

AT LONDON,
Printed by I. R. for N. L. and are to be fold at his
fhoppe vnder Saint Dunftons Church in

Two books are essential to the library of any English-speaking household; one of these is the Bible and the other is the works of William Shakespeare. These books form part of the house furnishings, not as reading material generally, but as the symbols of religion and culture—sort of a twentieth-century counterpart of the ancient Roman household gods. This symbolic status has done a great deal of damage both to religion and to Shakespeare.

Whatever Shakespeare may have been, he was not a deity. He was a writer of popular plays, who made a good living, bought a farm in the country, and retired at the age of about forty-five to enjoy his profits as a gentleman. The difference between Shakespeare and the other popular playwrights of his time was that he wrote better plays —plays that had such strong artistic value that they have been popular ever since. Indeed, even today, if Shakespeare could col-

6

William to Shakespeare

lect his royalties, he would be among the most prosperous of playwrights.

During the eighteenth century but mostly in the nineteenth, Shakespeare's works became "immortal classics," and the cult of Shakespeare-worship was inaugurated. The plays were largely removed from their proper place on the stage into the library where they became works of literature rather than drama and were regarded as long poems, attracting all the artistic and psuedo-artistic atmosphere surrounding poetry. In the nineteenth century this attitude was friendly but later, and especially in the early twentieth century, a strange feeling arose in the English-speaking world that poetry was sissy stuff, not for men but for "pansies" and women's clubs. This of course is sheer nonsense.

This outline will present a detailed analysis of the play and background information which will show the play in its proper perspective. This means seeing the play in relation to the other plays, to the history of the times when they were written, and in relation to the theatrical technique required for their successful performance.

G. B. Harrison's book *Introducing Shakespeare,* published by Penguin Books, will be of value for general information about Shakespeare and his plays. For reference material on the Elizabethan Theater, consult E. K. Chambers, *The Elizabethan Theatre* (four volumes). For study of the organization and production methods of this theater see *Henslowe's Diary* edited by W. W. Greg. Again for general reading the student will enjoy Margaret Webster's *Shakespeare Without Tears,* published by Whittlesey House (McGraw-Hill) in 1942.

The remainder of the Introduction will be divided into sections discussing Shakespeare's life, his plays, and his theater.

LIFE OF WILLIAM SHAKESPEARE

From the standpoint of one whose main interest lies with the plays themselves, knowledge of Shakespeare's life is not very important. Inasmuch as it treats of the period between 1592 and 1611, when the plays were being written, knowledge of his life is useful in that it may give some clues as to the topical matters introduced into the plays. For instance, the scene of Hamlet's advice to the players (Act III Scene ii) takes on an added significance when considered along with the fame and bombastic style of Edward Alleyn, the then famous actor-manager of the Lord Admiral's Players (the most powerful rivals of Shakespeare's company).

This biography is pieced together from the surviving public records of the day, from contemporary references in print, and from the London Stationer's Register. It is by no means complete. The skeletal nature of the biographical material available to scholars has led commentators in the past to invent part of the story to fill it out. These parts have frequently been invented by men who were more interested in upholding a private theory than in telling the truth, and this habit of romancing has led to a tradition of inaccurate Shakespearian biography. For this reason this outline may be of use in disposing of bad traditions.

In the heyday of the self-made man, the story developed that Shakespeare was a poor boy from the village, virtually uneducated, who fled from Stratford to London to escape prosecution for poaching on the lands of Sir Thomas Lucy, and there by his talent and a commendable industry raised himself to greatness. This rags-to-riches romance was in the best Horatio Alger tradition but was emphatically not true. The town records of Stratford make it clear that John Shakespeare, father of the playwright, was far from a pauper. He was a wealthy and responsible citizen who held in turn several municipal offices. He married (1557) Mary Arden, the daughter of a distinguished Catholic family. William, their third son, was baptized in the Parish Church in 1564. He had a good grammar school education. Ben Jonson's remark that Shakespeare had "small Latin and less Greek" did not mean the same in those days, when the educated man had a fluent command of

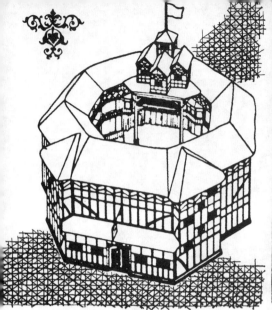

Exterior view of "The Globe"

Shakespeare's London

Interior view of "The Globe"

an introduction to Shakespeare

Latin and probably at least a reading knowledge of Greek, as it does now when classical scholars are few. The remark has been construed by the Horatio Alger people as meaning that Shakespeare reached London a semi-literate bumpkin; it is nonsense. It means merely that Shakespeare was not a university man, as most of the writers were, and that the University Wits were taking out their jealousy in snobbery and pointing out that Shakespeare used less purely literary symbolism than they did.

Shakespeare married Ann Hathaway when he was eighteen years old. She was some years older than he and the marriage seems to have been a rather hasty affair. Five months after the marriage, Suzanna, the first child, was born. Two years later, in 1585, twins Hamnet and Judith were baptized.

No one knows when Shakespeare came to London. The first mention of him occurs in the bad-tempered pamphlet which Robert Greene, one of the University Wits and a famous playwright, wrote just before his death. Greene complains of "an upstart crow, beautified with our feathers, that with his tiger's heart wrapped in a player's hide, supposes he is as well able to bombast out a blank verse as the best of you; and being an absolute Yohannes factotum, is in his own conceit the only Shakescene in a country." This was written in 1592 and indicates not only that Shakespeare was in London at the time, but that he was writing plays and beginning to make such a name for himself as to call forth the jealous apprehension of an established writer.

The next year, 1593, was a year of plague, and by order of the Lord Mayor and the Aldermen, the theaters were closed. The players, disorganized by this action, went on tour outside of London. During this year Shakespeare's two long poems, *Venus and Adonis* and *The Rape of Lucrece,* were entered in the Stationer's Register. Both were dedicated to the Earl of Southampton.

The public theaters had not been established very long. The first of these, called the Theatre, was built for James Burbage in 1576. By 1594, there were three such theaters in London, the two new houses being the Curtain and the Rose. By 1594, also, the three most celebrated of the writers, Kyd, Greene, and Marlowe were dead, and Shakespeare had already a considerable reputation. Before this date the theaters had been largely low class entertainment and the plays had been of rather poor quality. Through the revival of classical drama in the schools (comedies) and the Inns of Court (tragedies), an interest had been created in the stage. The noblemen of the time were beginning to attend the public theaters, and their tastes demanded a better class of play.

Against the background of this

FLUVIUS

South Warke 3 4 5

increasing status and upper-class popularity of the theaters, Shakespeare's company was formed. After the 1594 productions under Alleyn, this group of actors divided. Alleyn formed a company called the Lord Admiral's Company which played in Henslowe's Rose Theatre. Under the leadership of the Burbages (James was the owner of the Theatre and his son Richard was a young tragic actor of great promise), Will Kemp (the famous comedian), and William Shakespeare, the Lord Chamberlain's company came into being. This company continued throughout Shakespeare's career. It was renamed in 1603, shortly after Queen Elizabeth's death, becoming the King's players.

The company played at the Theatre until Burbage's lease on the land ran out. The landlord was not willing to come to satisfactory terms. The company moved across the river and built the new Globe theater. The principal sharers in the new place were Richard and Cuthbert Burbage each with two and a half shares and William Shakespeare, John Heminge, Angustus Phillips, Thomas Pope, and Will Kemp, each with one share.

Burbage had wanted to establish a private theater and had rented the refectory of the old Blackfriars' monastery. Not being allowed to use this building he leased it to a man called Evans who obtained permission to produce plays acted by chil-

dren. This venture was so successful as to make keen competition for the existing companies. This vogue of child actors is referred to in *Hamlet,* Act II Scene ii.

The children continued to play at Blackfriars until, in 1608, their license was suspended because of the seditious nature of one of their productions. By this time the public attitude towards the theaters had changed, and Burbage's Company, now the King's players, could move into the Blackfriars theater.

Partners with the Burbages in this enterprise were - Shakespeare, Heminge, Condell, Sly, and Evans. This was an indoor theater, whereas the Globe had been outdoors. The stage conditions were thus radically altered. More scenery could be used; lighting effects were possible. Shakespeare's works written for this theater show the influence of change in conditions.

To return to the family affairs of the Shakespeares, records show that in 1596 John Shakespeare was granted a coat of arms and, along with his son, was entitled to call himself "gentleman." In this year also, William Shakespeare's son Hamnet died. In 1597 William Shakespeare bought from William Underwood a sizable estate at Stratford, called New Place.

Shakespeare's father died in 1601, his mother, in 1608. Both of his daughters married, one in 1607, the other in 1616.

During this time, Shakespeare

went on acquiring property in Stratford. He retired to New Place probably around 1610 although this date is not definitely established, and his career as a dramatist was practically at an end. *The Tempest,* his last complete play, was written around the year 1611.

The famous will, in which he left his second best bed to his wife, was executed in 1616 and later on in that same year he was buried.

THE PLAYS

Thirty-seven plays are customarily included in the works of William Shakespeare. Scholars have been at great pains to establish the order in which these plays were written. The most important sources of information for this study are the various records of performances which exist, the printed editions which came out during Shakespeare's career, and such unmistakable references to current events as may crop up in the plays. The effect of the information gathered in this way is generally to establish two dates between which a given play must have been written. In *Hamlet* for instance, there is a scene in which Hamlet refers to the severe competition given to the adult actors by the vogue for children's performances. This vogue first became a serious threat to the professional companies in about 1600. In 1603 a very bad edition was published, without authorization, of *The*

Queen Elizabeth

an introduction
to Shakespeare

Elizabethan types

Lute, standing cup, stoop

Tragical History of Hamlet, Prince of Denmark by William Shakespeare. These two facts indicate that *Hamlet* was written between the years of 1600 and 1603. This process fixed the order in which most of the plays were written. Those others of which no satisfactory record could be found were inserted in their logical place in the series according to the noticeable development of Shakespeare's style. In these various ways we have arrived at the following chronological listing of the plays.

1591   *Henry VI Part I*
        Henry VI Part II
        Henry VI Part III
        Richard III
        Titus Andronicus
        Love's Labour Lost
        The Two Gentlemen
          of Verona
        The Comedy of Errors
        The Taming of the Shrew

1594   *Romeo and Juliet*
        A Midsummer Night's
          Dream
        Richard II
        King John
        The Merchant of Venice

1597   *Henry IV Part I*
        Henry IV Part II
        Much Ado About Nothing
        Merry Wives of Windsor
        As You Like It
        Julius Caesar
        Henry V
        Troilus and Cressida

1601   *Hamlet*
        Twelfth Night
        Measure for Measure
        All's Well That Ends Well

        Othello

1606   *King Lear*
        Macbeth
        Timon of Athens
        Antony and Cleopatra
        Coriolanus

1609   *Pericles*

1611   *Cymbeline*
        The Winter's Tale
        The Tempest
        Henry VIII

At this point it is pertinent to review the tradition of dramatic form that had been established before Shakespeare began writing. Drama in England sprang at the outset from the miracle and morality plays of the medieval guilds. These dramatized Bible stories became increasingly less religious as time passed until finally they fell into disrepute. The next development was the writing of so-called *interludes.* These varied in character but often took the form of bawdy farce. As the renaissance gathered force in England, Roman drama began to be revived at the schools and the Inns of Court. Before long English writers were borrowing plots and conventions wholesale from the classic drama. The Italian model was the most fashionable and consequently was largely adopted, but many features of the old *interludes* still persisted, especially in plays written for the public theaters.

With the development among the nobility of a taste for the theater, a higher quality of work became in demand. Very few of

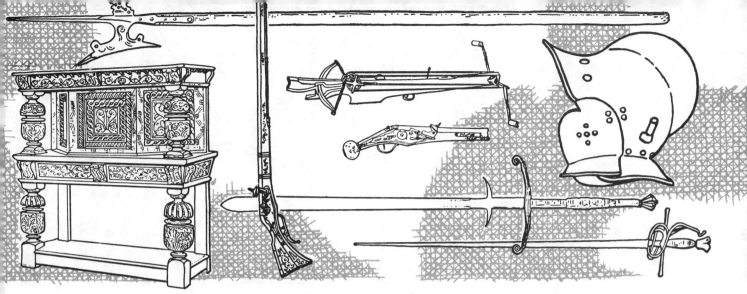

Court cupboard, crossbow, guns, sword, rapier, halberd, burgonet

the very early plays have survived. The reason for this is that the plays were not printed to be read; no one considered them worth the trouble. A play was strung together out of a set of stock characters and situations with frantic haste, often by as many as a dozen different men. These men who worked on plays did not regard their writing activity as of prime importance. They were primarily actors. With the cultivation of taste for better plays came the idea that the work of a playwright was an effort demanding special skill. The highborn audiences were interested in the plays themselves and began to include editions of their favorite plays in their libraries. With this demand for printed copies of the plays, the conception began of the dramatist as an artist in his own right, whether or not he acted himself (as most of them did).

By 1592, when Shakespeare began to make his personal reputation, a set of traditions had developed. This body of traditions gave Shakespeare the basic materials with which to work.

A special type of comedy writing had developed, centered around the name of John Lyly, designed for the sophisticated audience of the court and presented with lavish dances and decorative effects. This type of play was characterized by a delicately patterned artificiality of speech. The dialogue was studded with complicated references to Latin and Italian literature that the renaissance had made fashionable.

Shakespeare used this method extensively. In the early plays (before *The Merchant of Venice*) he was experimenting and wrote much that is nothing more than conventional. Later on, as his mature style developed, the writing becomes integral with and indispensable to the play and no longer appears artificial. In *Romeo and Juliet,* an early play, the following lines are spoken by Lady Capulet in urging Juliet to accept the Count Paris for her husband. These lines are brilliant but artificial, and the play seems to pause in order that this trick bit of word-acrobatics may be spoken.

> Read o'er the volume of young
> Paris' face,
> And find delight, writ there
> with beauty's pen.
> Examine every married lineament,
> And see how one another lends
> content:
> And what obscured in this fair
> volume lies,
> Find written in the margent of
> his eyes.
> This precious book of love, this
> unbound lover,
> To beautify him only needs a
> cover!

The other most important dramatic tradition was that of tragedy. The Elizabethan audiences liked spectacular scenes; they also had a great relish for scenes of sheer horror. This led to a school of tragic writing made popular by Kyd and Marlowe.

These plays were full of action and color and incredible wickedness, and the stage literally ran with artificial blood. Shakespeare's early tragedies are directly in this tradition, but later the convention becomes altered and improved in practice, just as that of comedy had done. The scene in *King Lear* where Gloucester has his eyes torn out stems from this convention. Lear, however, is a comparatively late play and the introduction of this scene does not distort or interrupt its organization.

Shakespeare's stylistic development falls into a quite well-defined progression. At first he wrote plays according to the habit of his rivals. He very quickly began experimenting with his technique. His main concern seems to be with tricks of language. He was finding out just what he could do. These early plays use a great deal of rhyme, seemingly just because Shakespeare liked writing rhyme. Later on, rhyme is used only when there is a quite definite dramatic purpose to justify it. Between the early plays and those which may be called mature (*The Merchant of Venice* is the first of the mature plays), there is a basic change in method. In the early works Shakespeare was taking his patterns from previous plays and writing his own pieces, quite consciously incorporating one device here and another there.

In the later period these tricks of the trade had been tested and

The world as known in 1600   Elizabethan coins

absorbed; they had become not contrived methods but part of Shakespeare's mind. This meant that, quite unconsciously, while his total attention was focused on the emotional and intellectual business of writing a masterpiece, he wrote in terms of the traditional habits he had learned and used in the earlier period. (*Henry IV, Julius Caesar, Henry V,* and *Hamlet* are the plays of this advanced stage.)

The group of plays between 1606 and 1609 shows a further new development. Having reached mastery of his medium in terms of dramatic technique (with *Othello*) and of power over the tension of thought in moving easily through scenes of comedy, pathos, and tragedy, he turned again to the actual literary quality of his plays and began to enlarge his scope quite beyond and apart from the theatrical traditions of his day. The early results of this new attempt are the two plays *King Lear* and *Macbeth*. The change in these plays is in the direction of concentration of thought. The attempt is, by using masses of images piled one on another, to convey shadings and intensities of emotion not before possible. He was trying to express the inexpressible. For example the following is from the last part of

an introduction
to Shakespeare

Lady Macbeth's famous speech in Act I, Scene v:

> Come, thick night,
> And pall thee in the dunnest smoke of hell,
> That my keen knife see not the wound it makes,
> Nor heaven peep through the blanket of the dark,
> To cry, hold, hold!

Compare the concentrated imagery of this speech with Hamlet's soliloquy at the end of Act III, Scene ii.

> 'Tis now the very witching time of night,
> When churchyards yawn, and hell itself breathes out
> Contagion to this world: now could I drink hot blood,
> And do such bitterness as the day
> Would quake to look on.

The sentiment of these two speeches is similar, but the difference in method is striking and produces a difference again in the type of effect. The *Lear-Macbeth* type of writing produces a higher tension of subtlety but tends to collect in masses rather than to move in lines as the lighter, more transparent writing of *Hamlet* does.

Shakespeare's last plays were conceived for the new indoor theater at Blackfriars and show this is in a more sophisticated type of staging. In *The Tempest,* last and most celebrated of these late comedies, there is dancing, and much complicated staging (such as the disappearing banquet, the ship at sea, and so on). The writing of plays for the

more distinguished audience of Blackfriars, and the increased stage resources there provided, influenced the form of the plays.

The writing of these plays forms a culmination. In his early apprenticeship Shakespeare had been extravagant in word-acrobatics, testing the limits of his technique. In the Lear-Macbeth period of innovation he had tried the limits of concentrated emotion to the point almost of weakening the dramatic effectiveness of the plays. In *The Tempest* his lines are shaken out into motion again. He seems to have been able to achieve the subtlety he was after in verse of light texture and easy movement, no longer showing the tendency to heaviness or opacity visible in *King Lear* and *Macbeth*.

THE THEATER

The first public theater in London was built in the year 1576 for James Burbage and was called simply The Theatre. Before this time players' companies had performed for the public in the courtyards of the city inns. For a more select public they frequently played in the great halls of institutions, notably the Inns of Court. The stage and auditorium of the Elizabethan theater were based on these traditions and combined features of both the hall and the inn-yard. The auditorium was small. There was a pit where the orchestra seats would be in a modern playhouse; this section was for the lowest classes who stood during the performances. Around the

12

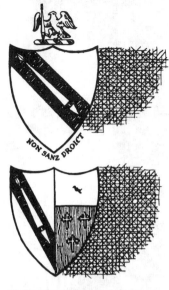

Shakespeare's Coat of Arms

Wood cut camp illustration

wall was a gallery for the gentry. The galleries and the tiring-house behind the fore-stage were roofed; the rest was open to the sky. The stage consisted of a very large platform that jutted out so that the pit audience stood on three sides of it. Behind this, under the continuation behind the stage of the gallery, was the inner stage; this was supplied with a curtain, but the open fore-stage was not. Above this inner stage was a balcony (really a continuation of the gallery), forming still another curtained stage. This gallery was used for kings addressing subjects from balconies, for the storming of walls, for Juliet's balcony and bedroom, for Cleopatra's monument and so on. Costumes and properties were extravagant (such as guillotines, fountains, ladders, etc.); extensive music was constantly used and such sound effects as cannon, drums, or unearthly screams were common; but there was no painted scenery as we know it; there was no darkness to focus attention on the stage, no facilities for stage-lighting. All these things are in marked contrast to the modern stage conventions and thus a serious problem of adaptation is posed when it comes to producing the plays under present day conditions.

The advantages are not all with the modern stage. It is true that the modern or picture stage can do more in the way of realistic effects, but this kind of realism is not important to good drama. In fact there has been a recent trend away from realistic scenery in the theater back to a conventional or stylized simplicity.

One effect of Shakespeare's stage upon his work was to make the scenes in the plays more person-scenes than place-scenes. As a matter of fact in many cases the places assigned in the texts to various scenes were not in the original and have only been added by an editor who did not understand this very fact.

It used to be said that *Antony and Cleopatra* could not be staged and was written to be read rather than acted. The grounds for this statement were that in the fourth act there were no less than fourteen scenes. To some, a scene means a change of place and requires a break in the play while scenery is shifted. To Shakespeare these scenes meant no such thing; they meant, simply, that there were fourteen different groupings of people, successively and without any break, carrying on the action of the play. The scene headings when added should have been (1) Caesar, (2) Antony and Cleopatra, (3) the common soldiers, etc., instead of (1) Before Alexandria, (2) Alexandria, a room in the palace, etc. By this you may see that with all its limitations, the Elizabethan stage had a measure of flexibility that the modern stage could envy.

Fashions in staging Shakespeare have altered radically in the last few years. At the close of the nineteenth century, Sir Herbert Beerbohm Tree staged a spectacular series of pageant productions. All the tricks of romantic realistic staging were used and, if necessary, the play was twisted, battered, and re-written to accommodate the paraphernalia.

The modern method is to produce the plays as nearly according to the text as possible and work out a compromise to achieve the sense of space and of flexibility necessary, yet without departing so far from the stage habits of today as to confuse or divert the audience. This technique was inaugurated by Granville-Barker in the early twentieth century. With the exception of such extravagant stunts as Orson Welles' production of *Julius Caesar* in modern dress (set in Chicago and complete with tommy-guns), the prevailing practice now is to use simple, stylized scenery adapted to the needs of producing the play at full length.

Much can be done in the way of learning Shakespeare through books, but the only sure way is to see a well produced performance by a good company of actors. Whatever genius Shakespeare may have possessed as a psychologist, philosopher, or poet, he was first of all a man of the theater, who knew it from the inside, and who wrote plays so well-plotted for performance that from his day up to the present, no great actor has been able to resist them.

Polonius and Hamlet

an introduction

DATE OF COMPOSITION

In July, 1602, the following was entered in the Stationers' Register: "*James Roberts* entered for his copy under the hands of Master Pasfeild and Master Waterson Warden a book called *The Revenge of Hamlet Prince of Denmark as it was lately acted by the Lord Chamberlain his servants*." An entry such as this meant that a certain printer, James Roberts in this case, claimed the copyright for publication of a new book. This entry is the first definite mention of Shakespeare's play. (The Lord Chamberlain's Servants was the company to which Shakespeare was attached.) The play must therefore have been both written and acted before this date.

The establishment of an earlier date when the play was clearly not yet written is less certain. In the autumn of the year 1598, a book by Francis Meres, called *Palladis Tamia*, was published. It contained a list of the chief English authors of the time and their outstanding works. Meres gave Shakespeare a very high place in this list and named twelve of his plays, six comedies and six trag-

edies. *Hamlet* does not appear. While this omission is not proof that the play was written after 1598, it seems unlikely that, in a list of Shakespeare's finest tragedies that included such clearly inferior works as *Titus Andronicus*, a very great play like *Hamlet* would be left out.

Besides the negative proof of Meres' list, scholars have been led to date the writing of *Hamlet* late in 1601 or early in 1602 by the references in Act II, Scene ii, to the loss of popularity of the adult actors which followed the fashionable success of the companies of child actors then operating. There were two of these juvenile companies. The first, the children of St. Paul's, began operations late in 1599; the second, the children of the Queen's Chapel, leased Blackfriars theater from Burbage (a colleague of Shakespeare's) in August, 1600.

SHAKESPEARE'S SOURCES FOR THE STORY

The story of Hamlet has been traced back to very early roots in the legends of Iceland, Ireland, and the Scandinavian countries. Tales of a Hamlet were gathered and appeared in

14

Ophelia: "He is dead and gone!"

o The Tragedy of Hamlet

the Danish chronicle of Saxo Grammaticus (thirteenth century). This account, in Latin, was printed in 1514. The story, in several different versions, seems to have been of some popularity. Belleforest, in his *Histories Tragiques* of 1582, a collection of tales in prose, printed a version based on Saxo with minor changes. (In Saxo the character corresponding to Polonius hid under the bed, in Belleforest he hides behind the arras.) This was translated into English as *The Historie of Hamlet* in 1608, graced with some phrases borrowed from Shakespeare. Shakespeare may have read the story in Saxo's Latin or Belleforest's French. That he was familiar with it in 1585 is suggested by his christening his son, born that year, Hamnet (this is one of several different spellings of Hamlet's name).

Besides these versions, there was an English play on the subject earlier than Shakespeare's. This play is lost, and the author of it is not certainly known, though it is believed to have been Thomas Kyd. It is mentioned in the introductory epistle to Greene's *Menaphon* by Nash in 1589, and was performed

under Henslowe's management in 1594.

In adapting the old story, Shakespeare made many changes, especially in characterization and dramatic effects, to fit it for effective stage presentation. For example, the killing of his uncle is only the middle of Hamlet's career in the saga. He then goes on to rule Denmark, marries two wives (at once), fights a war against another usurper, is betrayed by one of his wives, and killed. Hamlet's character in Saxo-Belleforest is that of a Viking hero, and his madness is entirely a trick by which he hoped to be able to get at his incestuous uncle.

Later printings of Shakespeare's *Hamlet* stem from the three earliest editions. These are the first (or bad) quarto (1603), the second (or good) quarto (1604-05), and the first folio (1623). The folio was a collection of all of Shakespeare's plays (except *Pericles*), and was published after Shakespeare's death as an authoritative edition by two of Shakespeare's fellow players, Heminge and Condell. For this collection Heminge and Condell used those manuscripts

in the possession of the company, then still functioning as The King's Servants. These manuscripts tended to include alterations made in the plays, either by Shakespeare or the actors, or other authors, which represent the play as it appeared on the stage, rather than as Shakespeare may have first written it.

In the case of *Hamlet*, most scholars agree that the second quarto (hereafter known as Q2), though rather sloppily printed, was taken from Shakespeare's manuscript, with two significant omissions which survive in the first folio (hereafter known as F), and that it therefore has more authority than either F or Q1 (first quarto). The two large omissions from Q2 are: that section of the talk between Hamlet, Rosencrantz, and Guildenstern (II,ii,240-69) that speaks of Denmark as the worst dungeon in the world (it was omitted probably because in 1604 the Queen of England, James I's wife, was a Danish princess), and that further section of the conversation (II,ii,336-59) dealing with the child players (probably omitted because in 1603 not only had the King become patron of

King Claudius

Shakespeare's company, but the Queen had become patron of the children acting at Blackfriars—for the King's actors to criticize the Queen's would be in doubtful taste).

Q1, though it has some interesting stage directions and some striking differences from the better texts, reads almost like a parody of them. Much research has aided most scholars in deciding that it was a stolen version assembled out of shorthand notes taken at a performance, plus some help from an unscrupulous actor either through memory or from scripts stolen from the theater, plus parts written by an inferior poet where memory failed. (Q1 was not printed under James Roberts' copyright, see above.) Its chief differences from Q2 and F are: that the "To be or not to be" soliloquy and the nunnery scene come at the beginning of II,ii, before Hamlet's conversation with Polonius ("you are a fishmonger"), and that Gertrude, after the closet scene, disclaims knowledge of Hamlet's father's murder, and agrees to ally herself with Hamlet (this alliance is born out by a later scene between Horatio and her, discussing Hamlet's return from the voyage to England).

F, on the other hand, omits a good deal of the more reflective passages, notably the big soliloquy in IV,iv.

Our text is based on Q2 with the omitted passages restored from F.

HAMLET AND THE NATURE OF TRAGEDY

The whole range of dramatic expression is bounded by the two great types of tragedy and comedy, a fact often symbolized by the two masks, one weeping, the other laughing, which frequently adorn theaters, playbooks, and programs. Tragedy deals with life's bitterness and defeat, and high tragedy with the extreme possibilities of these feelings. As each age of history has its own fundamental beliefs and values, so each has its own idea as to what life's greatest bitterness must be; hence, the definition of tragedy has had to be revised from time to time.

In England just before Shakespeare's time, a rather simple and broad definition was considered acceptable, based on the idea of fortune's wheel, which, in its continual revolution, raises up one man while another falls. A tragedy, under this scheme, involved the rise and fall of a great man (king or warrior or both) up to most fortunate success and down to utter defeat and death. The suffering in these plays was of a simple and massive kind, and, as little subtlety or complexity was required by the situation, little depth of character portrayal was attempted. But towards the end

of the sixteenth century, as Shakespeare was developing his craft, the need began to be felt for a deeper, more subtle, and more flexible tragic form. Ideas from the ancient Greeks (Aristotle) and Romans (Seneca) were adopted, blended, altered. A new tragic pattern began to emerge, very much richer and deeper than the old one, sounding intimately the depths of the human mind and spirit, the moral possibilities of human behavior, and displaying the extent to which men's destinies are interrelated one with another.

According to this scheme, an ideal tragedy would concern the career of a hero, a man great and admirable in both his powers and his opportunities. He should be a person high enough placed in society that his actions affect the well-being of many people. The plot should show him engaged in important or urgent affairs and should involve his immediate community in a threat to its security that will be removed only at the end of the action through his death. The hero's action will involve him in choices of some importance which, however virtuous or vicious in themselves, begin the spinning of a web of circumstances unforeseen by the hero which cannot then be halted and which brings about his downfall. This hostile destiny may be the result of mere

16

Laertes, his father, and his sister Ophelia

circumstance or ill luck, of the activities of the hero's enemies, of some flaw or failing in his own character, or of the operation of some supernatural agency that works against him. When it is too late to escape from the web, the hero-victim comes to realize everything that has happened to him, and in the despair or agony of that realization, is finally destroyed.

The effect of such a pattern is to gain the greatest possible response from the audience, so that it shares fully in the tragic emotions of pity or sympathy and fear or horror. These responses are gained through our fellow feeling for the sufferings of others, our deepest convictions as to right and wrong, truth and falsity, good and evil, our repugnance for ugliness and discord, and that heightened sense of the depth and dignity, the admirable possibilities, of the human spirit, which great tragedies somehow convey. It is perhaps this last element that makes tragedy, in spite of the bitter defeat it records, an enlivening and elevating experience rather than a depressing one.

Hamlet, though tragic in its effect, and among the best loved of all Shakespeare's plays, does not perfectly fit this pattern. Hamlet's greatness is an inward greatness of spirit; he is not overtly active in character; his power and his opportunity are very limited (his enemy has the obvious power). It is one of the great unsettled problems of the play that, rather than struggling towards his goal, Hamlet seems to delay and delay, to avoid it; he seems often to be unsettled as to what his goal really is. His very virtues are such as to weaken his capacity for forthright action. His nature, on the other hand, is interesting and attractive, his suffering is profound, and the pity and sympathy of the beholder are powerfully enlisted; so are the emotions of fear for Hamlet and horror at the dire events. The disorder of Denmark is made plain at the beginning, aggravated by the action, and dispelled at the end (in this sense Hamlet succeeds; the disjointed times are set right).

Besides these tragic attributes, the play is remarkable for its richness and variety, its fullness of interesting characters, each one a developed personality, its fullness of striking contrast. Preparations for war, revelry, intrigue, journeys to and from Wittenberg, Paris, Norway, Poland, England, a play within a play, an exciting duel scene, love, hatred, counselors, courtiers, grave diggers, follow each other through a story full of the most surprising twists and turns. The result of all this is an excitement and a tension not entirely of a tragic kind, not as pure nor as strictly unified as the highest tragedy demands. To say this is not to judge the play, but to indicate that it is a mixed work not exclusively devoted to a tragic pattern. Perhaps the printers of the first quarto were right in calling it not *The Tragedy of Hamlet* (as Q2 and F do), but *The Tragical History of Hamlet.*

THE STRUCTURE OF *HAMLET*

The act divisions found in this and almost all other modern texts of *Hamlet* are not Shakespeare's. They first appeared in 1676. They do not divide the action in any dramatically sensible way and should thus be regarded merely as a means of finding a given place in any standard edition.

With so many characters, so many interlocking story lines, such a variety of incidents and wealth of opinions, the play is structurally intricate to a remarkable degree. Anything said here must be oversimplified. Aside from the soliloquies and the scenes of pure action, there appear to be three main types of scenes in the play: 1) big ceremonial scenes involving the court (e. g., I,ii; the duel in V, ii), 2) domestic scenes concerned with parents and their children (e.g., I,iii; II,i; III,iv), and 3) scenes in which the overriding feature is Hamlet's trenchant, spontaneous, and generalized comments on life. In

17

"Alas, poor Yorick, I knew him."

some scenes one type may be superimposed on another (e. g., the play scene is a big ceremonial scene, but it is dominated by Hamlet's commentary).

The domestic scenes present the important theme of the relations of parents and children. Three parallel but contrasted families make up this strand of the action: the Polonius group, the Fortinbras group, and the Hamlet group. The theme of revenge for a slaughtered father is common to all three. In both Fortinbras' and Hamlet's case an uncle has filled somewhat the father's role. Each of these families sheds light on the other two, and the way in which their fortunes are interdependent is fascinating.

Hamlet's comments ("Nay, it is; I know not, seems,") serve to expose and irritate evil and hypocrisy at all points, whether in Claudius' court or in the mannerisms of the players. His business seems to be to lash about like a wittier version of an Old Testament prophet, bringing to bear on life the cutting beam of embittered idealism.

The ceremonial scenes are the great gathering points of the action. In each of them, lines of action that have been running parallel converge and mingle. Considered as a series, therefore, they vividly show forth the stages of the plot. In I,ii, Clau-

dius' court presents a silky surface, the world of "seems" in which the black figure of Hamlet is the only discord. The play scene in III,ii ends in the wild and disordered flight of the court, the world of seems unmasked. IV,iii, the ceremony of which is Claudius' formal declaration before his attendants of his course of action, is a businesslike and abbreviated assembly. Its strongest note is sounded in Hamlet's open contempt (IV,iii,18-38). Claudius is still slyly diplomatic, but he can no longer give the impression that all is well with the status quo. Ophelia's mad scene is really domestic in character, but her telling mockery of marriage and funeral makes it relevant to the ceremonial series. This mockery reflects back to the marriage of Gertrude and Claudius, to the love of Hamlet and Ophelia, and forward to Ophelia's own funeral. Ophelia's funeral, somber, curtailed, and marred by low brawling between Laertes and Hamlet, is a sad but honest ceremony. Claudius' part in it is confined to three curt commands. The duel scene represents Claudius' bid to re-establish the atmosphere of I,ii. The silky tone, the luxurious excess, the hypocrisy, all are back. Again Hamlet destroys the illusion, this time once and for all, but is himself caught and destroyed.

The plot really falls into three large sections. The first, the development of the true situation, occupies Act One. The progression is from vague foreboding and discontent to full knowledge, and in the case of Hamlet, to motivation. The second stage carries us to Hamlet's departure for England. It begins with intrigue, indirections, and uncertainty, building tension and suspense to the play scene, and the domestic scenes following it. Hamlet's attempt on the consciences of the Queen and King has succeeded, but at that crucial moment of Claudius' prayer, postpones his attempt on the King's life. The next move is the King's.

When Hamlet returns from his voyage, his attitude seems quite altered. In the meantime, Claudius and the court have been in "discord and dismay." The action begins to rise again towards the final conflict of Hamlet and toward his final clash with Claudius. Hamlet is ready ("The interim is mine;/ And a man's life's no more than to say 'One' "), but Claudius with his elaborate deceit moves first. Once again the strands of the action meet in a big scene.

ANACHRONISM

An anachronism is a confusion of historical periods. For example, though the Hamlet story came out of the seventh century, Hamlet, in the play, has been studying at Wittenberg, the famous protestant university founded in 1502. Such historical impossibilities are common to most of Shakespeare's plays. No one bothered over strict historical authenticity on the stage in Shakespeare's day, and such anachronisms went quite unnoticed. They have, however, one notable dramatic use. In the case of *Hamlet,* they lend a familiarity and an air of reality to the state of Denmark. As soon as the audience learns that Hamlet and Horatio studied at Wittenberg, they will know several things: that their education had been protestant, that they would likely be serious and thoughtful young men, that their belief with regard to ghosts would be either skeptical or that they would be spirits from Hell engaged in some mischief. Further, when Hamlet appears as a character of their own time, and some of the scenes discuss events and ideas with which they are familiar, and about which they have their own opinions, the audience finds an immediate and lively interest in and understanding of the setting and characters. The device of anachronism has been used by modern playwrights, too, notably George Bernard Shaw.

IRONY AND DRAMATIC IRONY

Irony is a special use of double meaning, as when someone makes a remark which, while clearly saying one thing, hints at a further and different meaning which only certain hearers would understand. The effect of such speech is often bitter and a bit sinister, always concentrated and full of suggestion. Irony may be of situation as well as of speech, as when Hamlet spares Claudius at his prayers (III, iii), thinking that Claudius is making his peace with God, while in fact, Claudius is merely discovering that he cannot repent and that to continue in villainous intrigue is his only course. The whole bent of Hamlet's mind, especially in his riddling speeches, is ironical. The device is very effective because of the note of grim humor, the sharp twist it can administer.

Dramatic irony is a special type. It depends on the fact that some characters in the play know more than others and that the audience can see more than any of them. Thus quite innocent remarks will have a by no means innocent meaning to the audience. One example of this is Claudius' speech to Laertes (IV,vii,33). He has diverted Laertes' revengeful energy onto Hamlet; then he says "You shortly shall hear more," meaning the news of Hamlet's death in England. But we know from IV,vi that Hamlet has returned and Claudius will hear more in a sense very different from his own meaning.

IMAGERY

Hamlet is rich in imagery. Much of the imagery is interrelated to form a pattern conveying to our senses a realization of Denmark's rottenness and Hamlet's disgust with it. One set of symbols concern disease ("goodness growing to a plurisy," "skin and film the ulcerous place," "the hidden imposthume of much wealth and peace"), another deals with rot and decomposition ("maggots in a dead dog," from graveyard scene), one with a rank overgrowing of weeds ("unweeded garden that grows to seed"). The weed series and the decomposition series are linked together ("the fat weed that rots on Lethe wharf"). Still another train of images concerns harlotry and cosmetics ("I have heard of your paintings too," "the harlot's cheek beautified with plastering art"). This set, too, is linked with the decomposition series ("tell her let her paint an inch thick, to this favor she must come at last"). Finally, the weed imagery is set against that of flowers which has its strongest presentation in Ophelia's mad scene.

These images and their relation are mentioned in the commentary as they occur. On them a good deal of our emotional response to the play depends.

THE LANGUAGE OF *HAMLET*

One mark of Shakespeare's progress as a writer is his increasing freedom and variety. In his later plays the verse is more flexible and less regular than in his early ones; weak and feminine endings become more common in the verse, and more and more run-on lines carry the rhythm and the meaning swiftly through several lines of verse. More and more, too, Shakespeare breaks his scansion; pauses in the lines become part of the rhythm and thus take the place of syllables.

Hamlet stands just after the middle of this development, and includes within itself examples of both the earlier style or at least an imitation of it and the later. If you compare the verse of the player's speech about Pyrrhus (II,ii, 448-513) which is perhaps an exaggeration of the earlier style, with Hamlet's soliloquy that ends the scene (II,ii, 543-601), the effect of this freer writing may be appreciated. (Actually, the Pyrrhus speech harks back even further to the style of Shakespeare's predecessor, Marlowe, but Shakespeare began by writing in a style very like Marlowe's; so the above comparison is not a misleading one.)

Another way in which Shakespeare's greater freedom and confidence with language shows is in his use of prose. You will have noticed already that, conventionally, prose was used in plays for the speech of clowns, people of the lower classes, for mad scenes and scenes of low comedy. This convention can be seen in *Hamlet* in a modified form. The grave diggers speak prose; Hamlet's mad scenes are in prose. On the other hand, the common soldiers speak verse; Hamlet sometimes speaks prose when he is being neither comic nor crazy (II,ii, 293-310; III,ii, 1-46; III,ii, 356-65; V,i, 196-208; V,ii, 211-17). Some of this prose is in its expressive power scarcely inferior to the verse (especially the "What a piece of work is man" speech, and the passage about Yorick).

It almost seems as if the swift variety of the action were mirrored in that of the language.

Bibliography

EDITIONS

A New Variorum Edition of Shakespeare, ed. Horace H. Furness. New York: J. B. Lippincott, 1871——. (Reprints by The American Scholar and Dover Publications.) Each play is dealt with in a separate volume of monumental scholarship.

The Yale Shakespeare, ed. Helge Kökeritz and Charles T. Prouty. New Haven: Yale University Press, 1955——. A multi-volume edition founded on modern scholarship.

COMMENTARY AND CRITICISM

Bentley, G. E. *Shakespeare and His Theatre.* Lincoln: University of Nebraska Press, 1964 (paperback). Illuminating discussion of the actual conditions under which, and for which, Shakespeare wrote.

Bradley, A. C. *Shakespearean Tragedy: Lectures on Hamlet, Othello, King Lear, Macbeth.* New York: Macmillan, 1904. (Paperback ed.; New York: Meridian Books, 1955.) A classic examination of the great tragedies.

Chambers, Edmund K. *William Shakespeare: A Study of Facts and Problems,* 2 vols. Oxford: Clarendon Press, 1930. Indispensable source for bibliographical and historical information.

Chute, Marchette. *Shakespeare of London.* New York: E. P. Dutton, 1949. A vivid account of Shakespeare's career in the dynamic Elizabethan metropolis.

Granville-Barker, Harley. *Prefaces to Shakespeare.* London: Sidgwick & Jackson, 1927-47. (2 vols.; Princeton: Princeton University Press, 1947.) Stimulating studies of ten plays by a scholarly man of the theater.

Harbage, Alfred. *Shakespeare's Audience.* New York: Columbia University Press, 1941. Revealing approach to Shakespeare as a practical man of the theater.

Knight, Wilson. *The Wheel of Fire.* London: Oxford University Press, 1930. Stresses the power of intuition to capture the total poetic experience of Shakespeare's work.

Spurgeon, Caroline. *Shakespeare's Imagery and What It Tells Us.* Cambridge: Cambridge University Press, 1935. A psychological study of the playwright's imagery as a means to understanding the man himself.

The Tragedy
of
Hamlet

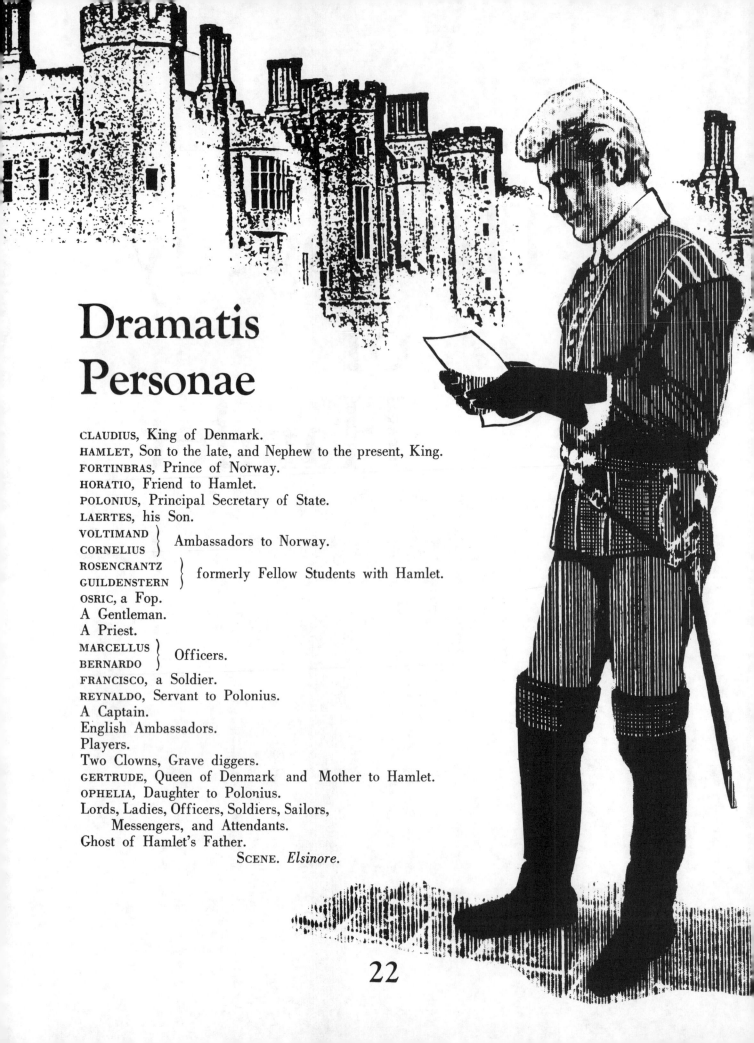

Dramatis Personae

CLAUDIUS, King of Denmark.
HAMLET, Son to the late, and Nephew to the present, King.
FORTINBRAS, Prince of Norway.
HORATIO, Friend to Hamlet.
POLONIUS, Principal Secretary of State.
LAERTES, his Son.
VOLTIMAND }
CORNELIUS } Ambassadors to Norway.
ROSENCRANTZ }
GUILDENSTERN } formerly Fellow Students with Hamlet.
OSRIC, a Fop.
A Gentleman.
A Priest.
MARCELLUS }
BERNARDO } Officers.
FRANCISCO, a Soldier.
REYNALDO, Servant to Polonius.
A Captain.
English Ambassadors.
Players.
Two Clowns, Grave diggers.
GERTRUDE, Queen of Denmark and Mother to Hamlet.
OPHELIA, Daughter to Polonius.
Lords, Ladies, Officers, Soldiers, Sailors,
      Messengers, and Attendants.
Ghost of Hamlet's Father.
                    SCENE. *Elsinore.*

HAMLET

ACT I SCENE I

The very first line of the play launches us into a world of mystery, surprise, and edginess. It is dark and cold; a sentry stands on duty as if tired after a long watch. Out of the darkness comes another figure, tense and anxious. Just as we expect the sentry to challenge the stranger, he challenges the sentry in accents full of alarm. What did he expect?

Francisco's heartsickness can be explained as the depression resulting from lonely and monotonous discomfort. On the other hand, it is like Bernardo's edginess in sounding a keynote of the play's atmosphere. The importance of this feeling of undefined evil will appear later on.

Notice the deft way in which, as this scene grows, the characters are grouped and distinguished. Francisco and Bernardo are simple soldiers on duty. Horatio and Marcellus, coming a moment later, make a separate group. Marcellus' address to the departing Francisco, "honest soldier," suggests somewhat superior rank; this impression is borne out in the rest of the scene by his talk which suggests a wider range of interests and a greater confidence in his own conclusions and by his knowledge of where Prince Hamlet may be found. Horatio, of course, will not be in military dress. His identity and the reason for his being present with the soldiers are revealed in line 42. Before that, his position of respect is shown by the way in which Marcellus seems to act as middleman between him and Bernardo (see ll. 23-9). More important than these differences of rank is the friendliness and lack of ceremony they show in conversation. These three like each other, call each other by first names, and listen with tolerance to each other's differing opinions.

Horatio's disbelief in ghosts marks him by Elizabethan standards as a person with very advanced ideas. Only a minority of an audience in 1602 would be so skeptical; most would believe in ghosts and would adopt, as Horatio tends to do later (I,iv,69), the protestant view that ghosts were devilish apparitions masking themselves in the likeness of a dead person in order to lead his survivors into evil. Such was the orthodox explanation in the English Church at the time.

The entry of the ghost in full armor is majestic and impressive. Its presence supplies the reason for Bernardo's jitters, while suggesting some profound mischief in the state. Lest the listener might not make this conclusion by him-

---

ACT ONE, scene one.

(ELSINORE. A PLATFORM BEFORE THE CASTLE)

FRANCISCO *at his post. Enter to him* BERNARDO.

Bernardo. Who's there?
Francisco. Nay, answer me. Stand and unfold yourself. 2
Bernardo. Long live the king! 3
Francisco. Bernardo?
Bernardo. He.
Francisco. You come most carefully upon your hour.
Bernardo. 'Tis now struck twelve; get thee to bed,
    Francisco.
Francisco. For this relief much thanks; 'tis bitter
    cold,
And I am sick at heart.
Bernardo. Have you had quiet guard?
Francisco.   Not a mouse stirring.
Bernardo. Well, good-night.
If you do meet Horatio and Marcellus,
The rivals of my watch, bid them make haste. 13
Francisco. I think I hear them. Stand, ho! Who is there?

Enter HORATIO *and* MARCELLUS.

Horatio. Friends to this ground.
Marcellus.   And liegemen to the Dane. 15
Francisco. Give you good-night.
Marcellus.   Oh! farewell, honest soldier: 16
Who hath reliev'd you?
Francisco.   Bernardo has my place.
Give you good-night.   [*Exit*
Marcellus.   Holla! Bernardo!
Bernardo.   Say,
What! is Horatio there?
Horatio.   A piece of him.
Bernardo. Welcome, Horatio; welcome, good Marcellus.
Horatio. What! has this thing appear'd again to-night?
Bernardo. I have seen nothing.
Marcellus. Horatio says 'tis but our fantasy, 23
And will not let belief take hold of him
Touching this dreaded sight twice seen of us: 25
Therefore I have entreated him along
With us to watch the minutes of this night;
That if again this apparition come,
He may approve our eyes and speak to it. 29
Horatio. Tush, tush! 'twill not appear.
Bernardo.   Sit down awhile,
And let us once again assail your ears,
That are so fortified against our story,
What we two nights have seen.
Horatio.   Well, sit we down,
And let us hear Bernardo speak of this.
Bernardo. Last night of all,
When yond same star that's westward from the pole 36
Had made his course to illume that part of heaven 37
Where now it burns, Marcellus and myself,
The bell then beating one,— 39

---

2. emphasis on "me."
   "unfold": reveal.

3. a watchword.

13. "rivals": partners.

15. "liegemen": loyal subjects.
    "the Dane": the King of the Danes.

16. God give you good night.

23. "fantasy": imagination.

25. "of": by.

29. "approve our eyes": verify what we ourselves see.

36. "pole": Polestar

37. "illume": illumine, light up.

39. "beating": striking.

23

HAMLET

ACT I SCENE I

self, Horatio announces it in, "This bodes some strange eruption to our state" (l.69). The fact that the skeptical Horatio has been converted adds further to our feeling of the ghost's actuality. The soldiers have secured a scholar to speak to the ghost (l.42) as a mark of their awe of it, because he might be expected to know from his study how to approach such supernatural agents, and because the ghost might have to be addressed in Latin, the language of religion. According to tradition, ghosts were unable to speak until spoken to.

When Horatio does speak, the ghost is offended because it is addressed in terms (ll.46-9) that imply that it is only assuming the form of the late king. Horatio changes his manner on its reappearance (ll. 130-8).

After expressing their wonder at the specter (note especially the almost gleeful triumph of Bernardo at seeing the skeptical scholar shaken [ll. 53-5]), the men drift into a discussion of the events that currently affect their lives, trying to explain the ghost's presence in terms of those eruptions in the state with which they are familiar. The information they impart is valuable to us in itself; Horatio's greater knowledge of state affairs indicates further the seniority of his rank. The conversation dispels the emotional tension of the scene while leading our minds into new matters so that the reappearance of the ghost comes as a dramatic surprise.

The following facts should be given special emphasis. The threat of warlike attack from Norway is real and urgent. Young Fortinbras is intent on gaining revenge on Denmark for his father's death. Just as young Fortinbras bears his father's name, so young Hamlet (l.170) bears his dead father's name (l.84). (See I,ii, 17-31 for further information.)

Both Bernardo (l.109) and Horatio are willing to accept the ghost as a portent, or as foreshadowing of a coming event. The belief that disturbances in Nature foretell and accompany disturbances in human affairs has its sources in astrology and religion. The universe, believers would say, is one creation, each part linked and related to all the others. Just as a pebble dropped into a pool will send ripples over its whole surface, so any disturbance in the universe will trouble the whole, and great disturbances like the murder of a king will trouble it greatly. That this belief was alive in Shakespeare's England

Enter GHOST

Marcellus. Peace! break thee off; look, where it comes again!

Bernardo. In the same figure like the king that's dead.

Marcellus. Thou art a scholar; speak to it, Horatio. 42

Bernardo. Looks it not like the king? mark it, 43
Horatio.

Horatio. Most like: it harrows me with fear and wonder.

Bernardo. It would be spoke to.

Marcellus.   Question it, Horatio. 45

Horatio. What art thou that usurp'st this time of night,
Together with that fair and war-like form
In which the majesty of buried Denmark 48
Did sometimes march? by heaven I charge thee, speak!

Marcellus. It is offended.

Bernardo.   See! it stalks away.

Horatio. Stay! speak, speak! I charge thee, speak!
[*Exit* GHOST.

Marcellus. 'Tis gone, and will not answer.

Bernardo. How now, Horatio! you tremble and look pale:
Is not this something more than fantasy?
What think you on 't? 55

Horatio. Before my God, I might not this believe 56
Without the sensible and true avouch 57
Of mine own eyes.

Marcellus.   Is it not like the king?

Horatio. As thou art to thyself:
Such was the very armour he had on
When he the ambitious Norway combated; 61
So frown'd he once, when in an angry parle 62
He smote the sledded Polacks on the ice. 63
'Tis strange.

Marcellus. Thus twice before, and jump at this dead hour, 65
With martial stalk hath he gone by our watch.

Horatio. In what particular thought to work I know not: 67
But in the gross and scope of my opinion, 68
This bodes some strange eruption to our state. 69

Marcellus. Good now, sit down, and tell me, he that knows, 70
Why this same strict and most observant watch
So nightly toils the subject of the land, 72
And why such daily cast of brazen cannon, 73
And foreign mart for implements of war, 74
Why such impress of shipwrights, whose sore task 75
Does not divide the Sunday from the week, 76
What might be toward, that this sweaty haste 77
Doth make the night joint-labourer with the day:
Who is't that can inform me?

Horatio.   That can I;
At least, the whisper goes so. Our last king,
Whose image even but now appear'd to us,
Was, as you know, by Fortinbras of Norway,
Thereto prick'd on by a most emulate pride, 83
Dar'd to the combat; in which our valiant Hamlet—
For so this side of our known world esteem'd him—
Did slay this Fortinbras; who, by a seal'd compact, 86

42. "scholar": i.e., having the necessary knowledge of Latin to exorcise a spirit. This was a common Elizabethan belief.

43. "mark": fake particular note of.

45. The belief was that a ghost could not open a conversation.

48. "the . . . Denmark": the late King of Denmark.

55. "on't": on it, of it.

56. "might": could.

57. "avouch": avouchment, verification.

61. "Norway": King of Norway.

62. "parle": parley.

63. "sledded Polacks": most probably Poles with sledges.

65. "jump": precisely.

67. i.e., what this may mean I know not.

68. "gross and scope": general conclusion.

69. "eruption": upheaval.

70. "Good now": short for "My good Horatio, now."

72. "toils": wearies.
"subject": subjects.

73. "cast": casting.

74. "foreign mart": marketing (purchasing) abroad.

75. "impress": impressment, conscription.

76. "divide": distinguish.

77. "toward": on foot, coming.

83. "prick'd": spurred.
"emulate": emulous, jealous.

86-95. i.e., it had been agreed prior to the combat that whichever won was to have the other's lands.

86. "seal'd compact": formal agreement.

24

HAMLET

ACT I SCENE I

and not merely a poet's convention is shown in the following extract from a news pamphlet of February 14, 1606. This article, after listing some strange sights seen at Carlstadt in Germany, goes on to say: "Such things together with the Earth's and Moon's late and horrible obscurations, the frequent eclipsations of the fixed bodies, within these four years more than ordinary, betoken new leagues, traitorous designments, catching at kingdoms, translation of empire, downfall of men in authority, emulation, ambition, innovations, factions, sects, schisms, and much disturbance."

It is delightfully in character that, whereas Bernardo relies on his common sense, Horatio cites an ancient and famous example from his readings in Plutarch or Strabo, two Greeks who wrote of the events surrounding Caesar's death. This reference would have been fresh in Shakespeare's mind since he had just finished writing JULIUS CAESAR in which Act One, Scene Three was devoted to strange disturbances in the universe. (For Horatio's love of things Roman, see also V,ii,344.)

Well ratified by law and heraldry,
Did forfeit with his life all those his lands
Which he stood seiz'd of, to the conqueror; 89
Against the which, a moiety competent 90
Was gaged by our king; which had return'd 91
To the inheritance of Fortinbras,
Had he been vanquisher; as, by the same co-mart,
And carriage of the article design'd, 94
His fell to Hamlet. Now, sir, young Fortinbras,
Of unimproved mettle hot and full, 96
Hath in the skirts of Norway here and there 97
Shark'd up a list of lawless resolutes 98
For food and diet to some enterprise
That hath a stomach in 't; which is no other— 100
As it doth well appear unto our state—
But to recover of us, by strong hand 102
And terms compulsative, those foresaid lands 103
So by his father lost. And this, I take it,
Is the main motive of our preparations,
The source of this our watch and the chief head 106
Of this post-haste and romage in the land. 107
    Bernardo. I think it be no other but e'en so;
Well may it sort that this portentous figure 109
Comes armed through our watch, so like the king
That was and is the question of these wars. 111
    Horatio. A mote it is to trouble the mind's eye. 112
In the most high and palmy state of Rome, 113
A little ere the mightiest Julius fell,
The graves stood tenantless, and the sheeted dead 115
Did squeak and gibber in the Roman streets; 116
As stars with trains of fire and dews of blood,
Disasters in the sun; and the moist star 118
Upon whose influence Neptune's empire stands
Was sick almost to doomsday with eclipse; 120
And even the like precurse of fierce events, 121
As harbingers preceding still the fates 122
And prologue to the omen coming on, 123
Have heaven and earth together demonstrated 124
Unto our climatures and countrymen. 125
               Re-enter GHOST
But, soft! behold! lo! where it comes again.
I'll cross it, though it blast me. Stay, illusion! 127
If thou hast any sound, or use of voice,
Speak to me:
If there be any good thing to be done,
That may to thee do ease and grace to me,
Speak to me:
If thou art privy to thy country's fate, 133
Which happily foreknowing may avoid, 134
O! speak!
Or if thou hast uphoarded in thy life
Extorted treasure in the womb of earth, 137
For which, they say, you spirits oft walk in death,
Speak of it: stay, and speak! [*Cock crows.*] Stop it,
    Marcellus.
    Marcellus. Shall I strike at it with my partisan? 140
    Horatio. Do, if it will not stand.
    Bernardo.   'Tis here!
    Horatio.   'Tis here! [*Exit* GHOST.
    Marcellus. 'Tis gone!

89. "seized of": possessed of; a legal term.

90. "moiety competent": sufficient portion.

91. "gaged": pledged.

94. "carriage . . . design'd": carrying out of the agreement.

96. "unimproved mettle": untried spirits

97. "skirts": outlying parts.

98. "Shark'd": gathered indiscriminately.
"lawless resolutes": desperadoes.

100. "hath . . . in't": calls for resolution, courage.

102. "But": than.
"of": from.

103. "terms compulsative": force.

106. "chief head": main purpose.

107. "romage": rummage, bustle.

109. "Well . . . sort": it is in keeping.

111. "question": subject.

112. "mote": speck of dust.

113-20. Compare JULIUS CAESAR, I,iii, 10-32, and II,ii, 16-23.

113. "palmy": flourishing.

115. "sheeted": shrouded.

116-17. Apparently something has been lost between lines 116 and 117, and it is impossible to get the original meaning of the passage.

118. "Disasters": ominous signs.
"moist star": moon—see next line.

120. "doomsday": the end of the world

121. "precurse": forerunning (Latin PRAE and CURSUS).

122. "harbingers": forerunners.

123. "omen": the ominous event or disaster.

124. i.e., heaven and earth have demonstrated these harbingers.

125. "climatures": regions.

127. Another common Elizabethan belief was that to cross the path of a ghost was to put one's self in its power.

133. "privy to": possessed of secret (private) knowledge of.

134. "happily": either (1) perchance (haply) or (2) luckily.

137. "Extorted": wrongfully acquired.

140. "partisan": long handled spear like a halberd carried by foot soldiers.

HAMLET

ACT I SCENE I

From line 149 to line 177 the poetry rises to a more musical or lyrical style suggesting at once the exaltation of their awe and the clearing of the air as the horizon lightens towards dawn.

Horatio

Finally at line 170, the hero's name is introduced to us. What will he think of his father's unquiet spirit? Thus the action is led forward to the meeting of Hamlet and Horatio. The first scene leaves us with a haunting sense of unexplained evil troubling both the dead and the living.

ACT I SCENE II

The warmth and color that floods the stage at the entrance of the Royal Court of Denmark (the Second Quarto text ushers it in with a flourish of trumpets) presents an interior in the greatest contrast to the bleak sentry post. The effect is one of almost exaggerated prosperity and well-being. The only disturbing factor to provide a link with the troubled mood of Scene One is the lone, sad-faced figure of a young man in black who keeps aloof. The King is a large and luxurious man. (He will later be called fat [IV,iii,24].) His speech is smooth and soothing, sometimes almost takes on a purring sound (ll. 42-50).

Until line 64, everything goes with ease and smoothness. We see in Claudius' method of handling young Fortinbras a further difference between him and his late brother. Here is the skilled diplomat instead of the gaunt and proud war hero.

We do it wrong, being so majestical,   143
To offer it the show of violence;
For it is, as the air, invulnerable,
And our vain blows malicious mockery.
   Bernardo. It was about to speak when the cock crew.
   Horatio. And then it started like a guilty thing
Upon a fearful summons. I have heard,
The cock, that is the trumpet to the morn,
Doth with his lofty and shrill-sounding throat
Awake the god of day; and at his warning,
Whether in sea or fire, in earth or air,
Th' extravagant and erring spirit hies   154
To his confine; and of the truth herein   155
This present object made probation.   156
   Marcellus. It faded on the crowing of the cock.
Some say that ever 'gainst that season comes   158
Wherein our Saviour's birth is celebrated,
The bird of dawning singeth all night long;
And then, they say, no spirit dare stir abroad;
The nights are wholesome; then no planets strike,   162
No fairy takes, nor witch hath power to charm,   163
So hallow'd and so gracious is that time.
   Horatio. So have I heard and do in part believe it.
But look, the morn in russet mantle clad   166
Walks o'er the dew of yon high eastern hill;
Break we our watch up; and by my advice
Let us impart what we have seen to-night
Unto young Hamlet; for, upon my life,
This spirit, dumb to us, will speak to him.
Do you consent we shall acquaint him with it,
As needful in our loves, fitting our duty?
   Marcellus. Let's do't, I pray; and I this morning know
Where we shall find him most conveniently. [*Exeunt.*

Scene two.

(THE COUNCIL CHAMBER)

Enter CLAUDIUS, *King of Denmark*, GERTRUDE, *the Queen*, Councillors, POLONIUS *and his son* LAERTES, VOLTIMAND *and* CORNELIUS, HAMLET *and* Attendants.

   King. Though yet of Hamlet our dear brother's death
The memory be green, and that it us befitted   2
To bear our hearts in grief, and our whole kingdom
To be contracted in one brow of woe,   4
Yet so far hath discretion fought with nature   5
That we with wisest sorrow think on him,   6
Together with remembrance of ourselves.
Therefore our sometime sister, now our queen,   8
Th' imperial jointress to this war-like state,   9
Have we, as 'twere with a defeated joy,   10
With one auspicious and one dropping eye,   11
With mirth in funeral and with dirge in marriage,
In equal scale weighing delight and dole,   13
Taken to wife: nor have we herein barr'd   14
Your better wisdoms, which have freely gone   15
With this affair along: for all, our thanks.

26

143. "majestical": majestic. What does this adjective modify?

154. "extravagant and erring": vagrant and wandering (both used in original Latin sense—a common device of Shakespeare).

155. "confine": prison.

156. "probation": proof.

158. "'gainst": in preparation for.

162. "strike": exert a malignant influence —a common belief.

163. "takes": infects.

166. "russet": to the Elizabethan this meant the warm gray tone of homespun cloth.

2. "green": fresh.

4. i.e., everyone in the kingdom ought to mourn.

5. "discretion": common sense. "nature": natural sorrow.

6-7. i.e., while we mourn the departed king, we must not forget the welfare of the state.

8. "sometime": former. "sister": sister-in-law. Notice how the dramatist is at pains to show as soon as possible the relationship between Claudius and Gertrude.

9. "jointress": partner.

10. "defeated": spoiled, marred.

11. i.e., rejoicing and sorrowing at the same time.

13. "dole": grief.

14. "barr'd": excluded, forbidden expression of.

15-16. "freely . . . along": approved the proceedings.

HAMLET

ACT I SCENE II

Though we admire this man's skill and ease of manner, there are several things to call his regime in question: 1) It would seem wrong to an Elizabethan audience that the crown should pass to old Hamlet's brother rather than to Prince Hamlet; 2) If Claudius' brother was as dear as line 1 suggests, how is it that sorrow bows so easily to wisdom? The whole business of weeping with one eye and smiling with the other seems doubtful; 3) The new King's marriage is a case of illegal incest (see paragraph below), and if his courtiers condone it, they condone a wrong, and the King might well thank them (l.16). Altogether, this man has slipped too quickly, too easily, and too completely into his brother's shoes.

Incest is the marriage of close relations. It is a carnal and unnatural act (cf. V,ii,385). The marriage of Gertrude and Claudius is a special case inasmuch as they are not blood relations. The objection in such cases is less physical than legal. The effect is to confuse the clear outline of family relationships upon which so much depends when questions of succession come up. Thus Claudius has become both brother and husband to Gertrude, and Hamlet is now both son and nephew to each.

The parallel between Hamlet and Fortinbras is strengthened here (ll. 28-31) by the fact that in Norway as in Denmark the deceased king has been succeeded by his brother rather than his son.

The new business begun in this scene all concerns the actions of three young men, Fortinbras (who seeks vengeance), Laertes (who wants to return to France), and Hamlet (whose attitude and dress threaten constantly the smiling ease of the court).

Hamlet's first three speeches give us the roots of his discontent: 1) He hates his uncle. 2) He is bitter about the marriage. 3) He recoils from falsity ("I know not 'seems'"). Hamlet's bitter drive cuts through the tone of Claudius' graceful utterance like a knife through cake. The Prince's wit, combined with the ironical turn of his melancholy, lead him to a frequent use of puns. "Too much i' the sun," is an example with more than two relevant meanings. The Second Quarto prints "sonne," suggesting the likelihood of the obvious pun on sun-son (cf. l.64), but "i' the sun" itself had the following meanings: exposure or homelessness, limelight (cf. II,ii,184). Burton's ANATOMY OF MELANCHOLY gives "long abode under the sun" as a common cause of the

---

Now follows, that you know, young Fortinbras, 17
Holding a weak supposal of our worth, 18
Or thinking by our late dear brother's death
Our state to be disjoint and out of frame, 20
Colleagued with the dream of his advantage, 21
He hath not fail'd to pester us with message,
Importing the surrender of those lands 23
Lost by his father, with all bands of law,
To our most valiant brother. So much for him.
Now for ourself and for this time of meeting. 26
Thus much the business is: we have here writ
To Norway, uncle of young Fortinbras,
Who, impotent and bed-rid, scarcely hears
Of this his nephew's purpose, to suppress
His further gait herein; in that the levies, 31
The lists and full proportions, are all made
Out of his subject; and we here dispatch
You, good Cornelius, and you, Voltimand,
For bearers of this greeting to old Norway,
Giving to you no further personal power
To business with the king more than the scope 37
Of these delated articles allow. 38
Farewell and let your haste commend your duty. 39
Cornelius. ⎱ In that and all things will we show our
Voltimand. ⎰ duty.
King. We doubt it nothing: heartily farewell.
            [*Exeunt* VOLTIMAND *and* CORNELIUS.
And now, Laertes, what's the news with you?
You told us of some suit; what is 't, Laertes? 43
You cannot speak of reason to the Dane, 44
And lose your voice; what wouldst thou beg, Laertes, 45
That shall not be my offer, not thy asking? 46
The head is not more native to the heart, 47
The hand more instrumental to the mouth, 48
Than is the throne of Denmark to thy father. 49
What wouldst thou have, Laertes?
Laertes.   Dread my lord, 50
Your leave and favour to return to France;
From whence though willingly I came to Denmark,
To show my duty in your coronation,
Yet now, I must confess, that duty done,
My thoughts and wishes bend again toward France
And bow them to your gracious leave and pardon. 56
King. Have you your father's leave? What says
    Polonius?
Polonius. He hath, my lord, wrung from me my slow
    leave
By laboursome petition, and at last
Upon his will I seal'd my hard consent: 60
I do beseech you, give him leave to go.
King. Take thy fair hour, Laertes; time be thine, 62
And thy best graces spend it at thy will. 63
But now, my cousin Hamlet, and my son,— 64
Hamlet. [*Aside.*] A little more than kin, and less
    than kind. 65
King. How is it that the clouds still hang on you?
Hamlet. Not so, my lord; I am too much i' the sun. 67
Queen. Good Hamlet, cast thy nighted colour off, 68
And let thine eye look like a friend on Denmark.
Do not for ever with thy vailed lids 70

---

17. "that you know": that (which) you know.

18. "weak supposal": poor opinion.

20. "disjoint . . . frame": disjointed and out of gear.

21. i.e., together with the hope of what he might gain.

23. "Importing": concerning.

26. "ourself": royal plural, used throughout the King's speeches. See line 18.

31. "gait": progress.

31-33. "levies . . . subject": the army he has raised has been from among his (the king of Norway's) subjects.

37. "scope": limit.

38. "delated articles": provisions set forth in their instructions.

39. "commend": literally, recommend; i.e., display your zeal for duty by your haste in the performance of it.

43. "suit": petition.

44. "of reason": with reason. "the Dane": see note 15 in Scene i.

45. "lose your voice": speak in vain.

46. i.e., that I am not ready to give unasked.

47. "native": closely related.

48. "instrumental": serviceable.

49. "the throne": i.e., the king.

50. "Dread": literally, dreaded; esteemed.

56. "pardon": permission.

60. "will": desire. "seal'd . . . consent": i.e., I reluctantly agreed to let him go.

62. "Take . . . hour": i.e., enjoy life while you are young; and/or, go whenever you like.

63. i.e., make use of your best accomplishments to spend your time as you desire.

64. "cousin": kinsman. This word was used for any near relation; here it would be nephew.

65. Hamlet, in the bitterness of his mood, plays on the words "kin" and "kind." The latter originated from the former and denoted the similarity of character, nature, or race within a family or tribe. Kind also could refer to natural affection between relatives.

67. "sun": another pun (son), indicating once more his dislike of the new relationship between himself and his uncle.

68. "nighted": black. Hamlet, alone of all the court, remains in deep mourning.

70. "vailed lids": downcast eyes.

HAMLET

ACT I SCENE II

disease. The way in which Hamlet conforms to the symptoms of melancholy will be shown from time to time as we go on.

If Hamlet's only cause of melancholy were his sorrow over the death of his father, there would be truth in Claudius' reprimand (ll. 87-106). Excessive mourning was, for instance, a fault to Heaven because, if the dead had gone to Heavenly bliss, a rational man would rejoice at his happiness rather than nursing his own grief. Such arguments as Gertrude and Claudius use are listed by Burton among the cures for mourning melancholy.

Lines 108-9 give us our first hint of the elective nature of the Danish throne (see III,ii, 346-7; V,ii, 65, 344-5). While this explains the possibility of Claudius' taking the throne, it does not make it likely. All four references to the election in the play stress the fact that the King's vote was of primary importance in securing the succession.

Wittenberg, Luther's university, was founded in 1502, and had become famous as a headquarter for thinkers and students of protestant confirmation or tendency.

The question is, why the King wants Hamlet to remain in the "cheer and comfort of our eye." He was glad enough to ship Laertes off to Paris. Can you suggest a reason?

Hamlet (l.120) does not answer Claudius but waits until his mother adds her wish. If you were acting the part, would you emphasize the defiance by stressing "you" (l. 120)? If you did so it would make Claudius' reply (l.121) sound all the more hollow and ridiculous.

For the King's drinking custom see I,iv, 7-22, and V,ii, 271-5.

Hamlet's first soliloquy has a special importance in showing us the extent of his disturbance before he knows of his father's ghost and its secret. The first thing to seize on is that Hamlet's stubbornness springs not from unmanly grief, but from noble fury and bitter shock. These are caused not from his father's death ("Ay, madam, it is common") but from his mother's criminal infidelity. He wears his black, then, to shame this thoughtless court into remembrance, and above all, his mother. They sense no shame and he cannot believe such indifference.

The inference is clear that Hamlet, taught by his own candor and purity, his idolization of his beloved parents (see ll. 140-5), and

---

Seek for thy noble father in the dust:
Thou know'st 'tis common; all that live must die,
Passing through nature to eternity.
Hamlet. Ay, madam, it is common.
Queen.　　　　　　　　　　　If it be,
Why seems it so particular with thee?　　　　　　75
Hamlet. Seems, madam! Nay, it is; I know not 'seems'.
'Tis not alone my inky cloak, good mother,
Nor customary suits of solemn black,
Nor windy suspiration of forc'd breath,　　　　　79
No, nor the fruitful river in the eye,
Nor the dejected haviour of the visage,　　　　　81
Together with all forms, modes, shows of grief,
That can denote me truly; these indeed seem,　　83
For they are actions that a man might play:　　　84
But I have that within which passeth show;
These but the trappings and the suits of woe.　　86
King. 'Tis sweet and commendable in your nature, Hamlet,
To give these mourning duties to your father:
But, you must know, your father lost a father;
That father lost, lost his; and the survivor bound
In filial obligation for some term
To do obsequious sorrow; but to persever　　　92
In obstinate condolement is a course　　　　　93
Of impious stubbornness; 'tis unmanly grief:
It shows a will most incorrect to heaven,
A heart unfortified, a mind impatient,　　　　　96
An understanding simple and unschool'd:
For what we know must be and is as common
As any the most vulgar thing to sense,　　　　　99
Why should we in our peevish opposition
Take it to heart? Fie! 'tis a fault to heaven,
A fault against the dead, a fault to nature,
To reason most absurd, whose common theme
Is death of fathers, and who still hath cried,　　104
From the first corse till he that died to-day,　　105
'This must be so.' We pray you, throw to earth
This unprevailing woe, and think of us　　　　107
As of a father; for let the world take note,
You are the most immediate to our throne;　　　109
And with no less nobility of love
Than that which dearest father bears his son
Do I impart toward you. For your intent　　　112
In going back to school in Wittenberg,　　　　113
It is most retrograde to our desire;　　　　　114
And we beseech you, bend you to remain　　　115
Here, in the cheer and comfort of our eye,
Our chiefest courtier, cousin, and our son.
Queen. Let not thy mother lose her prayers, Hamlet:
I pray thee, stay with us; go not to Wittenberg.
Hamlet. I shall in all my best obey you, madam.
King. Why, 'tis a loving and a fair reply:
Be as ourself in Denmark. Madam, come;　　　122
This gentle and unforc'd accord of Hamlet
Sits smiling to my heart; in grace whereof,
No jocund health that Denmark drinks to-day,
But the great cannon to the clouds shall tell,　126
And the king's rouse the heavens shall bruit again,　127

---

75. "particular": special concern.

79. i.e., profound sighs.

81. i.e., downcast countenance.

83. "seem": merely appear.

84. "play": act, as in a play.

86. "trappings": ornaments.

92. "obsequious sorrow": mourning for the dead.
pronunciation here: persev'er.

93. "obstinate condolement": grief which is contrary to the will of Heaven (explained by line 95).

96. "unfortified": not strengthened by religious consolation.

99. i.e., as any of the commonest things of our experience.

104. "still": always—a common Elizabethan use.

105. "corse": body. Do you detect any unconscious irony in the King's mention of "first corse"? It will be apparent when the ghost makes his revelation to Hamlet (see I,v, 39-40 and III,iii,37-8).

107. "unprevailing": futile.

109. i.e., you are next in line, the heir to the throne.

112. "impart": behave.

113. "school": university. Wittenberg was famous to Elizabethans as the birth place of the Protestant Reformation (1517), but since the university was not founded until 1502, its reference in the play is an anachronism.

114. "retrograde": contrary.

115. "bend you": incline yourself.

122. "Be as ourself in Denmark": Claudius is extending to Hamlet all the special privileges and prerogatives pertaining to a crowned prince.

126. It was a Danish custom to discharge a cannon when the King proposed a toast.

127. "rouse": draught of liquor, bumper, toast.
"bruit": echo.

28

HAMLET

perhaps the sober truth-seeking of Wittenberg, has built his view of life on an ideal. This fortunate world has collapsed without warning about him, and left him lost. Everything seems; nothing is but viciousness.

The result is a mournful or angry solitude, contempt for life (ll. 133-7), wish for death, and a tendency towards uncontrolled outbursts of emotion. All these are symptoms of melancholy. Even thus accounted for, the wish for suicide constitutes very strong revulsion. Many explanations are offered of the extremity of his feeling, for example: 1) the headlong convictions of youth; 2) melancholy (see above); 3) a mysterious sense of yet greater evil that he cannot define or locate (cf. Francisco I,i,9); 4) self-loathing brought on by the realization that the same blood enlivens his body as does his mother's (cf. III,i, 117-30). Further support for this last reason is produced by the likelihood that "solid" in line 129 should really be "sullied." (Q2 has "sallied" and F1, "solid"; but at II,i,39 Q2 has "sallies"; and F1 "sulleyes," i.e., "sullies." If F1 is assumed correct in the latter case, is seems likely that the former should have been "sulleyed.")

For the rank weed imagery (ll. 135-7), compare I,v,32-3; III,iii,37; III,iv,64-5,148,151-2; IV,vii,174.

Hamlet's change of mood when he recognizes Horatio is very striking. Time and again in the play we can watch this tendency in Hamlet to forget himself quickly in impulsive response to a new interest. The pleasure in his greeting (ll. 170-5) is spontaneous and delightful. It shows us the nervous vitality and immense variety of his personality. These are almost like glimpses of his unsaddened nature. They light up the charm and interest of his character. The identity of Horatio as Hamlet's fellow student is established in lines 164, 168, and 177, and the extent of their friendship may be measured by how quickly Hamlet speaks his is uppermost in his mind, and by Horatio's instantaneous understanding (l.179). Note how this encounter transforms and lightens Hamlet's bitterness.

Re-speaking earthly thunder. Come away.

[*Exeunt all except* HAMLET.

Hamlet. O! that this too too solid flesh would melt,

Thaw and resolve itself into a dew;   130

Or that the Everlasting had not fix'd

His canon 'gainst self-slaughter! O God! God!   132

How weary, stale, flat, and unprofitable

Seem to me all the uses of this world.   134

Fie on 't! Ah fie! 'tis an unweeded garden,   135

That grows to seed; things rank and gross in nature   136

Possess it merely. That it should come to this!   137

But two months dead: nay, not so much, not two:

So excellent a king; that was, to this,

Hyperion to a satyr; so loving to my mother   140

That he might not beteem the winds of heaven   141

Visit her face too roughly. Heaven and earth!

Must I remember? why, she would hang on him,

As if increase of appetite had grown

By what it fed on; and yet, within a month,

Let me not think on 't: Frailty, thy name is woman!   146

A little month; or ere those shoes were old

With which she follow'd my poor father's body,

Like Niobe, all tears; why she, even she,—   149

O God! a beast, that wants discourse of reason,   150

Would have mourn'd longer,—married with mine uncle,

My father's brother, but no more like my father

Than I to Hercules: within a month,

Ere yet the salt of most unrighteous tears   154

Had left the flushing in her galled eyes,   155

She married. O! most wicked speed, to post   156

With such dexterity to incestuous sheets.   157

It is not nor it cannot come to good;   158

But break, my heart, for I must hold my tongue!

Enter HORATIO, MARCELLUS *and* BERNARDO.

Horatio. Hail to your lordship!

Hamlet.   I am glad to see you well:

Horatio, or I do forget myself.

Horatio. The same, my lord, and your poor servant ever.

Hamlet. Sir, my good friend; I'll change that name with you.   163

And what make you from Wittenberg, Horatio?   164

Marcellus?

Marcellus. My good lord,—

Hamlet. I am very glad to see you. [*To* BERNARDO.] Good even, sir.

But what, in faith, make you from Wittenberg?

Horatio. A truant disposition, good my lord.

Hamlet. I would not hear your enemy say so,

Nor shall you do mine ear that violence,

To make it truster of your own report

Against yourself; I know you are no truant.

But what is your affair in Elsinore?

We'll teach you to drink deep ere you depart.   175

Horatio. My lord, I came to see your father's funeral.

Hamlet. I pray thee, do not mock me, fellow-student;

I think it was to see my mother's wedding.

Horatio. Indeed, my lord, it follow'd hard upon.

---

130. "resolve": dissolve.

132. "canon": law; here refers to the Sixth Commandment in the Bible.

134. "uses": usages, customs, and employment.

135. "Fie": interjection expressing sense of outraged propriety.

136. "rank": coarse.

137. "merely": entirely.

140. "Hyperion": the sun god. "satyr": half goat, half man—ugly and lecherous. Hamlet says that comparing his father to his uncle is like comparing Hyperion to Satyr.

141. "beteem": permit.

146. "Frailty . . . woman": woman is the epitome of frailty. Note Hamlet's bitter generalization based on his mother's behavior. It may go a long way toward explaining Hamlet's later treatment of Ophelia.

149. "Niobe": in Greek mythology a woman turned to stone while weeping for slain children; hence an inconsolable bereaved woman.

150. "wants": lacks—a common use with Shakespeare. "discourse of reason": ability to reason.

154. "unrighteous": insincere.

155. "flushing": redness. "galled": sore.

156. "post": hasten.

157. "dexterity": nimbleness. "incestuous": marriage to the brother of a dead husband was considered incestuous by both the Catholic and Protestant Churches.

158. This feeling of ill-omen is based on the incestuous action of his mother. It should be noted that Hamlet was sick in soul before he had even heard about the ghost. And of course he had no suspicion that his uncle might be a murderer.

163. i.e., I am your servant.

164. "make you from": are you doing away from.

175. A bitterly ironical reference to the drinking habits of the Court of Elsinore. This mood is reflected in his next two or three speeches as well.

HAMLET

There are two ways of speaking line 190: 1) quickly as if he thought Horatio were merely changing the subject. 2) Saw! (pause) Who?, as if awe-struck and incredulous. Which would you do?

Hamlet. Thrift, thrift, Horatio! the funeral bak'd
  meats
Did coldly furnish forth the marriage tables.
Would I had met my dearest foe in heaven   182
Or ever I had seen that day, Horatio!
My father, methinks I see my father.
 Horatio. O! where, my lord?
 Hamlet.   In my mind's eye, Horatio.   185
 Horatio. I saw him once; he was a goodly king.
 Hamlet. He was a man, take him for all in all,
I shall not look upon his like again.
 Horatio. My lord, I think I saw him yesternight.
 Hamlet. Saw who?
 Horatio. My lord, the king your father.
 Hamlet.   The king, my father!
 Horatio. Season your admiration for a while   192
With an attent ear, till I may deliver,   193
Upon the witness of these gentlemen,
This marvel to you.
 Hamlet.   For God's love, let me hear.
 Horatio. Two nights together had these gentlemen,
Marcellus and Bernardo, on their watch,
In the dead vast and middle of the night,
Been thus encounter'd: a figure like your father,
Armed at point exactly, cap-a-pe,   200
Appears before them, and with solemn march
Goes slow and stately by them: thrice he walk'd
By their oppress'd and fear-surprised eyes,
Within his truncheon's length; whilst they, distill'd   204
Almost to jelly with the act of fear,
Stand dumb and speak not to him. This to me
In dreadful secrecy impart they did,
And I with them the third night kept the watch;
Where, as they had deliver'd, both in time,   209
Form of the thing, each word made true and good,
The apparition comes. I knew your father;
These hands are not more like.
 Hamlet.   But where was this?   212
 Marcellus. My lord, upon the platform where we
  watch'd.
 Hamlet. Did you not speak to it?
 Horatio.   My lord, I did;
But answer made it none; yet once methought
It lifted up its head and did address
Itself to motion, like as it would speak;
But even then the morning cock crew loud,
And at the sound it shrunk in haste away
And vanish'd from our sight.
 Hamlet.   'Tis very strange.
 Horatio. As I do live, my honour'd lord, 'tis true;
And we did think it writ down in our duty
To let you know of it.
 Hamlet. Indeed, indeed, sirs, but this troubles me.
Hold you the watch to-night?
 Marcellus.⎫
 Bernardo. ⎭   We do, my lord.
 Hamlet. Arm'd, say you?
 Marcellus.⎫
 Bernardo. ⎭   Arm'd, my lord.

182. "dearest": bitterest.

185. "O! where, my lord?": What was Horatio thinking?

192. "Season your admiration": moderate your wonder. Shakespeare frequently uses admiration in its original (Latin) sense of wonder.

193. "attent": attentive.
 "deliver": report or express.

200. "cap-a-pe": fully armed from head to foot.

204. "truncheon": a general's baton.
 "distill'd": melted.

209. "deliver'd": reported. Compare line 193 above.

212. "These . . . like": i.e., the apparition as closely resembled your father as my hands do each other.

30

HAMLET

ACT I SCENE II

Notice the brilliant writing of the dialogue in lines 220-42, in which the staccato conversation fits beautifully into the poetic meter and gains force and excitement from it.

How would you read line 239? With what stance and gesture?

Hamlet, like Horatio, is in two minds about the ghost from the first (ll. 243-5 and 254; cf. I,i, 46-9 and commentary).

This time we must wait in suspense with Hamlet till midnight to meet the ghost. What can the ghost add to Hamlet's disturbance to make it greater?

Hamlet

ACT I SCENE III

This is the first of a series of domestic scenes. It is a splendid introduction to Polonius and his children who make up here a family group undisturbed as compared to those of Fortinbras and Hamlet. The whole framework of the scene seems designed to give us a sense of a normal or typical family. The

---

Hamlet.   From top to toe?
Marcellus.}
Bernardo.} My lord, from head to foot.
Hamlet. Then saw you not his face?
Horatio. O yes! my lord; he wore his beaver up.   229
Hamlet. What! look'd he frowningly?
Horatio. A countenance more in sorrow than in anger.
Hamlet. Pale or red?
Horatio. Nay, very pale.
Hamlet.   And fix'd his eyes upon you?
Horatio. Most constantly.
Hamlet.   I would I had been there.
Horatio. It would have much amaz'd you.
Hamlet. Very like, very like. Stay'd it long?
Horatio. While one with moderate haste might tell   237
   a hundred.
Marcellus.}
Bernardo.} Longer, longer.
Horatio. Not when I saw it.
Hamlet.   His beard was grizzled, no?   239
Horatio. It was, as I have seen it in his life,
A sable silver'd.
Hamlet.   I will watch to-night;   241
Perchance 'twill walk again.
  Horatio.   I warrant it will.   242
Hamlet. If it assume my noble father's person,
I'll speak to it, though hell itself should gape   244
And bid me hold my peace. I pray you all,
If you have hitherto conceal'd this sight,
Let it be tenable in your silence still;   247
And whatsoever else shall hap to-night,   248
Give it an understanding, but no tongue: 249
I will requite your loves. So, fare you well.   250
Upon the platform, 'twixt eleven and twelve,
I'll visit you.
All.   Our duty to your honour.
Hamlet. Your loves, as mine to you. Farewell.   253
   [*Exeunt* HORATIO, MARCELLUS, *and* BERNARDO.
My father's spirit (in arms!) all is not well;
I doubt some foul play: would the night were come!   255
Till then sit still, my soul: foul deeds will rise,
Though all the earth o'erwhelm them, to men's eyes.
                                          [*Exit.*

---

229. "beaver": the visor of the helmet, which could be lowered in battle.

237. "tell": count.

239. "grizzled": gray.

241. "sable silver'd": black streaked with white.

242. "warrant": guarantee.

244. "gape": open wide its mouth.

247. "tenable": held fast.

248. "hap": happen.

249. i.e., figure out the meaning of it for yourselves, but say nothing about it.

250. "requite": repay.

253. Compare Hamlet's correction here with that of line 163. He means that he wishes to be regarded as their friend to be loved as he loves them, rather than merely as a superior to be obeyed.

255. "doubt": suspect.

Scene three.

(A ROOM IN POLONIUS' HOUSE)

Enter LAERTES *and* OPHELIA.

Laertes. My necessaries are embark'd; farewell: 1
And, sister, as the winds give benefit
And convoy is assistant, do not sleep,   3
But let me hear from you.
Ophelia.   Do you doubt that?
Laertes. For Hamlet, and the trifling of his favour,
Hold it a fashion and a toy in blood,   6

---

1. "necessaries": baggage.

3. "convoy is assistant": a means of conveyance is available.

6. "toy in blood": trifling passion.

31

HAMLET

ACT I SCENE III

young man leaving home for the great world feels wise and important. The young girl is in love, and does not take her brother too seriously. The old father, fussy and full of advice, is anxious for the safety of his children, and suspicious of his daughter's young man. It would be a charming, delicately comic situation were it not for two things. First, in spite of the undoubted affection between these three, their whole relationship with each other is based upon suspicion and mistrust, felt and taught by Polonius, and shared by Laertes. Thus Laertes believes the worst of Hamlet; Polonius' famous advice to his son (ll. 58-81) is counsel of keeping up appearances based on caution and self-interest. Second, the young man Ophelia is forbidden to see is Hamlet, whose purity of nature and need for loyal affection we already realize. These facts alter our perspective. We see Polonius and Laertes unworthy men beside Hamlet, and we know that Ophelia's trust in Hamlet is justified. She too is ideally virtuous (cf. I,iii, 136, with I, ii, 120) and will, we feel, obey her father against her better nature; the result must be a cruel or even tragic distortion of feeling (see II,i; III,i; III,ii).

Yet Polonius is not a villain. He and Laertes stand midway between Hamlet's ideal purity and Claudius' smiling villainy. The former they don't believe in; the latter they don't imagine and are not equipped to cope with. The words of Hamlet concerning Rosencrantz and Guildenstern apply also here, " 'Tis dangerous when the baser nature comes/Between the pass and fell-incensed points/Of mighty opposites" (V,ii, 60-2). It is part of the function of tragedy to show us the heights and depths of human capability, thus removing the customary narrow baseness of our horizons.

The parallels and contrasts set up are quite important. Laertes and Hamlet present the intellectual and moral contrast symbolized by their destinations when they go abroad, Laertes to adventure in Paris, Hamlet to study in Wittenberg. (And we must not forget the third young man, fiery Fortinbras.) Ophelia and Gertrude, both women in love are also contrasted (cf. IV,v,182-3), but, ironically, Polonius' command will make Ophelia seem (false appearances again) as fickle. Do you think that Ophelia accepts the view that Hamlet is an ordinary young trifler, or does she keep her ideal whatever her father makes her do?

There are several contributions here to the trains of related im-

---

A violet in the youth of primy nature,   7
Forward, not permanent, sweet, not lasting,
The perfume and suppliance of a minute;   9
No more.
    Ophelia. No more but so?
     Laertes.   Think it no more:
For nature, crescent, does not grow alone   11
In thews and bulk; but, as this temple waxes,   12
The inward service of the mind and soul
Grows wide withal. Perhaps he loves you now,
And now no soil nor cautel doth besmirch   15
The virtue of his will; but you must fear,   16
His greatness weigh'd, his will is not his own,   17
For he himself is subject to his birth;   18
He may not, as unvalu'd persons do,
Carve for himself, for on his choice depends   20
The safety and the health of the whole state;
And therefore must his choice be circumscrib'd   22
Unto the voice and yielding of that body   23
Whereof he is the head. Then if he says he loves you,
It fits your wisdom so far to believe it   25
As he in his particular act and place
May give his saying deed; which is no further
Than the main voice of Denmark goes withal.   28
Then weigh what loss your honour may sustain,
If with too credent ear you list his songs,   30
Or lose your heart, or your chaste treasure open   31
To his unmaster'd importunity.   32
Fear it, Ophelia, fear it, my dear sister;
And keep you in the rear of your affection,   34
Out of the shot and danger of desire.
The chariest maid is prodigal enough   36
If she unmask her beauty to the moon;
Virtue herself 'scapes not calumnious strokes;
The canker galls the infants of the spring   39
Too oft before their buttons be disclos'd,   40
And in the morn and liquid dew of youth
Contagious blastments are most imminent.   42
Be wary then; best safety lies in fear:
Youth to itself rebels, though none else near.   44
    Ophelia. I shall th' effect of this good lesson keep,
As watchman to my heart. But, good my brother,
Do not, as some ungracious pastors do,   47
Show me the steep and thorny way to heaven,
Whiles, like a puff'd and reckless libertine,   49
Himself the primrose path of dalliance treads,   50
And recks not his own rede.
    Laertes.   O! fear me not.   51
I stay too long; but here my father comes.
        Enter POLONIUS.
A double blessing is a double grace;
Occasion smiles upon a second leave.   54
    Polonius. Yet here, Laertes! aboard, aboard, for
      shame!
The wind sits in the shoulder of your sail,
And you are stay'd for. There, my blessing with thee!   57
And these few precepts in thy memory
Look thou character. Give thy thoughts no tongue,   59
Nor any unproportion'd thought his act.   60
Be thou familiar, but by no means vulgar;   61

---

7. "primy": in its prime, youthful.

9. "suppliance of a minute": a minute's pastime.

11. "crescent": growing.

12. "temple": body; the temple of the soul.

15. "cautel": craft.

16. "will": desire.

17. "His greatness weigh'd": considering his high position.

18. "subject to ": controlled by.

20. "Carve": choose.

22. "circumscrib'd": restricted.

23. "voice and yielding": approval and acquiescence.
"body": people of the state.

25-8. i.e., you would be wise to believe it only to the extent that his position will allow him freedom to carry out his promises: which is only so far as public opinion in Denmark will support him.

28. "withal": with.

30. "credent": credulous.

31. "chaste treasure": precious chastity.

32. "unmaster'd importunity": uncontrolled and determined wooing.

34-5. i.e., don't allow your affections to get out of hand.

36. "chariest": most modest and virtuous.
"prodigal": wasteful, spendthrift.

39. i.e., the cankerworm damages the unopened buds.

40. "buttons": buds.
"disclos'd": opened.

42. "Contagious blastments": destructive blights.

44. i.e., youth tends to rebel against self-restraint, even though no one is near to tempt them.

47. "ungracious": lacking grace, depraved.

49. "puff'd": panting.
"libertine": licentious person.

50. i.e., himself enjoys all amorous pleasures.

51. "recks . . . rede": takes no care of his own counsel.

"fear me not": don't be afraid for me.

54. i.e., a happy chance allows a second leave-taking.

57. "stay'd": waited.

59. "character": inscribe.

60. "unproportion'd": unsuitable.

61. "vulgar": common.

32

HAMLET

ACT I SCENE III

agery. Hamlet's love is (ll. 7-9) a violet. Compare Laertes' shabby expectation with Hamlet's disillusion, expressed in images of weed and stubble (I,ii, 135-7). And see also Ophelia's violets (IV,v, 183-85). Lines 39-42 provide a link between images of flowers and of disease. The image of the woodcock and the springe (l.115) has its re-entry too (V,ii,310) with suitable irony; Laertes is caught in the toils of his own device.

Polonius

The friends thou hast, and their adoption tried, 62
Grapple them to thy soul with hoops of steel;
But do not dull thy palm with entertainment 64
Of each new-hatch'd, unfledg'd comrade. Beware 65
Of entrance to a quarrel, but, being in,
Bear 't that th' opposed may beware of thee.
Give every man thine ear, but few thy voice;
Take each man's censure, but reserve thy judgment. 69
Costly thy habit as thy purse can buy, 70
But not express'd in fancy; rich, not gaudy; 71
For the apparel oft proclaims the man,
And they in France of the best rank and station 73
Are most select and generous, chief in that.
Neither a borrower, nor a lender be;
For loan oft loses both itself and friend,
And borrowing dulls the edge of husbandry. 77
This above all: to thine own self be true,
And it must follow, as the night the day,
Thou canst not then be false to any man.
Farewell; my blessing season this in thee! 81
　Laertes. Most humbly do I take my leave, my lord.
　Polonius. The time invites you; go, your servants tend. 83
　Laertes. Farewell, Ophelia; and remember well
What I have said to you.
　Ophelia. 　　　　　'Tis in my memory lock'd,
And you yourself shall keep the key of it.
　Laertes. Farewell. 　　　　　[*Exit.*
　Polonius. What is 't, Ophelia, he hath said to you?
　Ophelia. So please you, something touching the
　　Lord Hamlet.
　Polonius. Marry, well bethought: 90
'Tis told me, he hath very oft of late
Given private time to you; and you yourself
Have of your audience been most free and bounteous.
If it be so,—as so 'tis put on me, 94
And that in way of caution,—I must tell you,
You do not understand yourself so clearly
As it behooves my daughter and your honour. 97
What is between you? give me up the truth.
　Ophelia. He hath, my lord, of late made many tenders 99
Of his affection to me.
　Polonius. Affection! pooh! you speak like a green girl, 101
Unsifted in such perilous circumstance. 102
Do you believe his tenders, as you call them?
　Ophelia. I do not know, my lord, what I should think.
　Polonius. Marry, I'll teach you: think yourself a baby,
That you have ta'en these tenders for true pay, 106
Which are not sterling. Tender yourself more dearly; 107
Or,—not to crack the wind of the poor phrase, 108
Running it thus,—you'll tender me a fool.
　Ophelia. My lord, he hath importun'd me with love
In honourable fashion. 111
　Polonius. Ay, fashion you may call it: go to, go to. 112
　Ophelia. And hath given countenance to his speech, 113
　　my lord,
With almost all the holy vows of heaven.
　Polonius. Ay, springes to catch woodcocks. I do know, 115
When the blood burns, how prodigal the soul 116

62. "adoption tried": friendship which has stood the test of time.

64-5. i.e., don't lose your power of discrimination by entertaining (entering into fellowship with) every new acquaintance you make.

65. "unfledg'd": literally, just out of the egg, i.e., immature.

69. "censure": opinion.

70. "habit": dress.

71. "express'd in fancy": showy.

73-4. i.e., it is particularly in their apparel that the French nobility display their taste and breeding.

77. "husbandry": thrift.

81. "season": ripen.

83. "tend": attend, wait.

90. "Marry": a common Elizabethan expletive for Mary, i.e., by the Virgin Mary.

94. "put on me": reported to me.

97. "behooves": is the duty of.

99. "tenders": offers.

101. "green": We still use this to mean inexperienced or foolish.

102. i.e., untested in such a dangerous affair as courtship.

106-09. "tenders . . . tender": Polonius makes a double pun: "tenders"—counters (like poker chips), "tender"—value, "tender"—show, offer.

107. "sterling": true currency.

108. "crack the wind of": overwork: an equestrian figure.

111. "fashion": a whim, not lasting; cf. l.6 above.

112. "go to": the Elizabethan equivalent of the modern "get along with you"; an expression of impatience.

113. "given . . . speech": given his words confirmation.

115. "springes": snares.
"woodcocks": foolish birds which are easily caught. Why do you suppose Polonius is so cynical?

116. "blood burns": passion is aroused. "prodigal": extravagantly.

Ophelia

ACT I SCENE IV

We are returned immediately to the setting and expectant mood of Scene One; the difference is that Hamlet can hardly wait for the apparition. The three are like any group who must kill time in pre-occupied expectation. They talk about the weather; they ask each other the time. Expectancy all over the theater rises as the time comes. Imagine the effect when the tense silence is broken suddenly by a flourish of trumpets and a cannon going off. The student or reader of these plays must constantly be picturing in his imagination the effects of spectacle and sound the stage directions indicate. A cannon shot less than one hundred feet from your ear can be a shattering enough experience if you expect it, but this is not the case here.

The drinking custom which now gives them a topic for conversation richer than the weather was of course prepared for above (I,ii, 125-8). Both here and later (V,ii, 271-5) it provides our most vivid dramatic symbol for the luxurious excess of Claudius and his court. We somehow feel the custom was not so much followed in Hamlet's father's days.

Lends the tongue vows: these blazes, daughter,   117
Giving more light than heat, extinct in both,
Even in their promise, as it is a-making,
You must not take for fire. From this time
Be somewhat scanter of your maiden presence;
Set your entreatments at a higher rate   122
Than a command to parley. For Lord Hamlet,
Believe so much in him, that he is young,
And with a larger tether may he walk   125
Than may be given you: in few, Ophelia,   126
Do not believe his vows, for they are brokers,   127
Not of that dye which their investments show,   128
But mere implorators of unholy suits,
Breathing like sanctified and pious bonds,   130
The better to beguile. This is for all: 131
I would not, in plain terms, from this time forth,
Have you so slander any moment's leisure,   133
As to give words or talk with the Lord Hamlet.
Look to 't, I charge you; come your ways.   135

Ophelia. I shall obey, my lord.   [*Exeunt.*

Scene four.

(THE PLATFORM)

Enter HAMLET, HORATIO, *and* MARCELLUS.

Hamlet. The air bites shrewdly; it is very cold.   1
Horatio. It is a nipping and an eager air.   2
Hamlet. What hour now?
Horatio.   I think it lacks of twelve.
Marcellus. No, it is struck.
Horatio. Indeed? I heard it not: then it draws near
    the season   5
Wherein the spirit held his wont to walk.   6
[*A flourish of trumpets, and ordnance shot off, within.*
What does this mean, my lord?
Hamlet. The king doth wake to-night and takes his rouse,   8
Keeps wassail and the swaggering up-spring reels;   9
And, as he drains his draughts of Rhenish down,   10
The kettle-drum and trumpet thus bray out   11
The triumph of his pledge.
Horatio.   Is it a custom?   12
Hamlet. Ay, marry, is 't:
But to my mind,—though I am native here
And to the manner born,—it is a custom   15
More honour'd in the breach than the observance.   16
This heavy-headed revel east and west   17
Makes us traduc'd and tax'd of other nations;   18
They clepe us drunkards, and with swinish phrase   19
Soil our addition; and indeed it takes   20
From our achievements, though perform'd at height,   21
The pith and marrow of our attribute.   22
So, oft it chances in particular men,
That for some vicious mole of nature in them,   24
As, in their birth,—wherein they are not guilty,
Since nature cannot choose his origin,—

117-20. i.e., these flashes (blazes) of passion must not be taken for true love (fire), for they are extinguished (extinct) as soon as they start.

122-23. "Set ... parley": when he asks you for an interview (entreatments), don't consider it as a command to negotiate (parley).

125. "larger tether": greater freedom.

126. "in few": in short.

127-31. i.e., his vows are not what they seem; they are merely go-betweens (implorators) whose purpose is to deceive you in the course of an unholy suit.

127. "brokers": salesmen.

128. "investments": garments.

130. "bonds": i.e., marriage bonds.

131. "beguile": betray.
     "This is for all": to sum up.

133. "slander ... leisure": abuse any moment of leisure.

135. "come your ways": come along; an everyday Elizabethan phrase.

1. "shrewdly": bitterly.

2. "eager": sharp.

5. "season": time of night.

6. "held ... walk": has been in the habit of walking.

8. "wake": hold a night of revel.
   "rouse": a toast in which all glasses must be drained before lowering.

9. "wassail": revelry, carousing.
   "up-spring": a high-kicking, wild German dance.
   "reels": is either a verb of which "up-spring" is the subject, or a noun modified by "up-spring."

10. "Rhenish": wine made in the Rhineland.

11-12. A Danish drinking custom. See also I, ii, 125-8.

11. "bray out": celebrate.

12. "The triumph of his pledge": victorious in celebration of the health he drinks.

15. "to the manner born": accustomed to it since a child.

16. i.e., it is a custom which would bring us more honor if we disregarded rather than kept it.

17. "heavy-headed": a transferred epithet. It is those who take part in the revel who become "heavy-headed" (thick-headed).

18. "traduc'd and tax'd": defamed and censored.
    "of": by.

19. "clepe": call.

19-20. "with swinish . . . addition": i.e., they smirch our honor by calling us swine.

20. "it": viz., drunkenness.

21. "though . . . height": though of the greatest merit.

22. "pith . . . attribute": essential part of our reputation.

24. "mole": blemish.

34

HAMLET

ACT I SCENE IV

Hamlet is led from his criticism of the custom to generalize about human nature (ll. 23-38), just as in I,ii, he was led from the contemplation of his mother's conduct to a generalization of woman's frailty. It is part of his character as a seeker after truth to induce principles from observations. Here as elsewhere his curious intelligence leads him along the path of ideas from his original preoccupation. It is perhaps at such moments that his nobility of mind chiefly shows. These lines (23-38) gain ironical force from their unconscious self-revelation (cf. III,ii, 66-75). What is Hamlet's "particular fault" that breaks "down the pales and forts of reason"?

The audience, or the reader, follows the line of Hamlet's thought and relaxes just as he and Horatio and Marcellus do, forgetting for a moment the ghost. Just at this moment it silently appears. Three times in this act the ghost enters, and each time Shakespeare has been able to take us by surprise, even when we most expect it.

The impact of line 39 is very much in the hands of the actor who, by his tone, inflection, and gesture can suggest anything from mere shock to something like prayer, can fuse or isolate the emotions of fear and love Hamlet feels. How would you speak the line? With what gesture?

Hamlet's recklessness of life (l. 65) is close to his wish for death (I,ii, 129-32) though not identical with it. This reckless expression should be recalled when Hamlet will accuse himself of cowardice (See III,i, 83; II,ii, 575, 571-3; IV,iv, 42-3).

Horatio has returned to his Protestant view of the ghost as tempter in disguise, a possibility that Hamlet himself (l.40) does not lose sight of even in the shock of first meeting. This uncertainty is important (see II,ii, 603-8).

Horatio's words (ll. 72-4) come ironically true, (depending on how you define madness).

Hamlet's violent struggle against the well-meant restraint of his friends provides just the right flurry of action for the moment. Without it, Hamlet's exit would be rather colorless. At the same time we see for the first time a Hamlet capable of sudden and purposeful violence, a man of impulsive temper and physical force who is not afraid to draw a sword (cf. III,iv, 23; V,ii, the duel).

By the o'ergrowth of some complexion, 27
Oft breaking down the pales and forts of reason,
Or by some habit that too much o'er-leavens
The form of plausive manners; that these men,
Carrying, I say, the stamp of one defect,
Being nature's livery, or fortune's star, 32
His virtues else, be they as pure as grace, 33
As infinite as man may undergo, 34
Shall in the general censure take corruption 35
From that particular fault: the dram of evil 36
Doth all the noble substance often dout,
To his own scandal.

Enter GHOST.

Horatio.   Look, my lord, it comes.
Hamlet. Angels and ministers of grace defend us!
Be thou a spirit of health or goblin damn'd, 40
Bring with thee airs from heaven or blasts from hell,
Be thy intents wicked or charitable,
Thou com'st in such a questionable shape 43
That I will speak to thee: I'll call thee Hamlet,
King, father; royal Dane, O! answer me:
Let me not burst in ignorance; but tell
Why thy canoniz'd bones, hearsed in death, 47
Have burst their cerements; why the sepulchre, 48
Wherein we saw thee quietly inurn'd, 49
Hath op'd his ponderous and marble jaws,
To cast thee up again. What may this mean,
That thou, dead corse, again in complete steel 52
Revisits thus the glimpses of the moon,
Making night hideous; and we fools of nature 54
So horridly to shake our disposition 55
With thoughts beyond the reaches of our souls?
Say, why is this, wherefore? what should we do?
          [*The* Ghost *beckons* HAMLET.
Horatio. It beckons you to go away with it,
As if it some impartment did desire 59
To you alone.
Marcellus.   Look, with what courteous action
It waves you to a more removed ground:
But do not go with it.
Horatio.   No, by no means.
Hamlet. It will not speak; then, will I follow it.
Horatio. Do not, my lord.
Hamlet.   Why, what should be the fear?
I do not set my life at a pin's fee; 65
And for my soul, what can it do to that, 66
Being a thing immortal as itself?
It waves me forth again; I'll follow it.
Horatio. What if it tempt you toward the flood, my lord, 69
Or to the dreadful summit of the cliff
That beetles o'er his base into the sea, 71
And there assume some other horrible form,
Which might deprive your sovereignty of reason 73
And draw you into madness? think of it;
The very place puts toys of desperation, 75
Without more motive, into every brain
That looks so many fathoms to the sea
And hears it roar beneath.
Hamlet. It waves me still. Go on, I'll follow thee.

27-30. i.e., by the overdevelopment of some quality which breaks down the restraints of reason, or by the acquisition of some habit which sours ("o'er-leavens"—ferments) sweet ("plausive"—agreeable) manners.

32. i.e., either inborn or the result of bad luck.

33. "His virtues else": his other virtues.

34. "undergo": sustain, or in other words, possess.

35. "general censure": public's judgment.

36-38. "the . . . scandal": a much disputed passage. Perhaps a line is missing. The general meaning seems to be that it takes only a small portion of evil to bring a scandal on the entire substance, however noble it may otherwise be.

40. "spirit of health": two possible meanings: (1) a saved (healthy) soul, not a lost one; or (2) a healing or beneficent spirit.
"goblin damn'd": damned fiend—an agent of the devil. Hamlet, from the very first, seems to question the authenticity of the ghost as the true spirit of his father.

43. "questionable": inviting question.

47. "canoniz'd": consecrated.
"hearsed": buried.

48. "cerements": winding-sheets.

49. "inurn'd": buried.

52. "complete steel": full armor.

54. "fools": dupes. Nature hides supernatural truth from our eyes.

55. "disposition": self-control.

59. "impartment": communication.

65. "a pin's fee": a pin's value.

66-67. "it" and "itself": both refer to the ghost.

69. "flood": sea. Elsinore is situated on the Danish coast.

71. "beetles o'er": overhangs.

73. i.e., which might dethrone your reason.

75. "toys of desperation": desperate fancies, or impulses—referring to the well-known impulse so many people have to jump off a high place.

35

HAMLET

ACT I SCENE IV

Line 90 has become so much a household saying that it is difficult to take as it comes on the stage. The remark has importance as the logical descendant of Francisco's speech (I,i, 9). (See also I,i, 69; I,ii, 254-7; I,v, 188-9.) Thus are we kept aware of vague feelings and strange portents in the public eye: "Foul deeds will rise,/ Though all the earth o'erwhelm them, to men's eyes."

ACT I SCENE V

This scene follows directly after the previous one with no break. Hamlet and the ghost, having left the stage by one of the two exit doors, reappear presently through the other door (or perhaps through the inner stage), just as, or even slightly before, Horatio and Marcellus follow them through the door by which they left the stage. The audience, due to the flexibility of Shakespeare's open stage, would accept the change of place semiconsciously in somewhat this form: The ghost leads Hamlet away. (Pause) Ah! Here they come. This must be the place to which the ghost has led him.

With respect to the ghost, Shakespeare's problem was delicate. The audience must feel that it is indeed the spirit of Hamlet's father, while at the same time admitting that Hamlet's and Horatio's suspicion that it may be the devil is understandable and well-founded. In devising this he could count on the fact that the traditional Roman Catholic belief in ghosts was older and simpler, and had a firmer hold on the popular imagination (though not the popular reason) than the newer more intellectual view of the Protestants. In emphasizing the Wittenberg connection of Hamlet and Horatio, he prepared the audience to expect a Protestant bias in their thought together with a scholarly respect for reason. Shakespeare then contrives that the ghost's language, like his visible presence, should carry the accents of dignity, sincerity, and authority; and should express gentleness (ll. 84-8) and sadness (ll.45-50). We are thus inclined to accept the ghost's account of his term in Purgatory (ll. 11-22) and his statement, "I

Marcellus. You shall not go, my lord.
Hamlet.   Hold off your hands!
Horatio. Be rul'd; you shall not go.
Hamlet.   My fate cries out,
And makes each petty artery in this body
As hardy as the Nemean lion's nerve. [*Ghost beckons.* 83
Still am I call'd. Unhand me, gentlemen,
                              [*Breaking from them.*
By heaven! I'll make a ghost of him that lets me: 85
I say, away! Go on, I'll follow thee.
                    [*Exeunt* Ghost *and* HAMLET.
Horatio. He waxes desperate with imagination.
Marcellus. Let's follow; 'tis not fit thus to obey him.
Horatio. Have after. To what issue will this come?
Marcellus. Something is rotten in the state of Denmark.
Horatio. Heaven will direct it.
Marcellus.   Nay, let's follow him.
                                        [*Exeunt.*

Scene five.

(ANOTHER PART OF THE PLATFORM)

Enter Ghost *and* HAMLET.

Hamlet. Whither wilt thou lead me? speak; I'll go
    no further.
Ghost. Mark me.
Hamlet.   I will.
Ghost.   My hour is almost come, 2
When I to sulphurous and tormenting flames
Must render up myself.
Hamlet.   Alas! poor ghost.
Ghost. Pity me not, but lend thy serious hearing
To what I shall unfold.
Hamlet.   Speak; I am bound to hear. 6
Ghost. So art thou to revenge, when thou shalt hear.
Hamlet. What?
Ghost. I am thy father's spirit;
Doom'd for a certain term to walk the night,
And for the day confin'd to fast in fires,
Till the foul crimes done in my days of nature 12
Are burnt and purg'd away. But that I am forbid.
To tell the secrets of my prison-house,
I could a tale unfold whose lightest word
Would harrow up thy soul, freeze thy young blood,
Make thy two eyes like stars start from their spheres, 17
Thy knotted and combined locks to part, 18
And each particular hair to stand on end, 19
Like quills upon the fretful porpentine: 20
But this eternal blazon must not be 21
To ears of flesh and blood. List, list, O list! 22
If thou didst ever thy dear father love—
Hamlet. O God!
Ghost. Revenge his foul and most unnatural murder.
Hamlet. Murder!
Ghost. Murder most foul, as in the best it is; 27

83. "hardy": strong.
"Nemean": the lion slain by Hercules.
"nerve": sinew.

85. "lets": hinders—still preserved in legal phraseology, e.g., without let or hindrance.

2. "Mark me": take special note of what I have to tell you.

6. "bound": obliged.

12. "nature": natural life.

17. "spheres": orbits as of planets (stars).

18. "knotted and combined locks": i.e., lying together in a mass.

19. "particular": individual.

20. "porpentine": porcupine.

21. "eternal blazon": description of eternity.

22. "List": listen.

27. "in the best": at best, i.e., even with the best cause.

HAMLET

ACT I SCENE V

am thy father's spirit'' (l.9).

"O my prophetic soul!" (l.40; cf. I,ii, 255).

"My most seeming virtuous queen" (l.46; cf. I,ii, 76).

Notice the hammering home of the key words, "murder" and "revenge" (ll. 25-31). Hamlet's speech which ends this passage (ll. 29-31) is most emphatic, yet his later actions contradict it (see III,iv, 106-10). This disagreement between Hamlet's promise and his performance is one of the play's crucial problems, and part of our task in this commentary must be to enable you to account for it. There is no reason to doubt Hamlet's sincerity at this point. We have already noticed on two occasions how quickly and wholeheartedly Hamlet throws himself into new situations to the exclusion of all else (see I,ii, 160-81; I,iv, 13-38). It is part of his sympathetic, finely balanced nature and grown melancholy to run so impulsively to extremes.

The ghost's employment (ll.32-3) of the rot and weed imagery serves to unite these two sets of images and to keep their echo alive in our ears (cf.I,ii, 135-7; I,iii, 39-40; I,iv,90). The speech will have an ironical twist in Hamlet's memory during the period when he does not stir.

The ghost's long narrative completes the tale of Claudius' villainy and Denmark's rottenness. Gauge the realization of the newly discovered extent of Claudius' hypocrisy in the young man who knew not "seems."

The ghost's dwelling on the physical details of the effect of the poison, (like leprosy which rots the body, before it dies) gives us a physical symbol of Claudius, and his canker's effect on Denmark (see V,ii, 69). For the common Elizabethan equation of the king's health with the nation's, see I,iii, 20-4 and III, iii, 11-23.

The great point the ghost makes of the horror of his being cut off without a chance to cleanse his soul and prepare it for death (confession, penance, prayer, absolution) has its echo in Hamlet's reasoning when he spares Claudius at his prayers (III,iii, 80-95).

This, Hamlet's second soliloquy, beginning line 92, (we shall not count the four lines at the end of Scene Two), continues the headlong enthusiasm of lines 29-31 ("Haste me to know 't, that . . . sweep to my revenge"), but now his excitement has mounted to that dangerous point beyond which it

---

But this most foul, strange, and unnatural. 28

Hamlet. Haste me to know't, that I, with wings as swift 29
As meditation or the thoughts of love,
May sweep to my revenge.

Ghost.   I find thee apt, 31
And duller shouldst thou be than the fat weed 32
That rots itself in ease on Lethe wharf, 33
Wouldst thou not stir in this. Now, Hamlet, hear:
'Tis given out, that sleeping in mine orchard,
A serpent stung me; so the whole ear of Denmark
Is by a forged process of my death 37
Rankly abus'd; but know, thou noble youth, 38
The serpent that did sting thy father's life
Now wears his crown.

Hamlet.   O my prophetic soul!
My uncle?

Ghost. Ay, that incestuous, that adulterate beast, 42
With witchcraft of his wit, with traitorous gifts,— 43
O wicked wit and gifts, that have the power
So to seduce!—won to his shameful lust
The will of my most seeming-virtuous queen.
O Hamlet! what a falling-off was there;
From me, whose love was of that dignity
That it went hand in hand even with the vow
I made to her in marriage; and to decline 50
Upon a wretch whose natural gifts were poor
To those of mine! 52
But virtue, as it never will be mov'd,
Though lewdness court it in a shape of heaven, 54
So lust, though to a radiant angel link'd,
Will sate itself in a celestial bed, 56
And prey on garbage.
But, soft! methinks I scent the morning air;
Brief let me be. Sleeping within mine orchard,
My custom always of the afternoon,
Upon my secure hour thy uncle stole, 61
With juice of cursed hebona in a vial, 62
And in the porches of mine ears did pour
The leperous distilment; whose effect 64
Holds such an enmity with blood of man
That swift as quicksilver it courses through
The natural gates and alleys of the body,
And with a sudden vigour it doth posset 68
And curd, like eager droppings into milk, 69
The thin and wholesome blood: so did it mine;
And a most instant tetter bark'd about, 71
Most lazar-like, with vile and loathsome crust 72
All my smooth body.
Thus was I, sleeping, by a brother's hand,
Of life, of crown, of queen, at once dispatch'd;
Cut off even in the blossoms of my sin, 76
Unhousel'd, disappointed, unanel'd, 77
No reckoning made, but sent to my account
With all my imperfections on my head:
O, horrible! O, horrible! most horrible!
If thou hast nature in thee, bear it not; 81
Let not the royal bed of Denmark be
A couch for luxury and damned incest. 83
But, howsoe'er thou pursu'st this act,
Taint not thy mind, nor let thy soul contrive 85

---

28. Twice the ghost uses the words "most unnatural." What is "most unnatural" about this particular murder?

29-30. A particularly fine simile. What could be swifter than thought, particularly if it is of love!

31. "apt": quick, ready.

32. "fat": thick, slimy, motionless.

33. "in ease": undisturbed.
"Lethe": the river of forgetfulness.

37. "forged process": false account.

38. "Rankly abus'd": greatly deceived.

42. "adulterate": adulterous.

43. "wit": cunning.

50. "decline": sink down both physically and morally.

52. "To": compared to.

54. "lewdness": sensuality, lust; the meaning here is though lust in the form of an angel woos it (virtue).

56. "sate . . . bed": weary of a heavenly union.

61. "secure": careless, unguarded.

62. "hebona": yew.

64. "leperous distilment": distillation producing leprosy.

68. "posset": curdle.

69. "eager": acid; cf. I, iv, 2.

71. "instant": immediate.
"tetter": skin eruption.
"bark'd about": encrusted, covered like bark on a tree.

72. "lazar-like": like leprosy.

76. i.e., cut off while in a state of sin and therefore in danger of eternal damnation.

77. "Unhousel'd": not having received the sacrament.
"disappointed": ill-equipped, unprepared.
"unanel'd": unanointed, not having received Extreme Unction (the last anointment of the dying).

81. "nature": natural feelings.

83. "luxury": lust.

85. "contrive": plot.

HAMLET

ACT I SCENE V

cannot be controlled and will spill over into frenzied speech and actions. With the other feelings that so move him, there is a kind of glee because his father's words give full justification to his hatred of Claudius, together with a command to act on it. He need no longer break his heart and hold his tongue (see I,ii, 159).

The content of the speech is in the nature of an elaborate vow of dedication. He addresses the whole universe to bear witness, and struggles to control his racing mind and collapsing body. He must remember; he will banish all else from his mind: studies, skills, entertainments. This separation from the old is emphasized later (l.167) when he refers to Horatio's philosophy. A few minutes before it was Hamlet's philosophy too.

But the first item he impresses on his newly erased memory is not his revenge, but, "O most pernicious woman!"

Having already imagined his memory as a table-book, he next takes out his own book. These ivory-paged notebooks were fashionable accessories carried by young gentlemen for recording memoranda and choice sayings. Most of the young gentlemen in the audience would carry one. His writing furiously in his tables seems a mad thing, the first really crazed action he commits. It is, in effect, an improvised ceremony putting a sort of final seal on his resolution. Most actors intensify this by having Hamlet swear on his sword, held up like a cross as he says lines 110-12. The above is the serious and symbolical side of his action. It has also a sort of wildly joking tone, making half-sane fun of Hamlet, the student, furiously recording the obvious in his notebook. This vein of treating the obvious as a great secret is carried on in his wild words to Horatio and Marcellus (ll. 123-4).

Compare the word "strange" (l.164) to l,i,69; l,ii,220; l,v,28.

During the remainder of the scene a number of curious things occur. Hamlet expresses a desire for secrecy and for solitude, both which we understand quite well. His insistence that the others swear "indeed" upon his sword is a continuation of the ceremonial impulse of the soliloquy. The rest is less easy. Why does he suddenly set Horatio at arm's length and mistrust him? The energy of his first excitement abates, and his words take on a sudden solidity and directness at lines 136-42. From this to the end, the excitement rises again, but is of a different

---

Against thy mother aught; leave her to heaven,
And to those thorns that in her bosom lodge,
To prick and sting her. Fare thee well at once!
The glow-worm shows the matin to be near,   89
And 'gins to pale his uneffectual fire;   90
Adieu, adieu! Hamlet, remember me.   [*Exit.*
  Hamlet. O all you host of heaven! O earth! What else?
And shall I couple hell? O fie! Hold, hold, my heart!
And you, my sinews, grow not instant old,
But bear me stiffly up! Remember thee!
Ay, thou poor ghost, while memory holds a seat
In this distracted globe. Remember thee!   97
Yea, from the table of my memory   98
I'll wipe away all trivial fond records,   99
All saws of books, all forms, all pressures past   100
That youth and observation copied there;
And thy commandment all alone shall live
Within the book and volume of my brain,
Unmix'd with baser matter: yes, by heaven!
O most pernicious woman!   105
O villain, villain, smiling, damned villain!
My tables,—meet it is I set it down,   107
That one may smile, and smile, and be a villain;
At least I'm sure it may be so in Denmark: [*Writing.*
So, uncle, there you are. Now to my word;   110
It is 'Adieu, adieu! remember me.'
I have sworn 't.
  Horatio. [*Within.*] My lord, my lord!
  Marcellus. [*Within.*]   Lord Hamlet!
  Horatio. [*Within.*]   Heaven secure him! 113
  Marcellus. [*Within.*] So be it!
  Horatio. [*Within.*] Hillo, ho, ho, my lord!   115
  Hamlet. Hillo, ho, ho, boy! come, bird, come.
        Enter HORATIO *and* MARCELLUS.
  Marcellus. How is 't, my noble lord?
  Horatio.   What news, my lord?
  Hamlet. O! wonderful.
  Horatio.   Good my lord, tell it.
  Hamlet. No; you will reveal it.
  Horatio. Not I, my lord, by heaven!
  Marcellus.   Nor I, my lord.
  Hamlet. How say you then, would heart of man once
    think it?
But you'll be secret?
  Horatio. }
  Marcellus. } Ay, by heaven, my lord.
  Hamlet. There's ne'er a villain dwelling in all Denmark
But he's an arrant knave.   124
  Horatio. There needs no ghost, my lord, come from
    the grave,
To tell us this.
  Hamlet.   Why, right; you are i' the right;
And so without more circumstance at all,   127
I hold it fit that we shake hands and part;
You, as your business and desire shall point you,—
For every man hath business and desire,
Such as it is,—and, for mine own poor part,
Look you, I'll go pray.
  Horatio. These are but wild and whirling words, my
    lord.

---

89. "matin": morning.

90. "'gins": begins.
"uneffectual": i.e., the daylight makes it ineffectual.

97. "globe": He holds his head with his hands.

98. "table": tablet; cf. l. 107 below.

99. "fond": foolish, trifling.

100. "saws": sayings, maxims, proverbs.
"forms": sketches.
"pressures": impressions.

105-6. To whom does each of these lines refer?

107. "My tables": cf. l. 98 above. Young men of education were in the habit of carrying ivory tablets for the purpose of recording good and worthwhile observations. See lines 99-101 above.
"meet": fitting, proper.

110. "word": either (1) watchword, or (2) motto.

113. "secure him": keep him from harm.

115. "Hillo, ho, ho": the falconer's cry to recall his hawk; hence "bird" in the following line.

124. "arrant": out-and-out.
"knave": scoundrel; really just another word for villain.

127. "circumstance": ceremony.

HAMLET

ACT I SCENE V

quality. Why does he speak so clownishly to the ghost's commands? What resolution prompts his planning to put on an antic disposition? By what train of thought or association does he arrive at the sense of lines 188-9?

As we read it, the "wild and whirling" words (ll. 119-32) are a defense. He cannot yet reduce his impression to a verbal expression, and catching at the levity of Horatio's falconer's cry (l.115), he carries it on till his mind steadies. Then his first concern is with secrecy. His antic replies to the ghost follow the forms of address used by sorcerers to the devil. Coming between line 138 and line 182, which contradict these two lines, are replies which must be most bewildering to Horatio and Marcellus. They may indicate Hamlet's mockery of Horatio's belief (see I,iv, 169-72), his own wavering conviction (see I,iv, 40-2), his desire to put Marcellus on a wrong scent, or a mere nervous flicker of hysteria (or of course, a mixture of these).

That Hamlet does assume false madness is true. His reason for doing so will best be discovered later on. Many feel that, reflecting back on his actions since the ghost's exit, he has come to realize how his emotional impulsiveness can break loose, and seeks in the antic disposition a means of explaining later outbursts.

The oddest revolution is expressed in those extremely important lines (188-9), with their echo of Francisco's, Horatio's, and Marcellus' misgivings about the state. First, Hamlet no longer conceives his task to be a simple revenge, but a setting right of the disjointed times. Second, he no longer looks forward to his task with impulsive enthusiasm, but with bitter resentment. Notice that after line 31, Hamlet never again utters the word revenge, and that what he records in his memory is the picture of smiling villainy. The simplest explanation of his sense of "cursed

Hamlet. I am sorry they offend you, heartily;
Yes, faith, heartily.

Horatio.   There's no offence, my lord.

Hamlet. Yes, by Saint Patrick, but there is, Horatio, 136
And much offence, too. Touching this vision here, 137
It is an honest ghost, that let me tell you; 138
For your desire to know what is between us,
O'ermaster 't as you may. And now, good friends, 140
As you are friends, scholars, and soldiers,
Give me one poor request.

Horatio. What is 't, my lord? we will.

Hamlet. Never make known what you have seen to-night.

Horatio. ⎫
Marcellus. ⎬ My lord, we will not.
       ⎭

Hamlet.   Nay, but swear 't.

Horatio.   In faith, 145
My lord, not I.

Marcellus.   Nor I, my lord, in faith.

Hamlet. Upon my sword. 147

Marcellus.   We have sworn, my lord, already.

Hamlet. Indeed, upon my sword, indeed.

Ghost. [*Beneath.*] Swear.

Hamlet. Ha, ha, boy! sayst thou so? art thou there,
    true-penny? 150
Come on,—you hear this fellow in the cellarage,— 151
Consent to swear.

Horatio.   Propose the oath, my lord.

Hamlet. Never to speak of this that you have seen,
Swear by my sword.

Ghost. [*Beneath.*] Swear.

Hamlet. Hic et ubique? then we'll shift our ground. 156
Come hither, gentlemen,
And lay your hands again upon my sword:
Never to speak of this that you have heard,
Swear by my sword.

Ghost. [*Beneath.*] Swear.

Hamlet. Well said, old mole! canst work i' the earth
    so fast?
A worthy pioner! once more remove, good friends. 163

Horatio. O day and night, but this is wondrous strange!

Hamlet. And therefore as a stranger give it welcome. 165
There are more things in heaven and earth, Horatio,
Than are dreamt of in your philosophy. 167
But come;
Here, as before, never, so help you mercy,
How strange or odd soe'er I bear myself,
As I perchance hereafter shall think meet
To put an antic disposition on, 172
That you, at such times seeing me, never shall,
With arms encumber'd thus, or this head-shake, 174
Or by pronouncing of some doubtful phrase,
As, 'Well, well, we know,' or, 'We could, an if we would;'
Or, 'If we list to speak,' or, 'There be, an if they might;' 177
Or such ambiguous giving out, to note 178
That you know aught of me: this not to do,
So grace and mercy at your most need help you, 180
Swear.

Ghost [*Beneath.*] Swear.   [*They swear.*

Hamlet. Rest, rest, perturbed spirit! So, gentlemen,

39

136-7. "Yes . . . too": It has been suggested that these words may have been spoken in an aside to Horatio, to whom Hamlet will later confide the truth.

137. "Touching": concerning.

138. "honest": true, i.e., not an agent of the devil; see I, iv, 40. There seems to be no doubt in Hamlet's mind at this point as to the ghost's authenticity. Explain then his later doubts.

140. "O'ermaster . . . may": overcome it as best you can. In other words, Hamlet says he has no intentions of enlightening them.

145-6. i.e., in faith, I will not reveal it.

147. "Upon my sword": "Mr. Garrick produced me a passage, I think, in Brantome, from which it appeared that it was common to swear upon the sword, that is, upon the cross which the old swords had upon the hilt" (Johnson).

150. "true-penny": a familiar phrase of affection—as we should say, "old boy" or "good chap."

151. "in the cellarage": the ghost's voice came from under the stage, or "cellarage" as it was called.

156. "Hic et ubique": here and everywhere.

163. "pioner": pioneer, miner. "remove": move.

165. "And . . . welcome.": welcome it in your mind without understanding it, as you would a stranger into your house.

167. The word "philosophy" was commonly used to mean natural philosophy or science.

172. "antic disposition": mad behavior.

174. "encumber'd": folded.

177. "There . . . might": i.e., there are those who could tell a story if only they were permitted.

178. "giving out": suggestion.

180. "grace and mercy": i.e., God's grace and mercy; cf. l. 169 above.

HAMLET

ACT I SCENE V

spite" is that he has a tragic glimpse of what his new knowledge and new purpose do to the life he had, in happier days, planned for himself (see commentary on V,ii).

With all my love I do commend me to you: 184
And what so poor a man as Hamlet is
May do, to express his love and friending to you   186
God willing, shall not lack. Let us go in together;
And still your fingers on your lips, I pray.
The time is out of joint; O cursed spite,
That ever I was born to set it right!
Nay, come, let's go together.   [*Exeunt.*

184. "me": myself. Hamlet requests the sympathy, understanding, and forebearance of his friends, suggesting that they will do this in return for the love he bears them.

186. "friending": friendship.

40

HAMLET

ACT II SCENE I

After the terrible communication delivered from father to son across the gulf of death, the picture here of Polonius attempting to spy on his son at a considerable distance is comical and even comfortable, especially when we learn that his motive is pure nosiness (l.73). Reynaldo's mission illustrates Polonius' mistrust of his son, and Polonius' idea of dishonor reveals (l.28) shabby morality. There is pathos, too, in this old fusspot. He is lonely separated from his son, and gropes in the dark with his baits of falsehood for contact with Laertes.

Polonius is not the only person who seems at this point to be rummaging in the dark. Hamlet, cut off from association with those he loved, broods in uncertainty. Claudius smiles over his royal rouse in ignorance of Hamlet's knowledge. It is a moment of poise.

This poise is first disturbed by the "affright" of Ophelia at Hamlet's silent visit. In her discription of the episode, where does one draw the line between genuine emotion and feigned madness? That is, is it Hamlet's aim through mad behavior to put Polonius on a wrong scent regarding the cause of his disorder, or is he simply taking this way, which will require no explanation, to take a last regretful look at a love that was?

ACT TWO, scene one.

(A Room in Polonius' House)

Enter POLONIUS *and* REYNALDO.

Polonius. Give him this money and these notes, 1
    Reynaldo.

Reynaldo. I will, my lord.

Polonius. You shall do marvellous wisely, good
    Reynaldo,
Before you visit him, to make inquiry
Of his behaviour.

Reynaldo.   My lord, I did intend it.

Polonius. Marry, well said, very well said. Look
    you sir,
Inquire me first what Danskers are in Paris; 7
And how, and who, what means, and where they keep, 8
What company, at what expense; and finding
By this encompassment and drift of question 10
That they do know my son, come you more nearer 11
Than your particular demands will touch it:
Take you, as 'twere, some distant knowledge of him; 13
As thus, 'I know his father, and his friends,
And, in part, him'; do you mark this, Reynaldo?

Reynaldo. Ay, very well, my lord.

Polonius. 'And, in part, him; but,' you may say, 'not
    well:
But if 't be he I mean, he's very wild,
Addicted so and so;' and there put on him 19
What forgeries you please; marry, none so rank 20
As may dishonour him; take heed of that;
But, sir, such wanton, wild, and usual slips
As are companions noted and most known 23
To youth and liberty.

Reynaldo.   As gaming, my lord?

Polonius. Ay, or drinking, fencing, swearing, quarreling,
Drabbing; you may go so far. 26

Reynaldo. My lord, that would dishonour him.

Polonius. Faith, no; as you may season it in the 28
    charge.
You must not put another scandal on him,
That he is open to incontinency; 30
That's not my meaning; but breathe his faults so quaintly 31
That they may seem the taints of liberty,
The flash and outbreak of a fiery mind,
A savageness in unreclaimed blood, 34
Of general assault.

Reynaldo.   But, my good lord,— 35

Polonius. Wherefore should you do this?

Reynaldo.   Ay, my lord, 36
I would know that.

Polonius.   Marry, sir, here's my drift; 37
And I believe it is a fetch of warrant: 38
You laying these slight sullies on my son, 39
As 'twere a thing a little soil'd i' the working, 40
Mark you,

1. "him": i.e., Laertes.
    "notes": letters.

7. "Danskers": Danes.

8. "what means": what their income is.
    "keep": lodge.

10. i.e., by this roundabout mode of inquiry.

11-12. "more nearer . . . touch it": i.e., without asking any direct questions find out more about him.

13. "Take": assume.

19. "put on him": charge him with.

20. "forgeries": inventions, viz., of misconduct.
    "rank": gross.

23. "companions noted": frequently observed as accompanying youth.

26. "Drabbing": associating with strumpets.

28. "Faith": a colloquial interjection meaning, in very truth.

28. "season": qualify.

30. "incontinency": debauchery. The explanation of the apparent contradiction between this and line 28 above is that Polonius does not mind Laertes drabbing, providing he does not do it too openly.

31. "quaintly": skillfully.

34. "unreclaimed": untamed.

35. "Of general assault": common to all men.

36. "Wherefore": why.

37. "drift": intention.

38. i.e., I believe it is a trick guaranteed to bring results.

39. "sullies": blemishes.

40. i.e., as if it were merely something slightly soiled by use.

41

HAMLET

ACT II SCENE I

Hamlet's feelings toward Ophelia must be mixed from the following ingredients: 1) his love for her (see V,i, 279-81); 2) his regret for a happy life that might have been ("O cursed spite"); 3) his disillusion and disgust with life (I,ii, 132-7); 4) his doubt of the constancy of women's love ("Frailty thy name is woman") reinforced as it has been by Ophelia's (to him) inexplicable rejection of his attentions (ll. 108-10); 5) his sense that under his new destiny there is no room for the sweets of love (I,v, 98-101). We may sense these feelings behind his piteous sigh (ll. 94-5), and judge that they provide his motive for visiting Ophelia, to take sad farewell and to show her what a monster she has made of him (see III,i, 140-1).

On the other hand, his love melancholy is too perfectly staged to be quite convincing. The Elizabethan figure of the melancholy lover, part comical, part pathetic, with his pale and drooping face, weak knees, fixed gaze, windy sighs, and disarranged clothing was a stock character in the popular imagination and would be recognized and identified by the audience as readily as it is by Polonius ("These indeed seem,/ For they are actions that a man might play" [I,ii, 83-4]). Now Hamlet's mental disturbance is not centered on Ophelia, as Claudius is quick to see (III,i, 165), but on much darker matters. We may conclude that while Hamlet's disappointment over Ophelia is keen, his guise of love-melancholy is put on. This example of the antic disposition (see I,v, 171-2) may be deliberately assumed to mislead Polonius (it certainly succeeds in doing so), or may be in that same spirit of self-mockery we noticed above when he wrote Claudius down in his notebook. Then he felt an uncontrollable impulse to express his resolution in a bitter caricature of the scholar with his notebook. Now he may well have felt a need to express the tragic distortion of his love in the same satirical vein, at once to act it out and to ridicule it. Hamlet has first been introduced to us as a scholar I,ii,) and lover (I,iii), but his study has not prepared him to understand evil, nor his love to comprehend infidelity, and now his destiny makes both seem trivial toys, "sweet, not lasting."

Your party in converse, him you would sound,   42
Having ever seen in the prenominate crimes
The youth you breathe of guilty, be assur'd,
He closes with you in this consequence;
'Good sir,' or so; 'friend,' or 'gentleman,'
According to the phrase or the addition   47
Of man and country.
   Reynaldo.   Very good, my lord.
   Polonius. And then, sir, does he this,—he does,—
What was I about to say? By the mass I was about
To say something: where did I leave?
   Reynaldo. At 'closes in the consequence.'
At 'friend or so,' and 'gentleman.'
   Polonius. At 'closes in the consequence,' ay, marry;
He closes with you thus: 'I know the gentleman;
I saw him yesterday, or t' other day,
Or then, or then; with such, or such; and, as you say,
There was a' gaming; there o'ertook in 's rouse;   58
There falling out at tennis;' or perchance,   59
'I saw him enter such a house of sale,'
Videlicet, a brothel, or so forth.   61
See you now;
Your bait of falsehood takes this carp of truth;   63
And thus do we of wisdom and of reach,   64
With windlasses, and with assays of bias,   65
By indirections find directions out: 66
So by my former lecture and advice
Shall you my son. You have me, have you not?   68
   Reynaldo. My lord, I have.
   Polonius.   God be wi' you; fare you well.
   Reynaldo. Good my lord!   70
   Polonius. Observe his inclination in yourself.   71
   Reynaldo. I shall, my lord.
   Polonius. And let him ply his music.
   Reynaldo.   Well, my lord.   73
   Polonius. Farewell!   [*Exit* REYNALDO.

Enter OPHELIA.

       How now, Ophelia! what's the matter?
   Ophelia. O! my lord, my lord, I have been so affrighted!
   Polonius. With what, in the name of God?
   Ophelia. My lord, as I was sewing in my closet,   77
Lord Hamlet, with his doublet all unbrac'd;   78
No hat upon his head; his stockings foul'd,
Ungarter'd, and down gyved to his ankle;   80
Pale as his shirt; his knees knocking each other;
And with a look so piteous in purport
As if he had been loosed out of hell
To speak of horrors, he comes before me.
   Polonius. Mad for thy love?
   Ophelia.   My lord, I do not know;   85
But truly I do fear it.
   Polonius.   What said he?
   Ophelia. He took me by the wrist and held me hard,
Then goes he to the length of all his arm,
And with his other hand thus o'er his brow,
He falls to such perusal of my face
As he would draw it. Long stay'd he so;   91
At last, a little shaking of mine arm,
And thrice his head thus waving up and down,

42-5. If the person you are questioning has ever seen Laertes guilty of the aforementioned (prenominate) crimes, be sure he will respond as follows.

47. "addition": title. See I, iv, 20.

58. "a'": a colloquial expression for "he." "o'ertook . . . rouse": drunk.

59. "falling out": quarreling.

61. "Videlicet": namely, viz.

63. "carp": a fish. Explain the figure.

64. "we . . . reach": i.e., we men of wisdom and breadth of understanding.

65. "windlasses": roundabout means. "assays of bias": This is a metaphor from the game of lawn-bowling: the weight in the bowl which causes it to follow a curved line is called the "bias." Hence the meaning of the phrase is "indirect attempts."

66. i.e., by indirect means we find out how to proceed.

68. "You have me": You understand me?

70. "Good my lord": This inversion of "My good lord" is frequent throughout the play. It was a common form of courtesy and respect.

71. "in": for.

73. "let . . . music": George Rylands suggests that this may mean, let him go his own way and enjoy himself. What support is there for this interpretation? Another reading is, give his own pretty story.

77. "closet": private room.

78. "doublet": a short, close-fitting coat which was fastened (braced) to the hose (short breeches) by laces. "When a man was relaxing or careless of appearance, he 'unbraced', as a modern man takes off his coat or unbuttons his waistcoat." (G. B. Harrison).

80. "down-gyved": fallen, like fetters, about his ankles.

85. Polonius' assumption is natural since Hamlet's appearance was the conventional one of a disappointed lover. Cf. Rosalind's description of a lover's appearance in AS YOU LIKE IT, III,ii, 397-400.

91. "As": as if.

HAMLET

ACT II SCENE I

Polonius is not merely misled, he is enlightened. He has seen what he had not imagined, that a young prince can be virtuous and sincere (II. 110-17). His sorrow for what he thinks he has caused does the old man credit; he is no villain. Thus Hamlet's first recorded action has captured the conscience of Polonius, and caused a small disruption of Denmark's false peace. One element in the unfolding action of the play is the inevitable spread of "discord and dismay" (see IV,i, 45) through the court as the evil comes to the surface and disrupts the world of "seems."

ACT II SCENE II

This scene in the castle lobby is the longest in the play, and one of the most characteristic in that its tensions and conflicts are such as can not immediately be expressed in action. It is a scene of secret intentions groping obscurely towards their goals by "indirections." In it Claudius and Polonius lay traps to catch at the cause of Hamlet's transformation, and they or their agents are met by the shafts of Hamlet's antic wit. We are given a deeper insight into the characters of Claudius, Gertrude, Polonius, and Hamlet, an opportunity to study the nature and effects of the antic disposition, and an outstanding example of Hamlet's variety of interest and impulsiveness of decision. One watches through most of this scene the fortunes of the world of appearances as both Claudius and Hamlet work on it, the one to protect it, the other to upset it.

The scene is best divided for study and comment as follows: 1) The second meeting of the court (to l.169); 2) Hamlet and Polonius (to l.221); 3) Hamlet, Rosencrantz and Guildenstern (to l.423); 4) Hamlet and the players (to l.551); 5) Hamlet's soliloquy.

He rais'd a sigh so piteous and profound
That it did seem to shatter all his bulk
And end his being. That done, he lets me go,
And with his head over his shoulder turn'd,
He seem'd to find his way without his eyes;
For out o' doors he went without their help,
And to the last bended their light on me.
   Polonius Come, go with me; I will go seek the king.
This is the very ecstasy of love,   102
Whose violent property fordoes itself   103
And leads the will to desperate undertakings
As oft as any passion under heaven
That does afflict our natures. I am sorry.
What! have you given him any hard words of late?
   Ophelia. No, my good lord; but, as you did command,
I did repel his letters and denied
His access to me.
   Polonius.   That hath made him mad.   110
I am sorry that with better heed and judgment
I had not quoted him; I fear'd he did but trifle,   112
And meant to wrack thee; but, beshrew my jealousy!   113
By heaven, it is as proper to our age   114
To cast beyond ourselves in our opinions   115
As it is common for the younger sort
To lack discretion. Come, go we to the king:
This must be known; which, being kept close, might   118
   move
More grief to hide than hate to utter love.
Come.   [*Exeunt.*

Scene two.

(A Room in the Castle)

Enter KING, QUEEN, ROSENCRANTZ, GUILDENSTERN, *and* Attendants.

King. Welcome, dear Rosencrantz and Guildenstern!
Moreover that we much did long to see you,   2
The need we have to use you did provoke
Our hasty sending. Something have you heard
Of Hamlet's transformation; so call it,
Sith nor the exterior nor the inward man   6
Resembles that it was. What it should be
More than his father's death, that thus hath put him
So much from the understanding of himself,
I cannot dream of: I entreat you both,
That, being of so young days brought up with him,   11
And sith so neighbour'd to his youth and humour,   12
That you vouchsafe your rest here in our court   13
Some little time; so by your companies
To draw him on to pleasures, and to gather,
So much as from occasion you may glean,   16
Whe'r aught to us unknown afflicts him thus,
That open'd lies within our remedy.   18
   Queen. Good gentlemen, he hath much talk'd of you;
And sure I am two men there are not living
To whom he more adheres. If it will please you   21

102. "ecstasy": frenzy.

103. "property": nature.
"fordoes": destroys.

110. "access": admittance.

112. "quoted": noted.

113. "beshrew": a plague upon.
"jealousy": suspicion.

114. "proper": natural.

115. "cast . . . ourselves": be too clever.

118-19. "which . . . love": Apparently Polonius felt that the King and Queen would consider Ophelia too low in station to be consort to Hamlet. Here he says that it is better to risk their displeasure than to conceal the cause of Hamlet's madness which might have more dire consequences.

2. "Moreover": besides.

6. "Sith": since.

11. "of . . . days": from such early days.

12. "neighbour'd": close to.
"humour": behavior. Some editors put "havior" in place of "humour."

13. "vouchsafe . . . rest": consent to remain.

16. "from occasion": by chance.

18. "open'd": revealed.

21. "To . . . adheres": whom he regards more highly.

43

HAMLET

ACT II SCENE II

(1)

The stage direction calls for Attendants who do not speak during the scene. Their presence is none the less dramatically important. Claudius' aim is to keep smooth the smiling surface of the court. As long as its members attend him, his words and actions are public and official, and must be guarded. As a court scene (Quarto two again ushers it in with a trumpet flourish), this one is subtly different from the last. Claudius is more intent and less at his spacious ease. Hamlet's madness has been noticed, and has had the effect, not of allaying, but of stirring the King's concern so that he has sent for Rosencrantz and Guildenstern to keep close tab on the wayward Prince.

The role assigned to Rosencrantz and Guildenstern (ll. 13-18) is like that assigned by Polonius to Reynaldo. (Recall in this connection Claudius' assumption of fatherly relationship to Hamlet in I,ii.) They are school friends of Hamlet, that is, childhood friends, not fellow students at Wittenberg. They thus come into contrast with Horatio (see III,ii, 64-6). Their replies to the King and Queen show their pliable dispositions and their tendency to fawn on their superiors. There is something loathsome in the whole tone of hollow and syrupy politeness oozing from the flattering unction of the dialogue (see ll. 33-4 and elsewhere). This hollowness is especially clear in the King's opening speech.

The Queen's speeches are interesting. They could stem from honest concern for her son's health and happiness. How much does she know of the truth? To what extent is she Claudius' accomplice; to what extent merely his mistress? Notice that it is she, not Claudius, who says, "amen" to the good wishes of Rosencrantz and Guildenstern towards Hamlet (ll. 38-9). Her quiet reply to the King in lines 56-7 seems sad and resigned. (These lines from 54 to 58 sound rather like asides not particularly intended to be heard by the remaining attendants.) If she knew of the murder of Hamlet's father, she would not be apt to say exactly what she does in these lines. Later she seems ready to accept Polonius' opinion (l.152). It is understandable that she should. Hamlet's love for Ophelia is news to her (l.113). If it causes his madness it removes blame from her own wrong, for if we assume her ignorance of the murder for a moment, the only evil consequence of her love for Claudius has been its effect on Hamlet.

The news from Norway reminds us of the career of young Fortin-

---

To show us so much gentry and good will   22
As to expend your time with us awhile,
For the supply and profit of our hope,   24
Your visitation shall receive such thanks
As fits a king's remembrance.
   Rosencrantz.   Both your majesties
Might, by the sovereign power you have of us,
Put your dread pleasures more into command
Than to entreaty.
   Guildenstern.   But we both obey,
And here give up ourselves in the full bent,   30
To lay our service freely at your feet,
To be commanded.
   King. Thanks, Rosencrantz and gentle Guildenstern.
   Queen. Thanks, Guildenstern and gentle Rosencrantz;
And I beseech you instantly to visit
My too much changed son. Go, some of you,
And bring these gentlemen where Hamlet is.
   Guildenstern. Heavens make our presence and our
      practices   38
Pleasant and helpful to him!
   Queen.   Ay, amen!
   [*Exeunt* ROSENCRANTZ, GUILDENSTERN, *and some*
                    Attendants.
          Enter POLONIUS.
Polonius. The ambassadors from Norway, my good
    lord,
Are joyfully return'd.
   King. Thou still hast been the father of good news. 42
   Polonius. Have I, my Lord? Assure you, my good liege,
I hold my duty, as I hold my soul,
Both to my God and to my gracious king;
And I do think—or else this brain of mine
Hunts not the trail of policy so sure
As it hath us'd to do—that I have found
The very cause of Hamlet's lunacy.
   King. O! speak of that; that do I long to hear.
   Polonius. Give first admittance to the ambassadors;
My news shall be the fruit to that great feast.   52
   King. Thyself do grace to them, and bring them in. 53
                  [*Exit* POLONIUS.
He tells me, my dear Gertrude, he hath found
The head and source of all your son's distemper.   55
   Queen. I doubt it is no other but the main;   56
His father's death, and our o'erhasty marriage.   57
   King. Well, we shall sift him.
   Re-enter POLONIUS, *with* VOLTIMAND *and* CORNELIUS.
            Welcome, my good friends!   58
Say, Voltimand, what from our brother Norway?
   Voltimand. Most fair return of greetings and desires.
Upon our first, he sent out to suppress   61
His nephew's levies, which to him appear'd
To be a preparation 'gainst the Polack;
But, better look'd into, he truly found
It was against your highness: whereat griev'd,
That so his sickness, age, and impotence
Was falsely borne in hand, sends out arrests   67
On Fortinbras; which he, in brief, obeys,
Receives rebuke from Norway, and, in fine,   69
Makes vow before his uncle never more

44

---

22. "gentry": courtesy.

24. i.e., for the fulfillment and profitable conclusion of our hope.

30. "in . . . bent": completely.

38. "practices": proceedings.

42. "still": always.

52. "fruit": dessert.

53. "grace": honor.

55. "distemper": mental disorder.

56. "the main": the principal cause of all.

57. The Queen's confident, straightforward explanation should be noted.

58. "sift him": find out what he (Polonius) knows.

61. "first": i.e., audience, or representation.

67. "borne in hand": imposed upon. "arrests": orders to stop.

69. "in fine": in the end.

HAMLET

ACT II SCENE II

bras. His ready acceptance of his uncle-father's instructions shows that his thirst for action is stronger than his desire for revenge. In this he appears in contrast to Hamlet. We learn to expect his march through Denmark (IV,iv), though not as a threat to Danish peace. Claudius' diplomacy has been successful.

Polonius' fussiness and windiness reach a height here as he leads up to his great discovery. Perhaps he is building suspense to dramatize his disclosure. Perhaps he is embarrassed by the prospect of reading Hamlet's love letter to the court. It does sound oddly funny thus repeated. This is the third major appearance of Polonius. With each one, the comic side of his character has been more prominent, as witness his precepts (I,iii, 59-80), his losing his way in his own elaboration (II,i, 49-51). The apex of his ridiculousness is reached in his interview with Hamlet below.

The art referred to in line 95 is the art of rhetoric or public speaking which statesmen especially studied, and in which Polonius is excessively proud of his skill.

Hamlet's love letter is of the conventional Elizabethan type, with a complimentary address, a verse, and a humble conclusion. Through the conventional framework, his character shows: his impatience with merely conventional versifying, his intense and wholehearted passion, his student-like use of the word "machine" which at the same time reflects his low estimation of the body as compared with the spirit.

Gertrude

To give the assay of arms against your majesty. 71
Whereon old Norway, overcome with joy,
Gives him three thousand crowns in annual fee,
And his commission to employ those soldiers,
So levied as before, against the Polack;
With an entreaty, herein further shown, [*Giving a paper.*
That it might please you to give quiet pass 77
Through your dominions for this enterprise,
On such regards of safety and allowance 79
As therein are set down.
King.   It likes us well; 80
And at our more consider'd time we'll read, 81
Answer, and think upon this business:
Meantime we thank you for your well-took labour. 83
Go to your rest; at night we'll feast together: 84
Most welcome home.
        [*Exeunt* VOLTIMAND *and* CORNELIUS.
Polonius.   This business is well ended.
My liege, and madam, to expostulate 86
What majesty should be, what duty is,
Why day is day, night night, and time is time,
Were nothing but to waste night, day, and time.
Therefore, since brevity is the soul of wit, 90
And tediousness the limbs and outward flourishes, 91
I will be brief. Your noble son is mad:
Mad call I it; for, to define true madness,
What is 't but to be nothing else but mad?
But let that go.
Queen.   More matter, with less art. 95
Polonius. Madam, I swear I use no art at all. 96
That he is mad, 'tis true; 'tis true 'tis pity;
And pity 'tis 'tis true; a foolish figure;
But farewell it, for I will use no art.
Mad let us grant him, then; and now remains
That we find out the cause of this effect, 101
Or rather say, the cause of this defect, 102
For this effect defective comes by cause; 103
Thus it remains, and the remainder thus.
Perpend. 105
I have a daughter, have while she is mine;
Who, in her duty and obedience, mark,
Hath given me this: now, gather, and surmise. 108
To the celestial, and my soul's idol, the most beauti-
        fied Ophelia.— 109
That's an ill phrase, a vile phrase; 'beautified' is a
vile phrase; but you shall hear. Thus:
In her excellent white bosom, these, &c.—
Queen. Came this from Hamlet to her?
Polonius. Good madam, stay awhile; I will be faithful.
        Doubt thou the stars are fire;
        Doubt that the sun doth move;
        Doubt truth to be a liar; 117
        But never doubt I love.
O dear Ophelia! I am ill at these numbers: I have 119
not art to reckon my groans; but that I love thee best,
O most best! believe it. Adieu.
        Thine evermore, most dear lady, whilst this
                machine is to him, 123
                        Hamlet.
This in obedience hath my daughter shown me;

45

71. "assay of arms": trial of arms.

77. "quiet pass": unmolested passage.

79. "regards" . . . allowance": safeguards and conditions.

80. "likes": pleases.

81. "more consider'd": i.e., when we have time for more consideration.

83. "well-took": well-handled.

84. No opportunity for feasting and revelry is lost upon Claudius.

86. "expostulate": debate.

90. "wit": wisdom. What delicious unconscious irony!

91. "flourishes": ornaments.

95. i.e., get down to cases and never mind the rhetoric.

96. Polonius is secretly pleased by what he considers to be the Queen's flattering reference to his rhetorical powers.

101. "effect": result.

102. "defect": viz., his madness.

103. i.e., his madness must have a cause.

105. "Perpend": ponder; an affected, pedantic word.

108. "surmise": guess the meaning.

109. "celestial": i.e., heavenly. "beautified": beautiful. Some suppose the whole letter is ironical. However, there seems to be no grounds for this; it is just the love letter of a young man, beginning in the usual fashion, containing a rather forced jingle for which he apologizes, and ending on a note of genuine passion. The student comes out in the word "machine." (Dover Wilson.)

117. "Doubt": suspect, but not so in the other lines of the verse.

119. "numbers": verses.

123. "machine": i.e., body.

HAMLET

ACT II SCENE II

In lines 133-4, Polonius claims his awareness of Hamlet's love, which is true, but suggests his own alertness as his means of discovering it, which is false (see I,iii, 91-5). The stages of Hamlet's decline that Polonius relates (ll. 146-50) are the stock progression of the symptoms of love-melancholy (cf. II,i, 75 ff. and commentary). There is something coarse and thoughtless in the phrase, "loose my daughter to him," that makes the Hamlet in us wince a little, and prepares us to accept the Prince's insinuation at line 174 (see commentary below).

The King's lines from line 151 on show us clearly that he is not convinced by Polonius, whatever Gertrude thinks. Line 155 even suggests that he has more general reservations about Polonius' judgment. Poor Polonius becomes less and less the counselor, and more and more the dupe.

The principal business of this part of the scene under the guise of benevolent concern, has been to launch two different sly devices for finding the cause of Hamlet's madness. In this enterprise the principal actor is Claudius, who thus shows his uneasiness.

And more above, hath his solicitings, 126
As they fell out by time, by means, and place, 127
All given to mine ear.
King.   But how hath she
Receiv'd his love?
Polonius.   What do you think of me?
King. As of a man faithful and honourable.
Polonius. I would fain prove so. But what might 131
    you think,
When I had seen this hot love on the wing,—
As I perceiv'd it (I must tell you that) 133
Before my daughter told me,—what might you,
Or my dear majesty, your queen here, think,
If I had play'd the desk or table-book, 136
Or given my heart a winking, mute and dumb, 137
Or look'd upon this love with idle sight; 138
What might you think? No, I went round to work, 139
And my young mistress thus I did bespeak: 140
'Lord Hamlet is a prince, out of thy star; 141
This must not be:' and then I prescripts gave her, 142
That she should lock herself from his resort,
Admit no messengers, receive no tokens.
Which done, she took the fruits of my advice; 145
And he, repulsed,—a short tale to make,—
Fell into a sadness, then into a fast,
Thence to a watch, thence into a weakness, 148
Thence to a lightness; and by this declension 149
Into the madness wherein now he raves,
And all we mourn for.
King.   Do you think 'tis this? 151
Queen. It may be, very like. 152
Polonius. Hath there been such a time,—I'd fain
    know that,—
That I have positively said, ' 'Tis so,'
When it prov'd otherwise?
King.   Not that I know.
Polonius. Take this from this, if this be otherwise:
    [*Pointing to his head and shoulder.*
If circumstances lead me, I will find
Where truth is hid, though it were hid indeed
Within the centre.
King.   How may we try it further? 159
Polonius. You know sometimes he walks four hours
    together
Here in the lobby.
Queen.   So he does indeed.
Polonius. At such a time I'll loose my daughter to him;
Be you and I behind an arras then; 163
Mark the encounter; if he love her not,
And be not from his reason fallen thereon,
Let me be no assistant for a state,
But keep a farm, and carters.
King.   We will try it. 167
Queen. But look, where sadly the poor wretch comes
    reading.
Polonius. Away! I do beseech you, both away.
I'll board him presently.
    [*Exeunt* KING, QUEEN, *and* Attendants.

126. "more above": moreover.

127. "fell out": occurred.

131. "fain": gladly.

133. "I . . . that": is parenthetical. At what pains Polonius is to advertise his shrewd perceptivity.

136. i.e. if I had kept this secret in my mind as a thing shut up in a desk or book.

137. i.e. had connived at the affair by saying nothing.

138. "with . . . sight": with an indifferent eye.

139. "round": straight.

140. "bespeak": address.

141. "star": sphere, i.e. station in life.

142. "prescripts": instructions, commands.

145. "took the fruits of": followed.

148. "Watch": sleeplessness.

149. "lightness": light-headedness. "this declension": these stages in decline.

151. "And . . . for": for which we all mourn.

152. "like": likely.

159. "centre": i.e. of the earth. "try it": test it.

163. "arras": tapestry, commonly hung in Medieval castles from ceiling to floor for the prevention of drafts.

167. "keep . . . carters": i.e. turn country squire.

HAMLET

ACT II SCENE II

(2)

Even Polonius, before Hamlet is done with him, sees some "method" in his madness. The method is to use whatever situation comes up as a starting point for bitter remarks on the state of the world. And as we listen to him unpack his heart with satire, we appreciate better the breadth of his distaste and the height of the ideal from which the world looks so ill. Thus one use of the antic disposition is to put Hamlet somewhat in the place of a jester who has license to expose the follies of life. It is an ideal position for sniping at the world of seems. No wonder Claudius is disturbed.

The tone in which Hamlet's remarks here are usually delivered is quick and light. Polonius's questions are in the carefully spineless style used by elders to address children when they are ill at ease with them and do not know what to say.

Some of Hamlet's remarks need explanation for a modern audience. "You are a fishmonger," for instance, in addition to its ordinary meaning, (itself undignified enough for Polonius), meant also a procurer, and a fishmonger's daughter was a harlot.

It was a very old belief that the sun's heat directly bred maggots in carrion flesh; "good kissing carrion," suggests an amorous pleasure in the process. The whole remark depicts Hamlet's revulsion from the physical facts of love, a revulsion that is part of his disgust at his mother. The linking of this disgust with Ophelia is a tragic irony. It is followed by an even more bitter version of the idea. Ophelia is now placed in the position of the dead dog (i.e., mere flesh). Polonius' caution is mocked in irony that must be unconscious on Hamlet's part. The words "i' the sun" had the popular meaning of homeless, unsheltered, or exposed to danger. A connection was made between this and the use of the phrase in the Psalm (Number 121) regularly used in the marriage service, "So that the sun shall not burn thee by day, nor the moon by night." (The King James Bible has "smite" instead of burn. Thus the word "sun" in connection with a maiden came to have the cant meaning of lust, and "i' the sun," exposed to lust (cf. I,ii, 67). Again whether by design or involuntarily, Hamlet confirms Polonius in his error as to the cause of his madness.

"Into my grave" recalls Hamlet's death-wish. (See I,ii, 129-32; I,v, 188-9.)

Lines 197-201 give us yet another symbol of physical decay (cf. I,v, 68-73).

Enter HAMLET, *reading.*

O! give me leave.   170

How does my good Lord Hamlet?

Hamlet. Well, God a-mercy.   172

Polonius. Do you know me, my lord?

Hamlet. Excellent well; you are a fishmonger.   174

Polonius. Not I, my lord.

Hamlet. Then I would you were so honest a man.

Polonius. Honest, my lord!

Hamlet. Ay, sir; to be honest, as this world goes, is to be one man picked out of ten thousand.

Polonius. That's very true, my lord.

Hamlet. For if the sun breed maggots in a dead dog, being a good kissing carrion,—Have you a daughter? 182

Polonius. I have, my lord.

Hamlet. Let her not walk i' the sun: conception is a blessing; but as your daughter may conceive, friend, look to 't.   186

Polonius. [*Aside.*] How say you by that? Still harp- 187 ing on my daughter: yet he knew me not at first; he said I was a fishmonger: he is far gone, far gone: and truly in my youth I suffered much extremity for love; very near this. I'll speak to him again. What do you read, my lord?

Hamlet. Words, words, words.

Polonius. What is the matter, my lord?   194

Hamlet. Between who?

Polonius. I mean the matter that you read, my lord.

Hamlet. Slanders, sir: for the satirical rogue says here that old men have grey beards, that their faces are wrinkled, their eyes purging thick amber and 199 plum-tree gum, and that they have a plentiful lack of wit, together with most weak hams: all which, sir, though I most powerfully and potently believe, yet I hold it not honesty to have it thus set down; for your- 203 self, sir, shall grow old as I am, if, like a crab, you could go backward.

Polonius. [*Aside.*] Though this be madness, yet there is method in 't. Will you walk out of the air, my 207 lord?

Hamlet. Into my grave?

Polonius. Indeed, that is out o' the air. [*Aside.*] How pregnant sometimes his replies are! a happi- 211 ness that often madness hits on, which reason and sanity could not so prosperously be delivered of. I 213 will leave him, and suddenly contrive the means of 214 meeting between him and my daughter. My honourable lord, I will most humbly take my leave of you.

Hamlet. You cannot, sir, take from me anything that I will more willingly part withal; except my life, ex- 218 cept my life, except my life.

Polonius. Fare you well, my lord.   [*Going.*

Hamlet. These tedious old fools!

Enter ROSENCRANTZ *and* GUILDENSTERN.

Polonius. You go to seek the Lord Hamlet; there he is.

Rosencrantz. [*To* POLONIUS.] God save you, sir!

     [*Exit* POLONIUS.

Guildenstern. Mine honoured lord!

Rosencrantz. My most dear lord!

Hamlet. My excellent good friends! How dost thou,

---

170. "board": accost.
"presently": immediately.

172. "God-a-mercy": by God's mercy, or as we would say, 'Thank God.'

174. "fishmonger": Hamlet is obviously putting on his antic disposition, and enjoying himself at Polonius' expense in the process. Whether he privately intends a deeper meaning for this word is questionable. Since Elizabethans sometimes used this word to denote "a seller of woman's virtue", it has been suggested that Hamlet may have been inferring that Polonius would not be above sacrificing his own daughter if it suited his purpose.

182. "carrion": flesh.

186. "look to't": take care.

187. "How . . . that": i.e., what do you know about that?

194. Hamlet deliberately takes the other meaning. Polonius was referring to subject matter.

199. "purging": discharging.
"amber": resin, hence any yellowish, gummy fluid.

203. "not honesty": not decent, proper.

207. "method": order, sense.

211. "pregnant" apt, significant.

211-12. "happiness": fortuitous elegance.

213. "prosperously . . . of": so successfully express (give birth to).

214. "suddenly": very soon, immediately.

218. "withal": with.

47

HAMLET

ACT II SCENE II

(3)

The warmth and pleasure of Hamlet's greeting to Rosencrantz and Guildenstern reminds us of his welcome for Horatio. (For a beautiful detail of characterization compare the greetings used to Hamlet by Horatio ["Hail to your lordship!" I,ii, 160], Rosencrantz, and Guildenstern [II.224-5]). The tone of the conversation, which they set, is not like Horatio's; it is light and witty, but they are not really saying anything. They merely make conversation. Hamlet has little respect for this butterfly style, although he strings along with it for a while. When they do not give a straight answer to his second leading question (l.238), his coolness gives way to the beginnings of mistrust. He turns then from banter to a dark melancholy strain at the word "prison." If he was playing the lunatic to Polonius with some relish, he is not doing so here. Frank by nature, Hamlet often drops his guard, or scorns it (cf. III,i, 150). This may be further seen in lines 378-82 of this scene.

Rosencrantz and Guildenstern are conscious of their mission, which is to find the cause of Hamlet's transformation. He gives them nothing to confirm their mistaken guess. It is ironical that Rosencrantz and Guildenstern, sent to sound out a madman, are sounded out by him instead (l. 284).

Guildenstern? Ah, Rosencrantz! Good lads, how do ye both?

Rosencrantz. As the indifferent children of the earth. 229

Guildenstern. Happy in that we are not over-happy; On Fortune's cap we are not the very button. 231

Hamlet. Nor the soles of her shoe?

Rosencrantz. Neither, my lord.

Hamlet. Then you live about her waist, or in the middle of her favours? 235

Guildenstern. Faith, her privates we. 236

Hamlet. In the secret parts of Fortune? O! most true; she is a strumpet. What news?

Rosencrantz. None, my lord, but that the world's grown honest.

Hamlet. Then is doomsday near; but your news is 241 not true. Let me question more in particular: what have you, my good friends, deserved at the hands of Fortune, that she sends you to prison hither?

Guildenstern. Prison, my lord!

Hamlet. Denmark's a prison.

Rosencrantz. Then is the world one.

Hamlet. A goodly one; in which there are many confines, wards, and dungeons, Denmark being one 249 o' the worst.

Rosencrantz. We think not so, my lord.

Hamlet. Why then, 'tis none to you; for there is nothing either good or bad, but thinking makes it so: to me it is a prison.

Rosencrantz. Why, then your ambition makes it one; 255 'tis too narrow for your mind.

Hamlet. O God! I could be bounded in a nutshell, and count myself a king of infinite space, were it not that I have bad dreams. 259

Guildenstern. Which dreams, indeed, are ambition, for the very substance of the ambitious is merely 261 the shadow of a dream.

Hamlet. A dream itself is but a shadow.

Rosencrantz. Truly, and I hold ambition of so airy and light a quality that it is but a shadow's shadow.

Hamlet. Then are our beggars bodies, and our mon- 266 archs and outstretched heroes the beggars' shadows. 267 Shall we to the court? for, by my fay, I cannot reason. 268

Rosencrantz. ⎱
Guildenstern. ⎰ We'll wait upon you. 269

Hamlet. No such matter; I will not sort you with 270 the rest of my servants, for, to speak to you like an honest man, I am most dreadfully attended. But, in 272 beaten way of friendship, what make you at Elsinore? 273

Rosencrantz. To visit you, my lord; no other occasion.

Hamlet. Beggar that I am, I am even poor in thanks; but I thank you: and sure, dear friends, my thanks are too dear a halfpenny. Were you not sent for? Is it 277 your own inclining? Is it a free visitation? Come, come, 278 deal justly with me: come, come; nay, speak. 279

Guildenstern. What should we say, my lord?

Hamlet. Why anything, but to the purpose. You were sent for; and there is a kind of confession in your looks which your modesties have not craft enough to colour: 283 I know the good king and queen have sent for you.

Rosencrantz. To what end, my lord?

229. i.e., so-so, middling well.

231. "button": i.e., at the very top.

235. "favours": attractions, charms.

236. "privates": intimates.

241. "doomsday": the day of judgment.

249. "confines": cells.
"wards": cells.

255. "ambition": Rosencrantz thinks perhaps it is thwarted ambition which is the cause of Hamlet's distemper.

259. "bad dreams": Could this be a reference to the haunting thoughts of his father's murder?

261. "substance...ambitious": successes of the ambitious man.

262. "shadow . . . dream": imperfect realization of his desires.

266-7. "Then . . . shadows": i.e., "Kings, the type of ambition, must then be to their anti-type, beggars, as shadows are to the bodies which cast them" (George Rylands).

267. "outstretched": aspiring.

268. "fay": faith.
"reason": argue.

269. i.e., we will be your attendants at court. Hamlet purposely takes the more literal meaning.

270. "No . . . matter": not at all.
"sort": class.

272. Hamlet may here refer to the constant spying on him, or it may be another reference to his thoughts (as "bad dreams" above).

273. "beaten . . . friendship": speaking as friend to friend.
"what . . . Elsinore": What are you doing at Elsinore?

277. "too . . . halfpenny": not worth a halfpenny.

278. "free visitation": voluntary visit.

279. Apparently Rosencrantz and Guildenstern here hesitate to answer.

283. "modesties": senses of fitness.
"colour": conceal.

HAMLET

ACT II SCENE II

The justly admired prose of lines 297-314 is a notable example of Shakespeare's flexibility of style. It is spoken not in jest, but in earnest, and is a highly expressive summing up of Hamlet's change since his mother's remarriage. Was it his further disappointment in his old schoolfellows that prompted this pessimistic utterance? It seems as if only Horatio, of all the people Hamlet meets in the play, does not give him reason to be disgusted with mankind (see III,ii,55-75).

As Hamlet begins to converse about the players, all traces of both his antic disposition and his real melancholy disappear. He shows such a close knowledge of the players' affairs and a keen interest in them. A new side of his nature begins to show itself. To Hamlet the scholar, the lover, and the wit is added Hamlet the patron of drama. It is a notable feature of the play that we continue to discover new resources in Hamlet right up to the last scene. Thus we are continually surprised and delighted by his variety, and our admiration for him grows, yet it is difficult to predict his actions. This distraction of Hamlet's interest is a strong example of his tendency to follow new interests with impulsive energy (cf. I,ii; I,v).

The subject from line 341 to line 365 is the crisis in the fortunes of the adult acting companies caused (during the time this play was written) by the establishment and popularity of children's companies. The children who acted in these plays were almost entirely choirboys (see ll. 348-50). The most popular company was that of the Children of the Queen's Chapel, who played in Blackfriars Theatre beginning in 1600. The other company was the Children of St. Paul's, who began somewhat earlier. Besides the novelty of these ventures, there were other reasons for their suc-

Hamlet. That you must teach me. But let me conjure you, by the rights of our fellowship, by the consonancy of our youth, by the obligation of our ever-preserved love, and by what more dear a better proposer could charge you withal, be even and direct with me, whether you were sent for or no! 286 287 288 289 290

Rosencrantz. [*Aside to* GUILDENSTERN.] What say you?

Hamlet. [*Aside.*] Nay, then, I have an eye of you. If you love me, hold not off. 294

Guildenstern. My lord, we were sent for.

Hamlet. I will tell you why; so shall my anticipation prevent your discovery, and your secrecy to the king and queen moult no feather. I have of late,—but wherefore I know not,—lost all my mirth, forgone all custom of exercises; and indeed it goes so heavily with my disposition that this goodly frame, the earth, seems to me a sterile promontory; this most excellent canopy, the air, look you, this brave o'erhanging firmament, this majestical roof fretted with golden fire, why, it appears no other thing to me but a foul and pestilent congregation of vapours. What a piece of work is a man! How noble in reason! how infinite in faculty! in form, in moving, how express and admirable! in action how like an angel! in apprehension how like a god! the beauty of the world! the paragon of animals! And yet, to me, what is this quintessence of dust? man delights not me; no, nor woman neither, though, by your smiling, you seem to say so. 297 304 305 309 310 311 312

Rosencrantz. My lord, there was no such stuff in my thoughts.

Hamlet. Why did you laugh then, when I said, 'man delights not me?'

Rosencrantz. To think, my lord, if you delight not in man, what lenten entertainment the players shall receive from you: we coted them on the way; and hither are they coming, to offer you service. 320 321

Hamlet. He that plays the King shall be welcome; his majesty shall have tribute of me; the adventurous Knight shall use his foil and target; the Lover shall not sigh gratis; the Humorous Man shall end his part in peace; the Clown shall make those laugh whose lungs are tickle o' the sere; and the Lady shall say her mind freely, or the blank verse shall halt for't. What players are they? 325 326 328 329

Rosencrantz. Even those you were wont to take delight in, the tragedians of the city.

Hamlet. How chances it they travel? their residence, both in reputation and profit, was better both ways. 333

Rosencrantz. I think their inhibition comes by the means of the late innovation. 335 336

Hamlet. Do they hold the same estimation they did when I was in the city? Are they so followed?

Rosencrantz. No, indeed they are not.

Hamlet. How comes it? Do they grow rusty?

Rosencrantz. Nay, their endeavour keeps in the wonted pace: but there is, sir, an aery of children, little eyases, that cry out on the top of question, and are most tyrannically clapped for 't: these are now the fashion, and so berattle the common stages,—so they 341 342 343 344 345

286. "That . . . me": i.e., you will have to tell me that.

286-7. "conjure": solemnly appeal to.

287. "fellowship": comradeship.

288. "consonancy": concord.

289-90. "better proposer": more skillful asker. (He may have Claudius in mind.)

290. "even": straightforward.

294. i.e., if that is the way things are, I will keep my eye on you.

297-99. "so . . . feather": i.e., thus it will be unnecessary for you to tell me and you need not betray the confidence of the King and Queen.

304. "canopy": covering.

305. "firmament": sky. "fretted": ornamented.

309. "faculty": active quality or virtue. "moving": movement. "express": perfectly modeled for its purpose.

310. "apprehension": understanding.

311. "paragon": flower of perfection.

312. "quintessence": perfection.

320. "lenten": meager, as in Lent. "entertainment": welcome.

321. "coted": overtook.

325. "foil and target": fencing rapier and small shield.

326. "gratis": for nothing. "Humorous Man": the player of character parts.

328. "tickle . . . sere": made to laugh easily.

329. "halt": limp.

333-54. This is a topical reference (one of several in Hamlet) to the stage war between the children's companies and the companies of adult actors which was raging at the time the play was written (see commentary).

333. "travel": go on tour. "residence": acting in the city.

335. "inhibition": curtailment.

336. "late innovation": recent change in the established order of things.

341-2. "endeavour . . . pace": they try as hard as ever.

342. "aery": nest.

343. "eyases": young hawks. "cry . . . question": are heard above all others.

344. "tyrannically": outrageously.

345. "berattle": abuse. "common stages": ordinary theaters (where the adult professional players performed).

HAMLET

ACT II SCENE II

cess. They played not in the public theaters but in so-called private theaters. Since these were indoor playhouses, performances could take place in the evening, and opportunities for lighting and more spectacular staging were indulged. The town riff-raff were excluded from these performances, and naturally the gentry found it pleasanter to sit with an audience of their own class. The plays, too, were of a more sophisticated kind, designed to tickle the fancy of a selected audience and to give the boys opportunity to display their excellent musical talent. The subjects of the plays tended more and more towards daring satire of public events of the times, a fact that furthered the lively interest they provoked.

The aristocratic section of the audience, though smaller in numbers than the "penny stinkards," provided the main source of both income and protection by which the players were sustained. Thus the success of the children was a real threat to actors who depended on the profession for their income (the children did not), and who were constantly in conflict with the authority of the City Council, which, largely Puritan in its views, was opposed to play-acting.

Anachronistic passages like this make the ancient society represented in the play seem timeless. By identifying seventh-century Denmark with sixteenth-century England, Shakespeare opens up the satirical possibilities of his theme. Thus Denmark's rottenness becomes also that of Elizabethan England, or of any time.

The signboard of the Globe Theatre, opened by Shakespeare's company in 1599, represented Hercules carrying the world on his shoulders.

An argument is the plot of a play. A playwright would offer the argument to a manager, and produce the complete manuscript of the play after the contract was signed.

Hamlet's relapse into melancholy (ll. 366-371) reflects his disillusion at human inconstancy onto the public, disloyal alike to their pleasures and their monarchs.

Compare "more than natural" in line 369 with "unnatural" in I,v,28.

On Polonius' entry, note how Hamlet relapses into his antic disposition. In speaking of the ancient Roman actor Roscius, who could scarcely be called news, he mocks the staleness of Polonius' message and also his habit of ap-

call them,—that many wearing rapiers are afraid of 346
goose-quills, and dare scarce come thither.

Hamlet. What! are they children? who maintains 'em? how are they escoted? Will they pursue the 349
quality no longer than they can sing? will they not say 350
afterwards, if they should grow themselves to common players,—as it is most like, if their means are 352
not better,—their writers do them wrong, to make them exclaim against their own succession? 354

Rosencrantz. Faith, there has been much to-do on both sides: and the nation holds it no sin to tarre them to con- 356
troversy: there was, for a while, no money bid for argu- 357
ment, unless the Poet and the Player went to cuffs 358
in the question.

Hamlet. Is it possible?

Guildenstern. O! there has been much throwing about of brains.

Hamlet. Do the boys carry it away? 363

Rosencrantz. Ay, that they do, my lord; Hercules 364
and his load too.

Hamlet. It is not very strange; for my uncle is King of Denmark, and those that would make mows at him 367
while my father lived, give twenty, forty, fifty, a hundred ducats a-piece for his picture in little. 369
'Sblood, there is something in this more than na- 370
tural, if philosophy could find it out. 371

[*Flourish of trumpets within.*

Guildenstern. There are the players.

Hamlet. Gentlemen, you are welcome to Elsinore. Your hands, come then; the appurtance of welcome 374
is fashion and ceremony: let me comply with you in 375
this garb, lest my extent to the players—which, I tell 376
you, must show fairly outward—should more appear like entertainment than yours. You are welcome; but 378
my uncle-father and aunt-mother are deceived.

Guildenstern. In what, my dear lord?

Hamlet. I am but mad north-north-west: when the 381
wind is southerly I know a hawk from a handsaw. 382

Enter POLONIUS.

Polonius. Well be with you, gentlemen!

Hamlet. Hark you, Guildenstern; and you too; at each ear a hearer: that great baby you see there is not yet out of his swaddling-clouts. 386

Rosencrantz. Happily he's the second time come to them; for they say an old man is twice a child.

Hamlet. I will prophesy he comes to tell me of the players; mark it. You say right, sir; o' Monday morning; 'twas so indeed.

Polonius. My lord, I have news to tell you.

Hamlet. My lord, I have news to tell you. When Roscius was an actor in Rome,— 394

Polonius. The actors are come hither, my lord.

Hamlet. Buz, buz! 396

Polonius. Upon my honour,—

Hamlet. Then came each actor on his ass,—

Polonius. The best actors in the world, either for 399
tragedy, comedy, history, pastoral, pastoral-comical, historical-pastoral, tragical-historical, tragical-comical-historical-pastoral, scene individable, or poem un- 402
limited: Seneca cannot be too heavy, nor Plautus too 403

346-7. "many wearing . . . goose-quills": many of the gallants are afraid of being ridiculed by the writers for the boy actors.

349. "escoted": paid.

350. "quality": acting profession.

352. "means": financial resources.

354. "exclaim . . . succession": abuse the profession to which they will succeed.

356. "tarre": urge.

357-8. "argument": plot of play.

358. "cuffs": battle.

363. "carry it away": win the day.

364-5. "Hercules . . . load": a reference to the Globe theater whose sign was Hercules carrying the globe on his shoulders.

367. "mows": grimaces. Hamlet is not surprised at the sudden revolution of popular favor.

369. "picture in little": miniature.

370. " 'Sblood": by God's blood, a common oath.

371. "philosophy": science.

374. "appurtance": proper accompaniment.

375. "fashion and ceremony": formal ceremony.

375-6. "comply . . . garb": put it into practice in this way, i.e., by shaking hands.

376. "extent": extending of formal ceremony.

378. "entertainment": welcome.

381. i.e., on one point (of the compass) only.

382. "hawk . . . handsaw": i.e., I am not so mad as you think.
"hawk": (the second quarto spells it, "hauke") may be hack, a tool of the ax family.

386. "clouts": clothes.

394. "Roscius": the most famous of ancient Roman actors.

396. "Buz, buz": a slang expression for, tell me something I don't know.

399-405. Polonius may be reading from the official license of the players which they have given to him on arrival.

402. "scene individable": i.e., preserving the unities.

402-3. "poem unlimited": viz., a play which observed none of the ancient rules.

403. "Seneca" and "Plautus": Roman writers of tragedy and comedy.

HAMLET

ACT II SCENE II

proaching his points with wordy definitions (see II,ii, 86-105). "Buz" is Oxford University slang for, Tell us what we don't know.

Jephthah (Judges 11:38) sacrificed his virgin daughter as a result of having sworn a foolish oath. The story was a popular one. Not only does the ballad Hamlet quotes survive, but a play on the subject, by Dekker and Munday, was acted in London not long before by the Lord Admiral's Servants, the strongest rivals of Shakespeare's company (see below).

(4)

The extent of Hamlet's familiarity with the theater may be measured by his acquaintance with these players, the extent of his enjoyment of the theater by the warmth of his welcome.

"My young lady" will be a boy actor. Actresses did not appear on the public stage in England until the Restoration (1660). Thus all of Shakespeare's female roles were performed by boys with unchanged voices, a fact that accounts for much of their style and character, and also for the small number of women in any single play. The career of such a boy was necessarily very short.

"Cracked within the ring" refers to coins. The monarch's picture was framed by a circular border, the ring, which was somewhat in from the edge of the coin. If a coin got cracked so that the crack extended within this ring, it was no longer legal tender.

A "chopine" is a shoe with a very high heel, worn by Italian ladies of fashion of the day.

The extent of Hamlet's patronage of the theater, formidable evidence of his varied interests and capacities, is vividly demonstrated here. He has heard a reading of a play before it was acted and had his share in judging it (and his judgement [ll. 437-48] is that of a connoisseur). Furthermore, to the admiration of Polonius and the players, he remembers thirteen lines of a speech from the play.

The Pyrrhus speech itself is carefully written in a style unlike the body of the play. It is high-sounding, bombastic, and exaggerated, full of brave ringing words and far-fetched comparisons. Its rhythm, too, is stiff and drumming. These features are dramatically

---

light. For the law of writ and the liberty, these are 404
the only men.

Hamlet. O Jephthah, judge of Israel, what a trea- 406
sure hadst thou!

Polonius. What a treasure had he, my lord?

Hamlet. Why
> One fair daughter and no more, 410
> The which he loved passing well.

Polonius. [*Aside.*] Still on my daughter.

Hamlet. Am I not i' the right, old Jephthah?

Polonius. If you call me Jephthah, my lord, I have a
daughter that I love passing well.

Hamlet. Nay, that follows not.

Polonius. What follows, then, my lord?

Hamlet. Why,
> As by lot, God wot. 419

And then, you know,
> It came to pass, as most like it was.—

The first row of the pious chanson will show you 422
more; for look where my abridgment comes. 423

Enter four or five Players.

You are welcome, masters; welcome, all. I am glad to
see thee well: welcome, good friends. O, my old friend! 425
Why, thy face is valanced since I saw thee last: comest 426
thou to beard me in Denmark? What! my young 427
lady and mistress! By 'r lady, your ladyship is nearer
heaven than when I saw you last, by the altitude of a
chopine. Pray God, your voice, like a piece of uncur- 430
rent gold, be not cracked within the ring. Masters, 431
you are all welcome. We'll e'en to 't like French
falconers, fly at anything we see: we'll have a speech
straight. Come, give us a taste of your quality; come, 434
a passionate speech.

First Player. What speech, my good lord?

Hamlet. I heard thee speak me a speech once, but it
was never acted; or, if it was, not above once; for
the play, I remember, pleased not the million; 'twas
caviare to the general: but it was—as I received it, 440
and others, whose judgments in such matters cried in 441
the top of mine—an excellent play, well digested in 442
the scenes, set down with as much modesty as cun- 443
ning. I remember one said there were no sallets in the 444
lines to make the matter savoury, nor no matter in the 445
phrase that might indict the author of affectation; but
called it an honest method, as wholesome as sweet,
and by very much more handsome than fine. One 448
speech in it I chiefly loved; 'twas Aeneas' tale to Dido 449
and thereabout of it especially, where he speaks of
Priam's slaughter. If it live in your memory, begin 451
at this line: let me see, let me see:—
> The rugged Pyrrhus, like the Hyrcanian beast,— 453

'tis not so, it begins with Pyrrhus:—
> The rugged Pyrrhus, he, whose sable arm, 455
> Black as his purpose, did the night resemble
> When he lay couched in the ominous horse, 457
> Hath now this dread and black complexion smear'd
> With heraldry more dismal; head to foot 459
> Now is he total gules, horridly trick'd 460
> With blood of fathers, mothers, daughters, sons,
> Bak'd and impasted with the parching streets, 462

51

---

404. "law of writ": classical plays.
"liberty": modern plays.

406. "Jephthah": See commentary.

410-11. "One . . . well": Hamlet quotes from a ballad on Jephthah still extant in Percy's RELIQUES.

419. "wot": knows.

422. "row": line.
"pious chanson": Godly ballad.

423. "abridgment": cutting short, i.e., interruption.

425. "old friend": i.e., the leading player.

426. "valanced": bearded.

427-8. "young lady": Since female parts on the Elizabethan stage were taken by trained boy actors, this is a reference to one of them.

430. "chopine": a high-heeled shoe. In other words, the boy had grown.

430-31. "uncurrent gold": bad gold coin.

431. "cracked . . . ring": Seeing how much the boy has grown, Hamlet is afraid his voice may be changing.

434. "quality": skill as an actor.

440. "caviare . . . general": too great a delicacy for the common herd.

441-2. "cried . . . mine": surpassed mine.

442. "digested": composed.

443. "modesty": moderation, hence also good taste.

444. "sallets": tasty bits.

445-6. "no . . . phrase": nothing in the language.

448. "fine": subtle.

449. "Aeneas' . . . Dido": the story of the sack of Troy as told to Queen Dido by Aeneas; see Virgil's AENEID.

451. "Priam": the King of Troy.

453. "Pyrrhus": the son of Achilles and one of the Greeks concealed in the famous wooden horse.
"Hyrcanian beast": tiger.

455. "sable": black.

457. "ominous horse": see note 453 above. Ominous is here used in the sense of fateful, i.e., for the Trojans.

459. "heraldry": painting, or insignia.

460. "total gules": completely red.
"trick'd": painted.

462. "impasted": made into a paste (i.e., the slain, not Pyrrhus).

HAMLET

ACT II SCENE II

suitable because they make this speech sound more stagey than its context. There is more to this technical achievement, however. It is in imitation of the heroic style of Christopher Marlowe, greatest of Shakespeare's predecessors, whose plays were still in the repertoire of the Lord Admiral's Servants (see above). Shakespeare had begun his own career in imitation of this style, but quickly developed his own more flexible and varied manner. Marlowe had written a tragedy on the subject of Aeneas' sojourn in Carthage, entitled DIDO, QUEEN OF CARTHAGE, and, although that play has no passage exactly parallel to this speech, the inference that Shakespeare here challenges comparison with Marlowe, or even that the players represent a sort of caricature of the Lord Admiral's Servants, is not far-fetched. (See also III,ii, 1-47 and commentary.)

Notice how appropriate the Pyrrhus speech is to Hamlet's underlying preoccupation. In it the collapse of a state follows upon the slaughter of its old king, but special note is taken of the faithfulness in grief of the Queen ("come to Hecuba"). The aptness even extends to verbal echo as in "strumpet fortune" (see l. 238 above).

That lend a tyrannous and damned light
To their vile murders: roasted in wrath and fire,
And thus o'er-sized with coagulated gore,   465
With eyes like carbuncles, the hellish Pyrrhus   466
Old grandsire Priam seeks.
So proceed you.
  Polonius. 'Fore God, my lord, well spoken; with
good accent and good discretion.   470
  First Player.   Anon, he finds him
Striking too short at Greeks; his antique sword,
Rebellious to his arm, lies where it falls,
Repugnant to command. Unequal match'd,   473
Pyrrhus at Priam drives; in rage strikes wide;
But with the whiff and wind of his fell sword
The unnerved father falls. Then senseless Ilium,   476
Seeming to feel this blow, with flaming top
Stoops to his base, and with a hideous crash   478
Takes prisoner Pyrrhus' ear: for lo! his sword,   479
Which was declining on the milky head   480
Of reverend Priam, seem'd i' the air to stick:
So, as a painted tyrant, Pyrrhus stood,   482
And like a neutral to his will and matter,   483
Did nothing.
But, as we often see, against some storm,   485
A silence in the heavens, the rack stand still,   486
The bold winds speechless and the orb below   487
As hush as death, anon the dreadful thunder
Doth rend the region; so, after Pyrrhus' pause,
Aroused vengeance sets him new a-work;
And never did the Cyclops' hammer fall   491
On Mars's armour, forg'd for proof eterne,   492
With less remorse than Pyrrhus' bleeding sword   493
Now falls on Priam.
Out, out, thou strumpet, Fortune! All you gods,
In general synod, take away her power;   496
Break all the spokes and fellies from her wheel,   497
And bowl the round nave down the hill of heaven,   498
As low as to the fiends!
  Polonius. This is too long.
  Hamlet. It shall to the barber's, with your beard.
Prithee, say on: he's for a jig or a tale of bawdry,   502
or he sleeps. Say on; come to Hecuba.   503
  First Player. But who, O! who had seen the mobled   504
    queen—
  Hamlet. 'The mobled queen?'—
  Polonius. That's good; 'mobled queen' is good.
  First Player. Run barefoot up and down, threat'ning
    the flames
With bisson rheum; a clout upon that head   508
Where late the diadem stood; and, for a robe,
About her lank and all o'er-teemed loins,   510
A blanket, in the alarm of fear caught up;
Who this had seen, with tongue in venom steep'd,   512
'Gainst Fortune's state would treason have pronounc'd:
But if the gods themselves did see her then,
When she saw Pyrrhus make malicious sport
In mincing with his sword her husband's limbs,
The instant burst of clamour that she made—
Unless things mortal move them not at all—
Would have made milch the burning eyes of heaven,   519

465. "o'er-sized . . . gore": painted over with congealed blood.

466. "carbuncles": precious stones of fiery red color.

470. "accent": enunciation, etc. "discretion": interpretation and understanding. "Anon": after a while.

473. "Repugnant . . . command": refusing to be used, owing to Priam's weakness.

476. "Ilium": Troy

478. "Stoops . . . base": collapses.

479. "Takes . . . ear": stuns Pyrrhus.

480. "declining": descending.

482. "painted": as in a painting, i.e., perfectly motionless.

483. "like . . . to": as if indifferent to. "matter": purpose.

485. "against": before.

486. "rack": cloud formations.

487. "orb": earth.

491. "Cyclops": the giant assistants to Vulcan.

492. "proof eterne": everlasting protection.

493. "remorse": pity.

496. "synod": council.

497. "fellies": felloes (of a wheel), i.e., sections of the rim.

498. "nave": hub.

502. "Prithee": I pray thee. "jig": a merry dance or tune.

503. "Hecuba": Priam's queen.

504. "mobled": muffled. This word has survived in Shropshire dialect.

508. "bisson rheum": blinding tears. "clout": rag.

510. "o'er-teemed": worn out with childbearing.

512-13. "Who . . . pronounc'd": Anyone seeing this would have bitterly pronounced treason against Fortune's tyranny.

519. "milch": milky, moist.

HAMLET

Why does Hamlet caution the player against mocking Polonius when he himself has been doing so every chance he gets?

Notice how Hamlet shakes off the King's leeches, and then note their wail of comical frustration (ll. 549-51).

(5)

When Hamlet says with such obvious relief, "Now I am alone," we realize how steadily he has been besieged with inquiry throughout this long scene.

This, the third and longest so far of Hamlet's soliloquies, is the first passage in which he reproaches himself with inaction. It is an extraordinarily varied speech, full of rhetoric and contradiction. He accuses himself of cowardice, surely a false charge. He speaks of being "unpregnant" of his cause when he has in fact just finished arranging a plan of action (see ll. 539-46 above). Hamlet's emotions rise and fall. In the first section of the speech he works himself up to an emotional crisis designed to rival that of the player in the Pyrrhus speech and issuing in the violent name-calling of lines 584-6. Its effect is not to diminish but to increase his self-contempt (ll. 587-92). Then, emotionally deadlocked, he forcibly steadies his mind (l. 593) to give a rational account of what he has decided to do.

And passion in the gods.

Polonius. Look! wh'er he has not turned his colour and has tears in 's eyes. Prithee, no more.

Hamlet. 'Tis well; I'll have thee speak out the rest soon. Good my lord, will you see the players well bestowed? Do you hear, let them be well used; for 525 they are the abstracts and brief chronicles of the time: 526 after your death you were better have a bad epitaph than their ill report while you live.

Polonius. My lord, I will use them according to their desert. 530

Hamlet. God's bodikins, man, much better; use every 531 man after his desert, and who shall 'scape whipping? Use them after your own honour and dignity: the less they deserve, the more merit is in your bounty. Take them in.

Polonius. Come, sirs.

Hamlet. Follow him, friends: we'll hear a play to-morrow.

[*Exit* POLONIUS, *with all the* Players *but the* First.]
Dost thou hear me, old friend; can you play The Murder of Gonzago?

First Player. Ay, my lord.

Hamlet. We'll ha 't to-morrow night. You could, for a need, study a speech of some dozen or sixteen lines, 543 which I would set down and insert in 't, could you not?

First Player. Ay, my lord.

Hamlet. Very well. Follow that lord; and look you mock him not. [*Exit* First Player.] [*To* ROSEN-CRANTZ *and* GUILDENSTERN.] My good friends, I'll leave you till night; you are welcome to Elsinore.

Rosencrantz. Good my lord!

[*Exeunt* ROSENCRANTZ *and* GUILDENSTERN.
Hamlet. Ay, so, God be wi' ye! Now I am alone.
O! what a rogue and peasant slave am I:
Is it not monstrous that this player here,
But in a fiction, in a dream of passion, 555
Could force his soul so to his own conceit 556
That from her working all his visage wann'd, 557
Tears in his eyes, distraction in 's aspect, 558
A broken voice, and his whole function suiting 559
With forms to his conceit? and all for nothing! 560
For Hecuba!
What's Hecuba to him or he to Hecuba
That he should weep for her? What would he do
Had he the motive and the cue for passion 564
That I have? He would drown the stage with tears,
And cleave the general ear with horrid speech, 566
Make mad the guilty and appal the free, 567
Confound the ignorant, and maze indeed 568
The very faculties of eyes and ears.
Yet I,
A dull and muddy-mettled rascal, peak, 571
Like John-a-dreams, unpregnant of my cause, 572
And can say nothing; no, not for a king,
Upon whose property and most dear life 574
A damn'd defeat was made. Am I a coward? 575
Who calls me villain? breaks my pate across? 576
Plucks off my beard and blows it in my face?

525. "bestowed": provided for.

526. "abstracts . . . chronicles": condensed histories (hence socially useful).

530. "desert": rank.

531. "God's bodikins": an oath; literally, by God's little body.

543. "study": learn.

555. "dream of passion": imaginary emotion.

556. "conceit": imagination.

557. "her working": "her" refers to "conceit"; i.e., the effect of imagination. "wann'd": paled.

558. "distraction": frenzy. "aspect": countenance.

559. "function": behavior.

560. "With . . . conceit": to the shape of his imagination.

564. "cue": signal.

566. "general ear": ears of the audience.

567. "free": innocent.

568. "Confound": confuse or amaze.

571. "mettled": spirited. "peak": mope.

572. "unpregnant . . . cause": inactive in my duty.

574. "property": personality, life.

575. "defeat": destruction.

576. "pate": head.

HAMLET

ACT II SCENE II

Self-hatred is not a new feeling with Hamlet, who is only too aware of his heredity, melancholy, weakness, and lack of preparation for life (see I,ii, 129-34; 153). What happens here is that, watching the player, Hamlet confuses reality and make believe. He marvels at the force of imagination that can produce real emotion from a make believe grief. For a moment he sees life as a theater (ll.563-9) in which speech is a form of action. It is only when he tries to outdo the actor that he sees the futility of speech except on the stage. His realization of the power of illusion has two results: 1) He sees that he himself may be the victim of the Devil's playacting (ll. 603-8). 2) He sees how Claudius may be stirred by the player's make believe into self-betrayal.

Hamlet's self reproach is justified. Until the players chanced to arrive, he had planned nothing definite against Claudius (he'd been reading books and playing the lunatic instead). Further, now that he has acted, his attempt is not on the King's life but on his conscience.

Tweaks me by the nose? gives me the lie i' the throat,
As deep as to the lungs? Who does me this, ha?
'Swounds, I should take it, for it cannot be 580
But I am pigeon-liver'd, and lack gall 581
To make oppression bitter, or ere this
I should have fatted all the region kites 583
With this slave's offal. Bloody, bawdy villain! 584
Remorseless, treacherous, lecherous, kindless villain! 585
O! vengeance!
Why, what an ass am I! This is most brave
That I, the son of a dear father murder'd,
Prompted to my revenge by heaven and hell,
Must, like a whore, unpack my heart with words,
And fall a-cursing, like a very drab, 591
A scullion! Fie upon 't! foh! 592
About, my brain; hum, I have heard, 593
That guilty creatures sitting at a play
Have by the very cunning of the scene
Been struck so to the soul that presently 596
They have proclaim'd their malefactions; 597
For murder, though it have no tongue, will speak
With most miraculous organ. I'll have these players 599
Play something like the murder of my father
Before mine uncle; I'll observe his looks;
I'll tent him to the quick: if he but blench 602
I know my course. The spirit that I have seen
May be the devil: and the devil hath power
To assume a pleasing shape; yea, and perhaps
Out of my weakness and my melancholy—
As he is very potent with such spirits—
Abuses me to damn me. I'll have grounds 608
More relative than this: the play's the thing 609
Wherein I'll catch the conscience of the king. [*Exit.*

580. "'Swounds": by God's wounds, another common oath.

581. "pigeon-liver'd": "lily-livered," i.e., a coward.
"gall": spirit.

583. "the region kites": the kites of the air. The kite is a bird of prey of the falcon family.

584. "this slave's offal": this slave's (i.e., the King's) guts.

585. "kindless": unnatural.

591. "drab": slut.

592. "scullion": the lowest form of the kitchen servants.

593. "About": to work.

596. "presently": immediately.

597. "malefactions": crimes.

599. "With . . . organ": through the most miraculous instruments.

602. "tent . . . quick": probe him to the very soul.
"blench": flinch.

608. "Abuses . . . me": deludes me in order that my soul may be damned by the committing of a sin (viz., murder).

609. "More . . . this": more conclusive than the word of a ghost.

54

HAMLET

ACT III SCENE I

The opening of this scene bears a family resemblance to that of the previous one (II,ii). The place is the same. The same speaking characters appear. The business of the scene is the continuation of Claudius' and Polonius' attempt to find the cause of Hamlet's madness. Claudius is noticeably less guarded in his expression of his attitude towards Hamlet. Before, remember, he professed a kindly interest in curing Hamlet and providing pastime for him, and veiled thus his desire to pump him. Now he begins questioning Rosencrantz and Guildenstern very pointedly, implies that he considers Hamlet's madness put on, and asserts that he regards it as dangerous. It would be tempting to stress the private nature of this scene, since there are no attendants indicated in the stage direction, as the reason for this new directness in the King; but in both the Second Quarto and the First Folio the presence of these attendant lords is called for. The reason why they were later removed was probably a matter of stage management. It is awkward to bring a whole crowd on stage for a passage of only twenty-eight lines unless they have something fairly important to do. This is one case where the modern text is preferred over the original, since it makes better sense dramatically.

It is the Queen who recalls the amiable purpose of raising Hamlet's spirits, a further indication of her affection for her son and her genuine desire that everyone should be happy. Together with her words to Ophelia (ll. 37-42), this reinforces our opinion that, though weak and soft, she cannot fully be the King's accomplice.

ACT THREE, scene one.

(A Room in the Castle)

Enter KING, QUEEN, POLONIUS, OPHELIA, ROSENCRANTZ, *and* GUILDENSTERN.

King. And can you, by no drift of conference,   1
Get from him why he puts on this confusion,
Grating so harshly all his days of quiet   3
With turbulent and dangerous lunacy?
    Rosencrantz. He does confess he feels himself
       distracted;
But from what cause he will by no means speak.
    Guildenstern. Nor do we find him forward to be   7
       sounded,
But, with a crafty madness, keeps aloof,
When we would bring him on to some confession
Of his true state.
    Queen.   Did he receive you well?
    Rosencrantz. Most like a gentleman.
    Guildenstern. But with much forcing of his dis-   12
       position.
    Rosencrantz. Niggard of question, but of our demands   13
Most free in his reply.
    Queen.   Did you assay him   14
To any pastime?
    Rosencrantz. Madam, it so fell out that certain players
We o'er-raught on the way; of these we told him,   17
And there did seem in him a kind of joy
To hear of it: they are here about the court,
And, as I think, they have already order
This night to play before him.
    Polonius.   'Tis most true;
And he beseech'd me to entreat your majesties
To hear and see the matter.
    King. With all my heart; and it doth much content me
To hear him so inclin'd.
Good gentlemen, give him a further edge,   26
And drive his purpose on to these delights.
    Rosencrantz. We shall, my lord.
     [*Exeunt* ROSENCRANTZ *and* GUILDENSTERN.
    King.   Sweet Gertrude, leave us too;
For we have closely sent for Hamlet hither,   29
That he, as 'twere by accident, may here
Affront Ophelia.   31
Her father and myself, lawful espials,   32
Will so bestow ourselves, that, seeing, unseen,
We may of their encounter frankly judge,
And gather by him, as he is behav'd,   35
If 't be the affliction of his love or no
That thus he suffers for.
    Queen.   I shall obey you.
And for your part, Ophelia, I do wish
That your good beauties be the happy cause
Of Hamlet's wildness; so shall I hope your virtues
Will bring him to his wonted way again,   41

---

1. "drift of conference": roundabout methods.

3. "Grating": disturbing.

7. "forward . . . sounded": willing to be questioned.

12. i.e., it took some effort on his part to be civil to us.

13-14. "Niggard . . . reply": i.e., not asking many questions but freely replying to ours. Is this true?

14. "assay": attempt to induce.

17. "o'er-raught": overtook.

26. "edge": encouragement.

29. "closely": secretly.

31. "Affront": confront, encounter.

32. "lawful espials": spies who are justified in their action.

35. "by . . . behav'd": i.e., by his behavior.

41. "wonted way": normal state.

55

HAMLET

ACT III SCENE I

Claudius' 'aside is our first evidence of his sense of guilt. As such, it is most important. It shows us what we could not before know, that he has a conscience to be caught by Hamlet's play. It proves, lest we should share Hamlet's wavering doubt, that the ghost spoke the truth. At the same time it rounds out Claudius' character suddenly, by showing us the torment behind the smile. He, too, is aware of the difference between reality and appearance. The imagery also is significant. It links this little speech with Gertrude's laxity, with Hamlet's distortion of Ophelia's character (see II,ii, 174, 184-5; III,i, 111-5,144-8; V,i, 217-9), and the cosmetic mask is a beautiful metaphor for the world of seems.

We now come to what we suppose is the most famous single speech in the play, Hamlet's fourth soliloquy. It gives us a glimpse of the sort of meditation that occupies Hamlet's solitary brooding. Its subjects, the death-wish and self-reproach, are nothing new. The difference is that no direct mention is made of his uncle-father and aunt-mother, the murder, or his revenge. The speech is calm and reflective in tone, almost impersonal as the thought ranges beyond himself to embrace every man's predicament in the world. It represents a Hamlet in search of nobility in life or death, unable to live at ease with life in the midst of its infamy, yet more in grief than anger. Perhaps weariness of spirit is what comes through as much as anything, a weariness that can see no effective action one man can take. The more he thinks, the more he doubts the use of action; the more he doubts, the more his will is puzzled. This is a tragic view of life, a universal clarity of vision coming to rest in pain and despair. But despair does not yet satisfy him; he feels both the duty and the need to act. We very soon see how, when confronted not with his world view but with a person he is intimately emotionally involved with, his irritable passion breaks out again. The result of the outbreak, as he must realize, is far from the nobility which had prompted the outbreak.

A good deal of one's interpretation of the nunnery scene hinges on the way lines 88-9 are spoken. They can be hard-boiled and ironical, or they can be tender and sincere. The first alternative gives us a Hamlet so settled in his disillusion that he can no longer be caught off guard, whose love has been utterly turned to hatred, and whose bitter words are meant to wound and degrade. The second

To both your honours.

Ophelia.   Madam, I wish it may.
                        [*Exit* QUEEN.

Polonius. Ophelia, walk you here. Gracious, so   43
   please you,
We will bestow ourselves. [*To* OPHELIA.] Read on
   this book;   44
That show of such an exercise may colour   45
Your loneliness. We are oft to blame in this,
'Tis too much prov'd, that with devotion's visage   47
And pious action we do sugar o'er
The devil himself.
   King. [*Aside.*]   O! 'tis too true;
How smart a lash that speech doth give my
   conscience!
The harlot's cheek, beautied with plastering art,
Is not more ugly to the thing that helps it   52
Than is my deed to my most painted word: 53
O heavy burden!
   Polonius. I hear him coming; let's withdraw, my
   lord.   [*Exeunt* KING *and* POLONIUS.
          Enter HAMLET.

Hamlet. To be, or not to be: that is the question: 56
Whether 'tis nobler in the mind to suffer
The slings and arrows of outrageous fortune,   58
Or to take arms against a sea of troubles,   59
And by opposing end them? To die: to sleep;
No more; and, by a sleep to say we end
The heart-ache and the thousand natural shocks
That flesh is heir to, 'tis a consummation
Devoutly to be wish'd. To die, to sleep;
To sleep: perchance to dream: ay, there's the rub;   65
For in that sleep of death what dreams may come
When we have shuffled off this mortal coil,   67
Must give us pause. There's the respect   68
That makes calamity of so long life;
For who would bear the whips and scorns of time,
The oppressor's wrong, the proud man's contumely,   71
The pangs of dispriz'd love, the law's delay,
The insolence of office, and the spurns   73
That patient merit of the unworthy takes,
When he himself might his quietus make   75
With a bare bodkin? who would fardels bear,   76
To grunt and sweat under a weary life,
But that the dread of something after death,
The undiscover'd country from whose bourn   79
No traveller returns, puzzles the will,   80
And makes us rather bear those ills we have
Than fly to others that we know not of?
Thus conscience does. make cowards of us all;   83
And thus the native hue of resolution   84
Is sicklied o'er with the pale cast of thought,   85
And enterprises of great pitch and moment   86
With this regard their currents turn awry,   87
And lose the name of action. Soft you now!   88
The fair Ophelia! Nymph, in thy orisons   89
Be all my sins remember'd.
   Ophelia.   Good my lord,   90
How does your honour for this many a day?
   Hamlet. I humbly thank you; well, well, well.

43. "Gracious": your grace.

44. "book": i.e., of devotions.

45. "exercise": i.e., religious exercise. "colour": give an excuse for.

47. "devotion's visage": the appearance of religious devotion.

52. "to . . . it": i.e., compared to the paint on her cheek.

53. "painted": fair-seeming, hence, by implication, false.

Stage direction: "Enter Hamlet": Hamlet is again reading, and is too absorbed to notice Ophelia.

56. "the question": i.e., the proposition put forward for argument.

58. "outrageous": cruel.

59. "sea": i.e., an endless turmoil.

65. "rub": impediment; a bowling figure, a rub being a roughness in the lawn causing a diversion in the course of the ball.

67. "shuffled . . . coil": i.e., cast off this mortal body, which, like a coil of rope, binds us to this earthly existence.

68. "respect": reason.

71. "contumely": insults.

73. "insolence of office": insolent behavior of officials.

73-4. "spurns . . . takes": the contemptuous treatment that men of merit have patiently to endure from the less worthy.

75. "quietus": release (from life), a legal term.

76. "bodkin": dagger. "fardels": burdens.

79. "bourn": boundary.

80. "puzzles the will": obstructs the resolution, or ability to act.

83. "conscience": reflection, i.e., speculation as to what the after-life may hold for us.

84. "native hue": natural color.

85. "cast": tinge.

86. "pitch and moment": height and importance.

87. "With this regard": on account of this. "awry": aside.

88. "Soft you now!": i.e., Hold on, now. Hamlet has just noticed Ophelia.

89. "Nymph": lovely maid. "orisons": prayers.

90. "Good my lord": See II, i, 70 and notes.

HAMLET

ACT III SCENE I

alternative gives us a Hamlet who still has not digested his bitter mistrust of others, and who, therefore, is always rediscovering evil and falsity as a, to him, most hateful second thought. His bitterness then becomes an expression of his own renewed pain.

"I never gave you aught," may mean, I am no longer the same man who gave you gifts, or You are not the same woman to whom I gave gifts.

Down to line 130 his bitterness is partly guilt and self-loathing (see ll. 117-9, 121-30). Notice that the first of these passages states clearly that his blood relationship with Gertrude and Claudius makes him shrink from his own "sullied flesh" (cf. I,ii, 129-32 and commentary; III,iv, 16).

There is a sharp alteration in Hamlet's manner following his sudden question about her father. After this his cruelty gains force, and his emotional pitch rises once more towards an uncontrollable or hysterical level. As this occurs, he again leaps from the single case to the general (l. 144), from Ophelia to womankind and from her marriage (l. 121-2, 136) to all marriages, and to his wild plan to end the human race in one generation by prohibiting marriage.

It is traditional to account in the staging for Hamlet's question (l. 131) and his change of manner by having Hamlet accidentally become aware that he is being spied on. If this occurs, Ophelia's, "At home, my lord," her only falsehood in the play, becomes to Hamlet damning evidence not only of her inconstancy, but her complicity with the King. Thus is Hamlet again tragically duped, and the ambiguous tenderness that hovered behind the earlier speeches (this was almost a love scene) is dispelled.

Now if it is true that Hamlet knows he is being spied upon, his "all but one," (l. 150) is a recklessly unguarded defiance, flung in the King's face. Hamlet, like the players (III,ii, 145), cannot keep counsel, but when driven by his bitter frenzy, tells all.

Ophelia. My lord, I have remembrances of yours, 93
That I have longed long to re-deliver;
I pray you, now receive them.
Hamlet.   No, not I;
I never gave you aught.
Ophelia. My honour'd lord, you know right well you did;
And, with them, words of so sweet breath compos'd
As made the things more rich: their perfume lost,
Take these again; for to the noble mind
Rich gifts wax poor when givers prove unkind. 101
There, my lord.
Hamlet. Ha, ha! are you honest? 103
Ophelia. My lord!
Hamlet. Are you fair?
Ophelia. What means your lordship?
Hamlet. That if you be honest and fair, your honesty 107
should admit no discourse to your beauty.
Ophelia. Could beauty, my lord, have better com- 109
merce than with honesty?
Hamlet. Ay, truly; for the power of beauty will
sooner transform honesty from what it is to a bawd 112
than the force of honesty can translate beauty into 113
his likeness: this was sometime a paradox, but the 114
time gives it proof. I did love you once. 115
Ophelia. Indeed, my lord, you made me believe so.
Hamlet. You should not have believed me; for virtue 117
cannot so inoculate our old stock but we shall relish
of it: I loved you not.
Ophelia. I was the more deceived.
Hamlet. Get thee to a nunnery: why wouldst thou
be a breeder of sinners? I am myself indifferent 122
honest; but yet I could accuse me of such things that
it were better my mother had not borne me. I am
very proud, revengeful, ambitious; with more of-
fences at my beck than I have thoughts to put them
in, imagination to give them shape, or time to act
them in. What should such fellows as I do crawling
between heaven and earth? We are arrant knaves, 129
all; believe none of us. Go thy ways to a nunnery.
Where's your father?
Ophelia. At home, my lord.
Hamlet. Let the doors be shut upon him, that he may
play the fool nowhere but in's own house. Farewell.
Ophelia. O! help him, you sweet heavens!
Hamlet. If thou dost marry, I'll give thee this plague
for thy dowry: be thou as chaste as ice, as pure as 137
snow, thou shalt not escape calumny. Get thee to a 138
nunnery, go; farewell. Or, if thou wilt needs marry,
marry a fool; for wise men know well enough what
monsters you make of them. To a nunnery, go; and 141
quickly too. Farewell.
Ophelia. O heavenly powers, restore him!
Hamlet. I have heard of your paintings too, well 144
enough; God hath given you one face, and you make
yourselves another: you jig, you amble, and you lisp, 146
and nickname God's creatures, and make your wan- 147
tonness your ignorance. Go to, I'll no more on 't: it
hath made me mad. I say, we will have no more
marriages; those that are married already, all but one, 150

93. "remembrances": love-tokens.

101. "wax": grow, become.

103. "honest": chaste, a regular meaning.

107-8. i.e., your chastity should have nothing to do with your beauty. Hamlet is implying, in his bitterness, that beautiful women are seldom chaste.

109-10. "commerce": association.

112. "bawd": brothel-keeper, a regular meaning.

113. "translate": transform.

114. "sometime a paradox": at one time an apparent contradiction.

115. "gives it proof": Is he thinking of his mother, or Ophelia, or both?

117-9. "virtue . . . it": i.e., no matter how we may try to engraft virtue onto our old stock (the old Adam in us), we shall always smack of original sin. Or Hamlet may be thinking of his own family as represented by Claudius and Gertrude. "It" would then refer to vice.

122-3. "indifferent honest": fairly virtuous.

129. "arrant knaves": out-and-out rascals.

137. "dowry": marriage portion.

138. "calumny": slander.

141. "monsters": beasts with horns, hence cuckolds. (A cuckold was supposed to wear invisible horns.)

144. "paintings": the use of make up by women goes back a long way.

146. "jig": dance lecherously.
    "amble": walk with exaggerated swing of hips.
    "lisp": talk affectedly, coquettishly.

147. "nickname": give indecent names to.

147-8. "make . . . ignorance": pretend that you are too naive to understand the meaning of your lewd nicknames and actions.

150. "but one": to whom is he referring?

57

HAMLET

ACT III SCENE I

Ophelia's beautiful speech after Hamlet's exit does more than express her sweet and selfless constancy; it gives us her picture of the old Hamlet. It is a feature of this play that we are not allowed an early glimpse of the hero in his full stature, but see him already brought low, and must piece out bit by bit his variety and pre-eminence. Ophelia's little portrait (note its flower image, and cf. III,iv, 42-3; IV, v, 175-85; etc.) suggests the renaissance ideal of the perfect prince, who was supposed to be thus fully rounded with social, military, scholarly, and artistic skills. We have part of this picture established: the courtly lover, the scholar, the patron of drama.

Claudius

ACT III SCENE II

During the first few moments of this scene, the stage must be dressed for the play within the play. This will involve seats for the court and whatever hangings and properties the players will require. The intelligence and imagination of both designer and director meet a challenge here. The court must watch the play, and we must be able to watch both, either at once or alternately. The scene is

---

shall live; the rest shall keep as they are. To a nunnery, go.　　　　　　　　　　　　　　　　　[*Exit.*

Ophelia. O! what a noble mind is here o'erthrown:
The courtier's, soldier's, scholar's, eye, tongue, sword;
The expectancy and rose of the fair state,　　　　　155
The glass of fashion and the mould of form,　　　　156
The observ'd of all observers, quite, quite down!
And I, of ladies most deject and wretched,
That suck'd the honey of his music vows,
Now see that noble and most sovereign reason,
Like sweet bells jangled, out of tune and harsh;
That unmatch'd form and feature of blown youth　　162
Blasted with ecstasy: O! woe is me,　　　　　　　163
To have seen what I have seen, see what I see!

Re-enter KING *and* POLONIUS.

King. Love! his affections do not that way tend;　165
Nor what he spake, though it lack'd form a little,
Was not like madness. There's something in his soul
O'er which his melancholy sits on brood;　　　　168
And, I do doubt, the hatch and the disclose　　　169
Will be some danger; which for to prevent,
I have in quick determination
Thus set it down: he shall with speed to England,
For the demand of our neglected tribute:　　　　173
Haply the seas and countries different　　　　　174
With variable objects shall expel　　　　　　　175
This something-settled matter in his heart,　　　176
Whereon his brains still beating puts him thus
From fashion of himself. What think you on 't?　178
Polonius. It shall do well: but yet do I believe
The origin and commencement of his grief
Sprung from neglected love. How now, Ophelia!
You need not tell us what Lord Hamlet said;
We heard it all. My lord, do as you please;
But, if you hold it fit, after the play,
Let his queen mother all alone entreat him
To show his grief: let her be round with him;　　186
And I'll be plac'd, so please you, in the ear　　187
Of all their conference. If she find him not,　　188
To England send him, or confine him where
Your wisdom best shall think.
King.　　　　　　　　It shall be so:
Madness in great ones must not unwatch'd go.
　　　　　　　　　　　　　　　　　　　　[*Exeunt.*

Scene two.

(A HALL IN THE CASTLE)

Enter HAMLET *and certain* Players.

Hamlet. Speak the speech, I pray you, as I pronounced it to you, trippingly on the tongue; but if you mouth it, as many of your players do, I had as lief the town-crier spoke my lines. Nor do not saw the air too much with your hand, thus; but use all gently: for in the very torrent, tempest, and—as I may say—whirlwind of passion, you must acquire and beget

---

155. "expectancy and rose": bright hope (i.e., as future king).

156. "glass": mirror.
"mould of form": pattern of manly beauty and behavior.

162. "unmatch'd": unmatchable.
"blown": in full blossom.

163. "Blasted . . . ecstasy": ruined by madness.

165. "affections": emotions.

168. "on brood": hatching.

169-70. "doubt . . . danger": suspect the result of his brooding will be dangerous.

173. "neglected tribute": money owed as a result of war with Denmark.

174. "Haply": perhaps.

175. "variable objects": various sights.

176. "something-settled": partly established; i.e., not yet incurable.

178. "fashion of himself": his normal self.

186. "grief": grievance.
"round": direct.

187-8. "in . . . conference": within hearing of all that is said.

188. "find him not": does not discover his secret.

1. "the speech": which he has written.

2. "trippingly": smoothly, easily.

3. "mouth": shout, or exaggerate enunciation.
"lief": soon.

58

HAMLET

ACT III SCENE II

very spectacular and exciting. It combines a court scene with further bitter improvisations by Hamlet. Thus it takes on the character of a duel between the King's world of appearances and Hamlet's disturbing truth. There is a delicate paradox in it, too. Claudius' world is a mask or make-believe; the players' world in their play is entirely make-believe. Out of the confrontation of two make-believes, one hiding what the other imitates, the truth is made to emerge.

In speaking to the player, Hamlet is coaching him how to speak the speech he has written to insert in their play (II,ii, 542-5). Once again we see him carried away from the particular to the general, as he rises to discourse on the purpose and technique of acting. It is commonly supposed that in these speeches Shakespeare has spoken his own conviction through Hamlet's mouth. His words imply a rejection of the old style of robust, high-flown acting still practised by Alleyn, leading tragedian with the Lord Admiral's Servants. This strutting, mouthing style was well suited to project the majestic, full-throated, but less flexible style of Marlowe (see the Pyrrhus speech II,ii, 455-520). When it came to Shakespeare's more natural mode with its immense variety of characters, each speaking in his own proper rhythm and inflection, judgment, moderation, and variation were called for. To perceive the variety compare Polonius' precepts (I,iii) with Claudius' opening speech (I,ii), Hamlet in soliloquy, and Ophelia (III,i, 153-63). Since the First Player does act in the older style (see II,ii, 455; and II. 262-3 below), the inference that these players are intended to represent the Lord Admiral's Servants is reasonably likely. (See also II,ii, 424-551 and commentary.)

When Horatio appears so readily at Hamlet's call, he is cast into sharp contrast with Rosencrantz and Guildenstern, who have just crossed the stage. It may be Hamlet's own perception of this contrast that sets off the glowing friendliness of his praise. Horatio is the only character, since Hamlet is deceived about Ophelia, who matches Hamlet's ideal of conduct. Horatio thus becomes a foil to the rest, both in our eyes and Hamlet's, throwing them into perspective and suggesting the heights, as they suggest the depths, of human capacity.

a temperance, that may give it smoothness. O! it 8
offends me to the soul to hear a robustious periwig- 9
pated fellow tear a passion to tatters, to very rags, to
split the ears of the groundlings, who for the most part 11
are capable of nothing but inexplicable dumb-shows 12
and noise: I would have such a fellow whipped for
o'er-doing Termagant; it out-herods Herod: pray 14
you, avoid it.
First Player. I warrant your honour.
Hamlet. Be not too tame neither, but let your own
discretion be your tutor: suit the action to the word,
the word to the action; with this special observance,
that you o'erstep not the modesty of nature; for any- 20
thing so overdone is from the purpose of playing, whose 21
end, both at the first and now, was and is, to hold, as
'twere, the mirror up to nature; to show virtue her
own feature, scorn her own image, and the very age and 24
body of the time his form and pressure. Now, this 25
overdone, or come tardy off, though it make the un- 26
skilful laugh, cannot but make the judicious grieve;
the censure of which one must in your allowance o'er- 28
weigh a whole theatre of others. O! there be players
that I have seen play, and heard others praise, and
that highly, not to speak it profanely, that, neither
having the accent of Christians nor the gait of Christian, pagan, nor man, have so strutted and bellowed
that I have thought some of nature's journeymen 34
had made men and not made them well, they imi-
tated humanity so abominably.
First Player. I hope we have reformed that
indifferently with us. 38
Hamlet. O! reform it altogether. And let those that
play your clowns speak no more than is set down
for them; for there be of them that will themselves
laugh, to set on some quantity of barren spectators to 42
laugh too, though in the mean time some necessary
question of the play be then to be considered; that's
villainous, and shows a most pitiful ambition in the 45
fool that uses it. Go, make you ready.
　　　　　　　　　　　　　　　　[*Exit* Players.
Enter POLONIUS, ROSENCRANTZ, *and* GUILDENSTERN.
How now, my lord! will the king hear this piece of
work?
Polonius. And the queen too, and that presently. 49
Hamlet. Bid the players make haste.
　　　　　　　　　　　　　　　　[*Exit* POLONIUS.
Will you two help to hasten them?
Guildenstern. ⎫
　　　　　　　 ⎬ We will, my lord.
Rosencrantz. ⎭
　　　　　　　[*Exeunt* ROSENCRANTZ *and* GUILDENSTERN.
Hamlet. What, ho! Horatio!

Enter HORATIO.

Horatio. Here, sweet lord, at your service.
Hamlet. Horatio, thou art e'en as just a man
As e'er my conversation cop'd withal. 56
Horatio. O! my dear lord,—
Hamlet.　　　　　　　Nay, do not think I flatter;
For what advancement may I hope from thee, 58
That no revenue hast but thy good spirits

8. "temperance": control.
9. "robustious": ranting.
9-10. "periwig-pated": bewigged.
11. "groundlings": the poorer and less critical section of the audience who stood in the pit.
12. "capable": of understanding. "inexplicable dumb-shows": the unintelligible pantomime preceding the play proper.
14. "Termagant . . . Herod": favorite characters in the old miracle plays, who were always portrayed as blustering tyrants.
20. "modesty": moderation.
21. "from": away from, contrary to.
24-5. "very . . . pressure": an exact reproduction of the age.
25. "form": shape. "pressure": imprint.
26. "come . . . off": slackly performed.
28. "which one": i.e., the judicious spectator. "allowance": estimation.
34. "journeymen": i.e., not master of their trade.
38. "indifferently": fairly well.
42. "barren": barren-witted.
45. "pitiful": contemptible.
49. "presently": immediately.

56. i.e., as ever I met.
58. "advancement": promotion.

HAMLET

ACT III SCENE II

Lines 69-75 belong with I,iv, 23-38. They are speeches in which Hamlet unconsciously reveals his own weaknesses (cf. also commentary to the conclusion of III,i, and V,ii, the duel).

Visualize once again with the aid of the stage direction the courtly pomp and pageantry of the entry of Claudius and his train to the strains of a Danish march. (Q2 brings the trumpets and kettle drums marching onto the stage. F1 adds "his guard carrying torches.")
The King's opening is again soothing and sweet, as in I,ii, but it is met by the straight-arm of Hamlet's mocking irony. He no longer feels bound to break his heart in silence. This partly calculated rashness gives Hamlet the upper hand for the first time. Claudius cannot speak out without danger. He keeps silence till after the first scene of the play, and it is Hamlet's bitter improvisation that drives the scene along.

Having dissociated himself from the King, he turns to Polonius. Such rudeness even in a lunatic must put the court on edge.

His next attack is in the same crushing bad taste, rebuffing his mother and cheapening Ophelia's beauty. Now for a while he puts us on edge too. His coarseness to Ophelia is really cruel and so grates on our ears that only our understanding of his mistake about her saves our sympathy. He is harder on this fragile and lovely girl than on anyone, and it is the force of disappointed love that generates his desire to wound her. How should that infinitely pathetic line, "You are merry, my lord?", be spoken?

By Hamlet's charge against his mother and his evocation of his father's memory, the mind of the whole court is turned back to the suspicious side of Claudius' behavior (cf. I,ii, 1-16), and a lot of Claudius' careful evasion of reality (cf. II,ii, 7-10) is undone. The relief in Claudius' mind at the players' entry will be considerable but short. It is hard to judge where the boundary falls in this scene between Hamlet's intention to disturb the court and the involuntary expression of his newly rising excitement.

The hobbyhorse, similar to our carnival horse composed of two men under a cloth, was a traditional part of the English May festivals. Its use (it was not a very moral beast) had been suppressed by puritan influence not long before the writing of the play. Hamlet quotes the refrain of a ballad on the subject.

To feed and clothe thee? Why should the poor be flattered?
No; let the candied tongue lick absurd pomp, 61
And crook the pregnant hinges of the knee 62
Where thrift may follow fawning. Dost thou hear? 63
Since my dear soul was mistress of her choice
And could of men distinguish, her election 65
Hath seal'd thee for herself; for thou hast been 66
As one, in suffering all, that suffers nothing, 67
A man that fortune's buffets and rewards
Hast ta'en with equal thanks; and bless'd are those
Whose blood and judgment are so well co-mingled 70
That they are not a pipe for fortune's finger 71
To sound what stop she please. Give me that man
That is not passion's slave, and I will wear him
In my heart's core, ay, in my heart of heart,
As I do thee. Something too much of this.
There is a play to-night before the king;
One scene of it comes near the circumstance
Which I have told thee of my father's death:
I prithee, when thou seest that act afoot,
Even with the very comment of thy soul 80
Observe mine uncle; if his occulted guilt 81
Do not itself unkennel in one speech, 82
It is a damned ghost that we have seen 83
And my imaginations are as foul
As Vulcan's stithy. Give him heedful note; 85
For I mine eyes will rivet to his face,
And after we will both our judgments join
In censure of his seeming. 88
Horatio.   Well, my lord:
If he steal aught the whilst this play is playing, 89
And 'scape detecting, I will pay the theft.

Hamlet. They are coming to the play; I must be idle: 91
Get you a place.

Danish march. A Flourish. Enter KING, QUEEN, POLONIUS, OPHELIA, ROSENCRANTZ, GUILDENSTERN, *and Others.*

King. How fares our cousin Hamlet?

Hamlet. Excellent, i' faith; of the chameleon's dish: 94
I eat the air, promise-crammed; you cannot feed 95
capons so.

King. I have nothing with this answer, Hamlet; 97
these words are not mine.

Hamlet. No, nor mine now. [*To* POLONIUS.] My lord, you played once i' the university, you say?

Polonius. That did I, my lord, and was accounted a good actor.

Hamlet. And what did you enact?

Polonius. I did enact Julius Caesar: I was killed i' the Capitol; Brutus killed me.

Hamlet. It was a brute part of him to kill so capital a calf there. Be the players ready?

Rosencrantz. Ay, my lord; they stay upon your pa- 108
tience.

Queen. Come hither, my good Hamlet, sit by me.

Hamlet. No, good mother, here's metal more at- 111
tractive.

Polonius. [*To the* KING.] O ho! do you mark that?

61. "candied": sugared with hypocrisy.

62. "pregnant": ready at the least opportunity to bend.

63. "Where . . . fawning": where gain will follow flattery.

65. "of": among.

66. "seal'd": fixed upon.

67. "suffering . . . suffers": putting up with.

70. "blood and judgment": passion and reason.

71-2. "pipe . . . please": a recorder or flute. The stops are the fingerholes.

80. "comment": close observation.

81. "occulted": hidden.

82. i.e., is not brought to light by one of the speeches in the play.

83. "damned ghost": (see II, ii, 609) i.e., a devil.

85. "stithy": smithy. "heedful note": careful observation.

88. "censure . . . seeming": judgment of his reaction.

89. "steal": conceal.

91. "be idle": seem crazy.

94-5. Hamlet takes the King's use of the word "fare" literally.

94. "chameleon's dish": The chameleon was supposed to feed on air.

95. "promise-crammed": stuffed with empty promises. To what is Hamlet referring?

97. i.e., I can make nothing of this answer.

108. i.e., they await your convenience.

111. "metal": substance, stuff.

60

HAMLET

ACT III SCENE II

The full irony of lines 145-6 may be realized by equating "tell" with reveal.

"In 1538," says Dowden, "the Duke of Urbino, married to a Gonzaga, was murdered by Luigi Gonzaga, who dropped poison in his ear." If Shakespeare knew of this it would be enough for him to model his play within the play on it; he would not have needed to adopt the Italian form of poisoning. In the old Danish story, the murder of Hamlet's father was done by open violence. It has often been pointed out that Claudius' type of villainy is more Italian than Northern: it is crafty, suave, and luxurious.

The play itself is written in a dramatic style yet older than that of the Pyrrhus speech, as if it were a period piece kept in the repertoire for country audiences who liked the ceremonial dumb show and the musical but monotonous chime of the rhymed couplets. The relatively long length of this play suggests that we are meant to devote attention to its lines. Such attention reveals a good deal of comment relative to the main story, partly ironical and partly giving poetic echo and emphasis to sentiments expressed by Hamlet and the King.

Hamlet. Lady, shall I lie in your lap?

        [*Lying down at* OPHELIA's *feet.*

Ophelia. No, my lord.

Hamlet. I mean, my head upon your lap?

Ophelia. Ay, my lord.

Hamlet. Do you think I meant country matters?

Ophelia. I think nothing, my lord.

Hamlet. That's a fair thought to lie between maid's legs.

Ophelia. What is, my lord?

Hamlet. Nothing.

Ophelia. You are merry, my lord.

Hamlet. Who, I?

Ophelia. Ay, my lord.

Hamlet. O God, your only **jig-maker.** What should a 127 man do but be merry? for, look you, how cheerfully my mother looks, and my father died within's two hours.

Ophelia. Nay, 'tis twice two months, my lord.

Hamlet So long? Nay, then, let the devil wear black, 132 for I'll have a suit of sables. O heavens! die two months ago, and not forgotten yet? Then there's hope a great man's memory may outlive his life half a year; but, by'r lady, he must build churches then, or else shall he suffer not thinking on, with the hobby-horse 137 whose epitaph is, 'For, O! for, O! the hobby-horse is forgot.'

Hautboys play. The dumb-show enters.

Enter a King and a Queen, *very lovingly; the* Queen *embracing him, and he her. She kneels, and makes show of protestation unto him. He takes her up, and declines his head upon her neck; lays him down upon a bank of flowers: she, seeing him asleep, leaves him. Anon comes in a fellow, takes off his crown, kisses it, and pours poison in the* King's *ears, and exit. The* Queen *returns, finds the* King *dead, and makes passionate action. The* Poisoner, *with some two or three* Mutes, *comes in again, seeming to lament with her. The dead body is carried away. The* Poisoner *wooes the* Queen *with gifts; she seems loath and unwilling awhile, but in the end accepts his love.*   [*Exeunt.*

Ophelia. What means this, my lord?

Hamlet. Marry, this is miching mallecho; it means 141 mischief.

Ophelia. Belike this show imports the argument of 143 the play.

Enter Prologue.

Hamlet. We shall know by this fellow: the players cannot keep counsel; they'll tell all.

Ophelia. Will he tell us what this show meant?

Hamlet. Ay, or any show that you'll show him; be not you ashamed to show, he'll not shame to tell you what it means.

Ophelia. You are naught, you are naught. I'll mark 151 the play.

Prologue.   For us and for our tragedy,

        Here stooping to your clemency,

        We beg your hearing patiently.

127. "your . . . jig-maker": i.e., I am the funniest man alive (ironic).

132-3. "let . . . sables": This is spoken ironically, as is his whole speech here. He says that since his father has been so long remembered the Devil should go into mourning, but he will get a suit trimmed with rich fur (sable), i.e., he will go out of mourning. There is also a suggestion (cf. IV,vii,79) that sables were appropriate to older men. His meaning then might partly be, I'm aging fast.

137. "not . . . on": not being thought of.

137-9. "hobby-horse . . . forgot": Hamlet quotes a line from a satirical ballad of the day directed against the Puritans who opposed the May Day celebrations in which the hobby horse was a familiar object.

Stage direction: "Hautboys": oboes.

141. "miching mallecho": slinking mischief.

143. "argument": plot.

151. "naught": naughty.

HAMLET

ACT III SCENE II

For Hamlet's application of lines 183-4 to his mother, see also III,iv, 28-9. He is mistaken about her too.

Some difficulty has been felt at Claudius' seemingly stupid question (II. 236-7). If Claudius has seen the dumb show, he will not need to ask it. (Some critics and directors suggest that the King was talking to someone and did not see the dumb show.) The purpose of the question is to attempt as tactfully as possible to halt the performance. Ever since the dumb show, the King has been struggling with doubts and fears. He does not know how much Hamlet knows. He is sure in his own mind that there were no witnesses to the murder. The parallel may be a coincidence. In any case, the court does not know anything; they will take it as simply an amusingly old-fashioned melodrama. If he can master his feelings and keep still, all may pass off without trouble. But the further the play progresses, as the protestations of the Player Queen hit home, and as Hamlet's remarks become more pointed and his excitement and scrutiny become intense, his own distress and fear move him. What can he gracefully do? In the face of such obvious insult and insinuation leveled in public at himself and Gertrude, to be silent now will look as guilty as to object. The effect of the whole first scene of the melodrama is that of a largely silent duel between Hamlet's provocation and Claudius' resistance. The whole point of this question in lines 236-7 is to show that for once the King cannot master the situation; his question coming thus ill-timed will sound just as odd to the court as to us.

Hamlet's reply to Claudius' distraught question is like a crow of triumph. The King's conscience is caught; the ghost spoke truth. Now all that remains is to goad Claudius into showing his guilt and distress.

Line 189 echoes many passages depicting Hamlet's revulsion from the physical side of love (cf. I,ii, 156-7; I,v, 55-7; II,ii, 181-5; III,iv, 91-4, 182-5).

Lines 192-219 give a reasoned account of how love wanes with time, and purpose may be lost. This is a most important theme in the play. The waning of love is one of the causes of Hamlet's disillusion, and the loss of purpose, of his self-reproach. Line 193 may remind us of the violence of Hamlet's soliloquy of dedica-

Hamlet. Is this a prologue, or the posy of a ring?　156
Ophelia. 'Tis brief, my lord.
Hamlet. As woman's love.　158
　　　　　Enter two Players, King *and* Queen.
Player King. Full thirty times hath Phoebus' cart　159
　　gone round
Neptune's salt wash and Tellus' orbed ground,　160
And thirty dozen moons with borrow'd sheen　161
About the world have times twelve thirties been,
Since love our hearts and Hymen did our hands　163
Unite commutual in most sacred bands.　164
Player Queen. So many journeys may the sun and
　　moon
Makes us again count o'er ere love be done!
But, woe is me! you are so sick of late,
So far from cheer and from your former state,
That I distrust you. Yet, though I distrust,　169
Discomfort you, my lord, it nothing must;
For women's fear and love holds quantity,　171
In neither aught, or in extremity.　172
Now, what my love is, proof hath made you know;
And as my love is siz'd, my fear is so.
Where love is great, the littlest doubts are fear;
Where little fears grow great, great love grows there.
Player King. Faith, I must leave thee, love, and
　　shortly too;
My operant powers their functions leave to do:　178
And thou shalt live in this fair world behind,
Honour'd, belov'd; and haply one as kind
For husband shalt thou—
Player Queen.　　　　O! confound the rest;
Such love must needs be treason in my breast:
In second husband let me be accurst;
None wed the second but who kill'd the first.
Hamlet. [*Aside.*] Wormwood, wormwood.　185
Player Queen. The instances that second marriage　186
　　move,
Are base respects of thrift, but none of love;　187
A second time I kill my husband dead,
When second husband kisses me in bed.
Player King. I do believe you think what now you
　　speak;
But what we do determine oft we break.
Purpose is but the slave to memory,　192
Of violent birth, but poor validity;　193
Which now, like fruit unripe, sticks on the tree,
But fall unshaken when they mellow be.
Most necessary 'tis that we forget
To pay ourselves what to ourselves is debt;
What to ourselves in passion we propose,
The passion ending, doth the purpose lose.
The violence of either grief or joy
Their own enactures with themselves destroy;　201
Where joy most revels grief doth most lament,
Grief joys, joy grieves, on slender accident.
This world is not for aye, nor 'tis not strange,　204
That even our love should with our fortunes change;
For 'tis a question left us yet to prove
Whe'r love lead fortune or else fortune love.
The great man down, you mark his favourite flies;

156. "posy . . . ring": i.e., as brief and silly as the inscription inside a ring.

158. A bitter observation arising out of his mother's behavior and his treatment at the hands of Ophelia.

159. "Phoebus' cart": the chariot of the sun.

160. "Neptune": god of the sea. "Tellus": goddess of earth. "orbed": spherical.

161. "borrow'd sheen": light borrowed from the sun.

163. "Hymen": god of marriage.

164. "commutal": mutually.

169. "distrust": am anxious about.

171. "quantity": equal proportion.

172. i.e., either nothing or too much.

178. "operant powers": bodily strength. "leave": cease.

185. "Wormwood": bitterness. (Wormwood is a plant with bitter qualities.)

186. "instances": arguments.

187. "respects of thrift": considerations of gain.

192. i.e., our purpose is soon forgotten.

193. "validity": strength.

201. "enactures": performances.

204. "aye": ever.

HAMLET

ACT III SCENE II

tion in I.v; line 207 suggests Gertrude. (Cf. also I,iii, 5-8, 14-7; II,ii, 366-71, 571-5; III,i, 83-8, 111-15; III,iv, 65-7, 106-10; IV,iv, soliloquy; and most remarkable of all, IV,vii, 110-22.)

Notice how line 235 may be aimed subtly at the Queen by placing a slight stress on the word "she'll."

What significance may there be in Lucianus' being, not brother, but nephew (Hamlet's relationship) to the King.

Puppet shows were popular entertainment. It was the custom to have a narrator, called the interpreter, who explained the action of the marionettes whenever it could not be made clear purely in action. As this metaphor is applied to Hamlet and Ophelia, who would be pulling the strings?

Hamlet's impatient outburst to the player continues, even in the midst of his main action, because of his dislike of the exaggerated acting style. In addition, regular theater-goers in the audience would recall the extent of Hamlet's knowledge of plays, because "The croaking raven doth bellow for revenge" is a misquotation from a popular play of the 1590's THE TRUE TRAGEDIE OF RICHARD THE THIRD, which had, "The screeking raven sits croaking for revenge. Whole herds of beasts come bellowing for revenge."

As he watches Claudius and his court, the whole false-seeming world fleeing away, Hamlet in hysterical triumph bursts, as he has before, into the quotation of apt snatches of ballads.

Damon and Pythias were legendary friends who changed the course of a tyrannical government by the example of their constancy to each other. "Pajock" (i.e., peacock) is much more apt here than the obvious rhyming word is. Claudius is no ass, but has many of the features attributed to peacocks. Here is a contemporary description: "He is vain, loves not his young, is inordinately lustful, swalloweth his own ordure, hath the voice of a fiend, the head of a serpent, and the pace of a thief."

Notice how the first three sections of this scene gather three main elements of Hamlet's character: 1) His lively interest and keen judgment in advising the player; 2) His warm and friendly nature in talking to Horatio; 3) His bitter wit, cruelty, and hysteria when confronted with those who have caused his disillusion.

The poor advanc'd makes friends of enemies.
And hitherto doth love on fortune tend,   210
For who not needs shall never lack a friend;
And who in want a hollow friend doth try
Directly seasons him his enemy.   213
But, orderly to end where I begun,
Our wills and fates do so contrary run
That our devices still are overthrown,   216
Our thoughts are ours, their ends none of our own:
So think thou wilt no second husband wed;
But die thy thoughts when thy first lord is dead.
   Player Queen. Nor earth to me give food, nor
          heaven light!
Sport and repose lock from me day and night!
To desperation turn my trust and hope!
An anchor's cheer in prison be my scope!   223
Each opposite that blanks the face of joy   224
Meet what I would have well, and it destroy!
But here and hence pursue me lasting strife,
If, once a widow, ever I be wife!
   Hamlet. If she should break it now!
   Player King. 'Tis deeply sworn. Sweet, leave me
          here awhile;
My spirits grow dull, and fain I would beguile   230
The tedious day with sleep.   [*Sleeps.*
   Player Queen.   Sleep rock thy brain;
And never come mischance between us twain! [*Exit.*
   Hamlet. Madam, how like you this play?
   Queen. The lady doth protest too much methinks. 234
   Hamlet. O! but she'll keep her word.
   King. Have you heard the argument? Is there no 236
offence in 't?
   Hamlet. No, no, they do but jest, poison in jest; no
offence i' the world.
   King. What do you call the play?
   Hamlet. The Mouse-trap. Marry, how? Tropically. 241
This play is the image of a murder done in Vienna:
Gonzago is the duke's name; his wife, Baptista. You
shall see anon; 'tis a knavish piece of work: but what 244
of that? your majesty and we that have free souls, it 245
touches us not: let the galled jade wince, our withers 246
are unwrung.   247

Enter Player *as Lucianus.*

This is one Lucianus, nephew to the king.
   Ophelia. You are a good chorus, my lord.   249
   Hamlet. I could interpret between you and your 250
love, if I could see the puppets dallying.   251
   Ophelia. You are keen, my lord, you are keen.   252
   Hamlet. It would cost you a groaning to take off 253
my edge.
   Ophelia. Still better, and worse.
   Hamlet. So you mis-take your husbands. Begin, 256
murderer; pox, leave thy damnable faces, and begin.
Come; the croaking raven doth bellow for revenge.
   Lucianus. Thoughts black, hands apt, drugs fit, and
          time agreeing;
Confederate season, else no creature seeing;   260
Thou mixture rank, of midnight weeds collected,
With Hecate's ban thrice blasted, thrice infected,   262

---

210. "tend": wait, depend.

213. i.e., immediately makes an enemy of him.
"seasons": brings to maturity.

216. "devices": plans.
"still": always.

223. "anchor": anchorite, hermit.
"my scope": all that is permitted me.

224. "blanks": blanches, makes pale.

230. "beguile": entertain.

234. Is the Queen speaking from self-knowledge, or is it simply unconscious irony?

236. "argument": plot of a play.

241. "Mouse-trap": Why this title?
"Tropically": figuratively a "trope" being a figure of speech.

244. "knavish": villainous—referring to the subject matter, viz., murder.

245. "free": innocent.

246-7. "let ... unwrung": i.e., let he who has a guilty conscience wince; it doesn't bother ours.

246. "galled jade": a nag with saddle sores.
"withers": the juncture of the shoulder bones of a horse.

247. "unwrung": uninjured.

249. "chorus": used in Greek drama to assist the audience in the interpretation of the play.

250. "interpret": the puppet master, like the chorus, explains what is happening as he manipulates the puppets.

251. "love": lover.
"dallying": fondling one another.

252. "keen": severe, sarcastic. Hamlet takes a more literal meaning as point of departure for his cruelly suggestive rejoinder.

253. "a groaning": i.e., a good deal of pain.

256. "So . . . husbands": a reference to the "for better, for worse" of the marriage service as well as to his previous speech.
"mis-take": a suggestion on Hamlet's part that women are not true to their marriage vows.

260. "Confederate season": suitable opportunity.
"else no creature": no other creature.

262. "Hecate's ban": the curse of Hecate, the goddess of witchcraft.

HAMLET

ACT III SCENE II

The remainder of the scene till the small soliloquy at the end is infused with Hamlet's sense of triumph. It shows through his treatment of Rosencrantz and Guildenstern. He is more direct and open in his distaste for them, but his sarcasm, though pointed, is less tight-lipped; he is enjoying himself.

Compare "start not so wildly from my affair" with I,v, 133.

In spite of his higher spirits, Hamlet holds Rosencrantz and Guildenstern at arm's length now with his repeated "Sir" and his intentional misunderstanding of their words. It is the same sort of mockery he has used on Polonius. Rosencrantz effects a change in the tone by his appeal to their old friendship. Hamlet's reply is a trifle puzzling. "Pickers and stealers," meaning hands, was apparently a fairly common colloquial expression. It came from the Church Catechism which says, "keep my hands from picking and stealing, and my tongue from evil speaking, lying and slandering." If you are not content to accept the speech as a simple declaration of friendship, it may have the following meanings: 1) I love you as much as I ever did 2) (accent on "So"). I love you as much as I do these my hands which I loathe and contemn ("by" meaning beside).

Thy natural magic and dire property, 263
On wholesome life usurp immediately.
     [*Pours the poison into the Sleeper's ears.*
Hamlet. He poisons him i' the garden for 's estate.
His name's Gonzago; the story is extant, and writ in
very choice Italian. You shall see anon how the murderer gets the love of Gonzago's wife.
Ophelia. The king rises.
Hamlet. What! frighted with false fire? 270
Queen. How fares my lord?
Polonius. Give o'er the play.
King. Give me some light: away!
All. Lights, lights, lights!
     [*Exeunt all except* HAMLET *and* HORATIO.
Hamlet. Why, let the striken deer go weep,
     The hart ungalled play;
     For some must watch, while some must sleep:
     So runs the world away.
Would not this, sir, and a forest of feathers, if the 279
rest of my fortunes turn Turk with me, with two Pro- 280
vincial roses on my razed shoes, get me a fellowship 281
in a cry of players, sir? 282
Horatio. Half a share.
Hamlet. A whole one, I.
     For thou dost know, O Damon dear, 285
     This realm dismantled was 286
     Of Jove himself; and now reigns here
     A very, very—pajock. 288
Horatio. You might have rhymed. 289
Hamlet. O good Horatio! I'll take the ghost's word
for a thousand pound. Didst perceive?
Horatio. Very well, my lord.
Hamlet. Upon the talk of the poisoning?
Horatio. I did very well note him.
     Re-enter ROSENCRANTZ *and* GUILDENSTERN.
Hamlet. Ah, ha! Come, some music! come, the
recorders! 296
     For if the king like not the comedy,
     Why then, belike he likes it not, perdy. 298
Come, some music!
Guildenstern. Good my lord, vouchsafe me a word
with you.
Hamlet. Sir, a whole history.
Guildenstern. The king, sir,—
Hamlet. Ay, sir, what of him?
Guildenstern. Is in his retirement marvellous
distempered. 306
Hamlet. With drink, sir?
Guildenstern. No, my lord, rather with choler. 308
Hamlet. Your wisdom should show itself more richer
to signify this to his doctor; for, for me to put him to his
purgation would perhaps plunge him into far more 311
choler.
Guildenstern. Good my lord, put your discourse into
some frame, and start not so wildly from my affair. 314
Hamlet. I am tame, sir; pronounce.
Guildenstern. The queen, your mother, in most
great affliction of spirit, hath sent me to you.
Hamlet. You are welcome.
Guildenstern. Nay, good my lord, this courtesy is

263. "dire property": dreadful power.

270. "false fire": i.e., a blank cartridge.

279. "forest of feathers": plumed hat much worn by players.

280. "turn Turk": turn bad.

280-1. "Provincial roses": rosettes for concealing the laces on shoes.

281. "razed": slashed for ornamentation. "fellowship": partnership.

282. "cry": pack.

285. "Damon": i.e., perfect friend.

286. "dismantled": robbed.

288. "pajock": peacock.

289. Presumably Horatio is thinking of "ass."

296. "recorders": flageolets; the pre-eighteenth-century form of flute.

298. "perdy": by God.

306. "distempered": disordered, upset. Hamlet deliberately interprets this as a physical disorder.

308. "choler": anger. Again Hamlet takes the meaning in its physical sense, viz., billiousness.

311. "purgation": It is probable that Hamlet intends a pun: (1) to administer a purgative to get rid of the bile, (2) to purge him of his guilt.

314. "frame": shape, order.

HAMLET

ACT III SCENE II

"We . . . us": (ll. 338-9) is the royal plural, as if his obedience (even to his mother) were a favor granted by a Prince.

For the origin of, "Sir, I lack advancement," see II,ii, 255-6.

The musty proverb (ll. 348-9) reads, "While the grass doth grow oft starves the seely steed." Its application would be, My ambition is not satisfied with a promise for the future.

The hunting metaphor shows Hamlet more suspicious of their friendly questions than their rudeness. The toil (trap) would be set downwind of a grazing stag. When the hunters then approached from windward, the stag, scenting them, would run into the trap.

The recorder, a popular musical instrument of the time, has been revived lately and may readily be seen and heard in music shops or on phonograph records. It is a whistle-flute with seven fingerholes and a thumb hole, having a range of two octaves and a bit, and a pure sweet tone. Recorders come in five standard sizes from high soprano to bass. Unlike the modern or side flute, it extends forward from the mouth like a clarinet. The commonest size (the alto) is about a foot and a half long. Hamlet's familiarity with the instrument adds music to his other accomplishments. Some skill at singing and playing was part of the equipment of a proper gentleman of the time ("The glass of fashion and the mould of form" [III,i, 156]).

Guildenstern's lack of skill makes him an incomplete man. Elsewhere Shakespeare offers a fuller statement of the significance of such a lack of music. See JULIUS CAESAR I,ii, and THE MERCHANT OF VENICE V,i, where Lorenzo says:

> The man that hath no music in himself,
> Nor is not moved with concord of sweet sounds,
> Is fit for treasons, stratagems, and spoils;
> The motions of his spirit are dull as night
> And his affections dark as Erebus:
> Let no such man be trusted.

not of the right breed. If it shall please you to make me a wholesome answer, I will do your mother's commandment; if not, your pardon and my return shall be the end of my business.

Hamlet. Sir, I cannot.

Guildenstern. What, my lord?

Hamlet. Make you a wholesome answer; my wit's diseased; but, sir, such answer as I can make, you shall command; or, rather, as you say, my mother: therefore no more, but to the matter: my mother, you say,—

Rosencrantz. Then, thus she says: your behaviour hath struck her into amazement and admiration. 332

Hamlet. O wonderful son, that can so astonish a mother! But is there no sequel at the heels of this mother's admiration? Impart.

Rosencrantz. She desires to speak with you in her closet ere you go to bed. 337

Hamlet. We shall obey, were she ten times our mother. Have you any further trade with us?

Rosencrantz. My lord, you once did love me.

Hamlet. So I do still, by these pikers and stealers. 341

Rosencrantz. Good my lord, what is your cause of distemper? you do surely bar the door upon your own liberty, if you deny your griefs to your friend. 344

Hamlet. Sir, I lack advancement. 345

Rosencrantz. How can that be when you have the voice 346 of the king himself for your succession in Denmark? 347

Hamlet. Ay, sir, but 'While the grass grows,'—the 348 proverb is something musty.

Enter Players, *with recorders.*

O! the recorders: let me see one. To withdraw with 350 you: why do you go about to recover the wind of me, 351 as if you would drive me into a toil? 352

Guildenstern. O! my lord, if my duty be too bold, 353 my love is too unmannerly.

Hamlet. I do not well understand that. Will you play upon this pipe?

Guildenstern. My lord, I cannot.

Hamlet. I pray you.

Guildenstern. Believe me, I cannot.

Hamlet. I do beseech you.

Guildenstern. I know no touch of it, my lord.

Hamlet. 'Tis as easy as lying; govern these ventages 362 with your finger and thumb, give it breath with your mouth, and it will discourse most eloquent music. Look you, these are the stops.

Guildenstern. But these cannot I command to any utterance of harmony; I have not the skill.

Hamlet. Why, look you now, how unworthy a thing you make of me. You would play upon me; you would seem to know my stops; you would pluck out the heart of my mystery; you would sound me from my lowest note to the top of my compass; and there is much 372 music, excellent voice, in this little organ, yet cannot 373 you make it speak. 'Sblood, do you think I am easier to be played on than a pipe? Call me what instrument you will, though you can fret me, you cannot 376 play upon me.

332. "admiration": wonder.

337. "closet": private room (see commentary).

341. "pickers and stealers": hands.

344. "deny . . . griefs": refuse to unburden yourself.

345. "advancement": promotion. Hamlet remembers his previous conversation with these two, regarding ambition.

346-7. "voice of the king": i.e., a powerful influence towards his election to the throne.

348. " 'While . . . grows' ": . . . the steed starves.

350. "withdraw": go aside.

351. "recover the wind": a hunting figure: to get to windward.

352. "toil": net.

353-4. "if . . . unmannerly": If I have been too forward in questioning you it is only because of the greatness of my affection for you.

362. "ventages": holes, stops.

372. "compass": the range of a musical instrument.

373. "this little organ": i.e., the recorder.

376. "fret": annoy, with a pun on the frets or bars on the fingerboard of a stringed instrument.

HAMLET

ACT III SCENE II

The brief soliloquy which ends the scene has an importance of its own. It is not like Hamlet, but is more in the style of a revenger's speech. His words (l.398) indicate that he feels a change in his spirit, a hardening, a new strain of willful cruelty taking the place of his gentle, frank, reflective self. We may notice a gradual increase in the harshness of his attitude developing throughout this act. Such an alteration is understandable and even necessary if he is to cope violently with evil (see III,iv and commentary).

Hamlet's first concerted action has ended in success. The conscience of the King has been caught, the ghost vindicated, and the world of false-seeming disorganized and put to flight.

ACT III SCENE III

The scene begins like III,i, with Claudius in conference with Rosencrantz and Guildenstern. This is the third such meeting (see II,ii, and III,i). With each one the tone of the King's conspiracy is darker, and each one is a more compact and furtive-looking group, here just the three.

Rosencrantz and Guildenstern who themselves "live and feed upon your majesty," are quick to second his purpose (see III,ii, 60-2). The long speech of Rosencrantz (ll. 11-23 expresses an opinion with which Queen Elizabeth's loyal citizens in the audience would heartily agree (cf. Laertes, I,iii, 18-21). As the mind is to the body, so the monarch is to the state. If Claudius were the king by right, Rosencrantz and Guildenstern would be justified in their conduct. We know, however, the falsity of Claudius, and Rosencrantz's speech takes on an ironical meaning. It was Hamlet's father whose "cease" had drawn ruin on Denmark. Now, under Claudius, Denmark is corrupted, as Marcellus said (I,iv,90).

Enter POLONIUS.

God bless you, sir!

Polonius. My lord, the queen would speak with you, and presently. 380

Hamlet. Do you see yonder cloud that's almost in shape of a camel?

Polonius. By the mass, and 'tis like a camel, indeed.

Hamlet. Methinks it is like a weasel.

Polonius. It is backed like a weasel.

Hamlet. Or like a whale?

Polonius. Very like a whale.

Hamlet. Then I will come to my mother by and by.
[*Aside.*] They fool me to the top of my bent. 389
[*Aloud.*] I will come by and by.

Polonius. I will say so. [*Exit.*

Hamlet. 'By and by' is easily said. Leave me, friends.
[*Exeunt all but* HAMLET.

'Tis now the very witching time of night, 393
When churchyards yawn and hell itself breathes out
Contagion to this world: now could I drink hot blood, 395
And do such bitter business as the day
Would quake to look on. Soft! now to my mother.
O heart! lose not thy nature; let not ever
The soul of Nero enter this firm bosom; 399
Let me be cruel, not unnatural;
I will speak daggers to her, but use none;
My tongue and soul in this be hyprocrites;
How in my words soever she be shent, 403
To give them seals never, my soul, consent! [*Exit.* 404

Scene three.

(A ROOM IN THE CASTLE)

Enter KING, ROSENCRANTZ, *and* GUILDENSTERN.

King. I like him not, nor stands it safe with us
To let his madness range. Therefore prepare you; 2
I your commission will forthwith dispatch,
And he to England shall along with you.
The terms of our estate may not endure 5
Hazard so dangerous as doth hourly grow
Out of his lunacies.

Guildenstern. We will ourselves provide. 7
Most holy and religious fear it is 8
To keep those many many bodies safe 9
That live and feed upon your majesty.

Rosencrantz. The single and peculiar life is bound 11
With all the strength and armour of the mind
To keep itself from noyance; but much more 13
That spirit upon whose weal depend and rest 14
The lives of many. The cease of majesty 15
Dies not alone, but, like a gulf doth draw 16
What's near it with it; it is a massy wheel, 17
Fix'd on the summit of the highest mount,
To whose huge spokes ten thousand lesser things
Are mortis'd and adjoin'd; which, when it falls, 20
Each small annexment, petty consequence, 21

---

380. "presently": immediately (by contrast with Hamlet's, "by and by").

389. "top . . . bent": the extent that I am willing to be fooled.

393. "witching time": when witchcraft ranges abroad.

395. "Contagion": infection.

399. "Nero": who killed his own mother.

403. "shent": rebuked.

404. "seals": i.e., to seal my words with action.

2. "range": roam freely.

5. "terms . . . estate": our position as head of the state.

7. "ourselves provide": make our preparations.

8. "fear": anxiety.

9. "many bodies": the King's subjects.

11. "peculiar": private.

13. "noyance": harm.

14. "weal": welfare.

15. "cease of majesty": death of a king.

16. "gulf": whirlpool.

17. "massy": massive.

20. "mortis'd": firmly joined.

21. "annexment . . . consequence": attachment, smallest thing connected with it.

HAMLET

ACT III SCENE III

The King's soliloquy is a measure of the extent to which his conscience has been caught. It is true that he has shown remorse before (III,i, 49-54), but it did not drive him to his knees then. The trouble is that, although he feels remorse and fears for his soul and his safety, he does not repent. What he wants is to add the luxury of a cleared conscience to his other pleasures: absolution without penance. He asks, as he kneels, for grace. If he succeeds he may rise a new man, but he fails (ll.87-8). When he rises he rises confirmed in villainy. Prayer has not served him; so evil must serve him according to the usual reasoning of hardened men: If I am damned, then all I have is this life, and nothing I do can make my punishment afterwards, if there is any afterward, worse; therefore, here goes.

The effect as Hamlet passes by is almost like sleepwalkers brushing each other in a dream. Neither really sees the other. Claudius misses his chance for grace; Hamlet, his chance for revenge. It is a moment of great irony on which the plot turns.

Attends the boisterous ruin. Never alone 22
Did the king sigh, but with a general groan. 23
   King. Arm you, I pray you, to this speedy voyage;
For we will fetters put upon this fear,
Which now goes too free-footed.
  Rosencrantz   } We will haste us.
  Guildenstern }
     [*Exeunt* ROSENCRANTZ *and* GUILDENSTERN.

        Enter POLONIUS.

Polonius. My lord, he's going to his mother's closet:
Behind the arras I'll convey myself 29
To hear the process; I'll warrant she'll tax him home; 30
And, as you said, and wisely was it said, 31
'Tis meet that some more audience than a mother,
Since nature makes them partial, should o'erhear
The speech, of vantage. Fare you well, my liege: 34
I'll call upon you ere you go to bed
And tell you what I know.
   King.   Thanks, dear my lord.
                        [*Exit* POLONIUS.
O! my offence is rank, it smells to heaven; 37
It hath the primal eldest curse upon 't; 38
A brother's murder! Pray can I not,
Though inclination be as sharp as will: 40
My stronger guilt defeats my strong intent;
And like a man to double business bound,
I stand in pause where I shall first begin,
And both neglect. What if this cursed hand
Were thicker than itself with brother's blood,
Is there not rain enough in the sweet heavens
To wash it white as snow? Whereto serves mercy
But to confront the visage of offence? 48
And what's in prayer but this two-fold force,
To be forestalled, ere we come to fall, 50
Or pardon'd, being down? Then, I'll look up;
My fault is past. But, O! what form of prayer
Can serve my turn? 'Forgive me my foul murder?'
That cannot be since I am still possess'd
Of those effects for which I did the murder, 55
My crown, mine own ambition, and my queen.
May one be pardon'd and retain the offence? 57
In the corrupted currents of this world 58
Offence's gilded hand may shove by justice,
And oft 'tis seen the wicked prize itself 60
Buys out the law; but 'tis not so above;
There is no shuffling, there the action lies 62
In his true nature, and we ourselves compell'd
Even to the teeth and forehead of our faults 64
To give in evidence. What then? what rests? 65
Try what repentance can: what can it not?
Yet what can it, when one can not repent?
O wretched state! O bosom black as death!
O limed soul, that struggling to be free 69
Art more engaged! Help, angels! make assay; 70
Bow, stubborn knees; and heart with strings of steel
Be soft as sinews of the new-born babe.
All may be well.   [*Retires and kneels.*

        Enter HAMLET.

Hamlet. Now might I do it pat, now he is praying; 74

22. "Attends": is included in.

23. "general groan": the grief of all his people.

29. "arras": a tapestry wall hanging (named for the place where they were made).

30. "process": proceedings. "tax him home": effectually take him to task.

31. as you said": Is this true?

34. "of vantage": from some place of vantage.

37. "rank": foul.

38. "primal . . . curse": viz., the one pronounced upon Cain for the murder of his brother. "Primal" here means original.

40. "will": desire.

48. "confront . . . offence": oppose sin face to face, like a champion.

50. "forestalled": prevented.

55. "effects": advantages.

57. "offence": the prize of sin.

58. "currents": courses, ways.

60. "wicked prize": proceeds of the crime.

62-3. "there . . . nature": the case is tried on its merits.

64. "teeth . . . forehead": in the very face of.

65. "rests": remains (to be done).

69. "limed": caught, as with bird lime.

70. "engaged": entangled. "assay": an attempt.

74. "pat": easily.

HAMLET

ACT III SCENE III

Refer to I,v, 76-80 in connection with lines 80-2 of this scene.

The question that fascinates scholars here is whether Hamlet's real reason for sparing Claudius is the one he gives. To some it sounds too far-fetched to be a natural influence on his action, to others it appears too savage an idea to spring from Hamlet's gentle nature.

We believe that Hamlet does resent, not the violence, but the ignobility of his duty; that he has a melancholy sense of the futility of this or any action; that he has come to some mistrust with his own impulsiveness; but that on the other hand he is a crueller and less delicate person than before, and believes what he says here.

The crucial decision is whether Hamlet felt an impulse to kill the King, which his second thoughts put aside, or whether he felt no impulse but only a dull sense of duty which he evades.

ACT III SCENE IV

This is the most intense of all the domestic scenes in the play and the climax of Hamlet's relationship to his mother. Neither he nor she is the same after it as before.

Gertrude, her first attack repulsed by Hamlet's unexpected firmness and point, takes refuge in maternal authority (l.14, which might be paraphrased, Remember whom you're speaking to, young man). When this is met with a direct charge of incest and a hoarse expression of revulsion (ll.15-6), she makes another motherly threat (l.17, which now would take the form of, Your father will see to you). From this point on it is Hamlet who bears the authority. At line 17 she makes as if to go to the door. Hamlet seizes her, thrusts her back into her chair, and stands over her with blazing eyes, sometimes portrayed even with his hand on his sword hilts.

In stabbing the eavesdropper, Hamlet acts again on impulse. Would his impulse have taken such a deadly form before? The situation is parallel to that at line 130 in the nunnery scene, but the emotional dynamics are more intense, and Hamlet's disgust has taken on a new dimension, a compact hardness and directness. The slaying of Polonius is, as Hamlet realizes, of great advantage to

---

And now I'll do 't: and so he goes to heaven;
And so am I reveng'd. That would be scann'd: 76
A villain kills my father; and for that,
I, his sole son, do this same villain send
To heaven.
Why, this is hire and salary, not revenge. 80
He took my father grossly, full of bread, 81
With all his crimes broad blown, as flush as May; 82
And how his audit stands who knows save heaven? 83
But in our circumstance and course of thought 84
'Tis heavy with him. And am I then reveng'd,
To take him in the purging of his soul,
When he is fit and season'd for his passage? 87
No.
Up, sword, and know thou a more horrid hent; 89
When he is drunk asleep, or in his rage,
Or in the incestuous pleasure of his bed,
At gaming, swearing, or about some act
That has no relish of salvation in 't;
Then trip him, that his heels may kick at heaven,
And that his soul may be as damn'd and black
As hell, whereto it goes. My mother stays: 96
This physic but prolongs thy sickly days. [*Exit.* 97
      The KING *rises and advances.*
King. My words fly up, my thoughts remain below:
Words without thoughts never to heaven go. [*Exit.*

Scene four.

(THE QUEEN'S APARTMENT)

Enter QUEEN *and* POLONIUS.

Polonius. He will come straight. Look you lay home 1
    to him;
Tell him his pranks have been too broad to bear with, 2
And that your Grace hath screen'd and stood between
Much heat and him. I'll silence me e'en here. 4
Pray you, be round with him.
  Hamlet. [*Within.*] Mother, mother, mother!
  Queen.   I'll warrant you;
Fear me not. Withdraw, I hear him coming.
      [POLONIUS *hides behind the arras.*
        Enter HAMLET.
  Hamlet. Now, mother, what's the matter?
  Queen. Hamlet, thou hast thy father much offended.
  Hamlet. Mother, you have my father much offended.
  Queen. Come, come, you answer with an idle tongue. 11
  Hamlet. Go, go, you question with a wicked tongue.
  Queen. Why, how now, Hamlet!
  Hamlet.   What's the matter now?
  Queen. Have you forgot me?
  Hamlet.   No, by the rood, not so: 15
You are the queen, your husband's brother's wife;
And,—would it were not so!—you are my mother.
  Queen. Nay then, I'll set those to you that can speak. 17
  Hamlet. Come, come, and sit you down; you shall
    not budge;

---

76. "That . . . scann'd": that demands closer examination.

80. "hire and salary": action deserving pay, a kind act.

81. "grossly": in a state of sin.

82. "broad blown": in full blossom. "flush": fresh.

83. "audit": account (with Heaven).

84. "circumstance . . . thought": the way we on earth look at things.

87. "season'd": ripe, ready.

89. "hent": literally grasp, hence a time for action.

96. "stays": waits for me.

97. "physic": medicine, viz., prayer. There may be a pun intended here.

1. "lay . . . him": tell him what's what (cf.III,iii, 29).

2. "broad": open and unrestrained.

4. "heat": anger. "silence me": hide myself.

11. "idle": foolish.

15. "rood": cross, crucifix.

17. "I'll . . . speak": a maternal threat (i.e., Your father will deal with you).

HAMLET

ACT III SCENE IV

Claudius, who now has lots of justification for dealing with Hamlet severely.

Notice that Hamlet believes his mother, since she loved Claudius adulterously before the murder (see I,v,42-6), to be his accomplice in it (II.29 and also III,ii,183-5). Her exclamation (I.30), along with other indications noted above (II,ii and III,i), seems to be a clear enough indication that she did not know of it.

For the rest of the scene until the ghost restrains him, Hamlet's expressive fury rises steadily towards hysterical incoherence as he lashes his mother with the full force of his disillusion and his inability to understand such a falling off. His words are full of forceful imagery, much of it thematic, and of echoes of earlier passages in the play. Gertrude is reduced from frightened defiance (II. 39-40, 51-2) to guilty anguish (II. 88-91, 94-6, 101). Hamlet, carried forward by his emotional energy, is by then out of control and cannot stop when his goal of making her see her evil is accomplished.

We see, and Hamlet must realize, that his action in this scene is disobedient to the ghost's command (I,v,84-8). That he proceeds anyway indicates the importance to him of having the matter out of the way. It is as if he feels that, however bitter it may be, they must understand each other clearly.

Lines 42-4, with their flower and infection imagery, refer both to Gertrude's love for his father and his love for Ophelia. These images have many links. For the rose and its corruption, see the following: I,ii, 135; I,iii,39-40; III,i,155; IV,v, 157. For flower imagery in general, refer to: I,iii,7; IV,v, 175-85 (Ophelia's mad scene); IV, vii, 168-75 (Ophelia's death); V,i, 248-50 (Ophelia's funeral). Notice how the flower imagery clusters around Ophelia and Hamlet's love for her. The image of the blister links with both disease and corruption motifs. For further information and corruption images see the following: I,iii,39-42; I,v,32-3, 57, 64-73; I,iv,90; II,ii, 65-7, 181-2, 197-201; III,i, 84-5, 163; III,ii, 167-81, 309-312; IV,iii, 20-39, 68; IV,iv, IV,vii, 115-7; V,i, 78-226, V,ii,69. Other examples in the present scene may be found at II.64-5, 90, 147-9, 153.

The use of the portraits has been handled in many ways, from full length paintings on the wall to no actual pictures at all. It is not likely that Hamlet would carry Claudius' picture. It is generally

---

You go not, till I set up a glass 19
Where you may see the inmost part of you.
 Queen. What wilt thou do? thou wilt not murder me?
Help, help, ho!
 Polonius. [*Behind.*]   What, ho! help! help! help!
 Hamlet. [*Draws.*] How now! a rat? Dead, for a 23
  ducat, dead! [*Makes a pass through the arras.*
 Polonius. [*Behind.*] O! I am slain.
 Queen. O me! what hast thou done?
 Hamlet. Nay, I know not: is it the king?
 Queen. O! what a rash and bloody deed is this!
 Hamlet. A bloody deed! almost as bad, good mother,
As kill a king, and marry with his brother.
 Queen. As kill a king!
 Hamlet.   Ay, lady, 'twas my word.
  [*Lifts up the arras and discovers* POLONIUS.
[*To* POLONIUS.] Thou wretched, rash, intruding fool,
 farewell!
I took thee for thy better; take thy fortune; 32
Thou find'st to be too busy in some danger.
Leave wringing of your hands: peace! sit you down,
And let me wring your heart; for so I shall
If it be made of penetrable stuff,
If damned custom have not brass'd it so 37
That it is proof and bulwark against sense. 38
 Queen. What have I done that thou dar'st wag thy
  tongue
In noise so rude against me?
 Hamlet.   Such an act
That blurs the grace and blush of modesty,
Calls virtue hypocrite, takes off the rose
From the fair forehead of an innocent love
And sets a blister there, make marriage vows 44
As false as dicers' oaths; O! such a deed
As from the body of contraction plucks 46
The very soul, and sweet religion makes
A rhapsody of words; heaven's face doth glow, 48
Yea, this solidity and compound mass, 49
With tristful visage, as against the doom, 50
Is thought-sick at the act.
 Queen.   Ay me! what act,
That roars so loud and thunders in the index? 52
 Hamlet. Look here, upon this picture, and on this;
The counterfeit presentment of two brothers. 54
See, what a grace was seated on this brow;
Hyperion's curls, the front of Jove himself, 56
An eye like Mars to threaten and command,
A station like the herald Mercury 58
New-lighted on a heaven-kissing hill, 59
A combination and a form indeed, 60
Where every god did seem to set his seal, 61
To give the world assurance of a man.
This was your husband: look you now, what follows.
Here is your husband; like a mildew'd ear, 64
Blasting his wholesome brother. Have you eyes?
Could you on this fair mountain leave to feed, 66
And batten on this moor? Ha! have you eyes? 67
You cannot call it love, for at your age
The hey-day in the blood is tame, it's humble, 69
And waits upon the judgment; and what judgment

---

19. "glass": looking glass.

23. "for a ducat": would stake a ducat on it.
"ducat": a coin.

32. "thy better": viz., the King.

37. i.e., if habitual vice hasn't made your heart impenetrable (brazen).

38. "sense": feeling.

44. "sets a blister": brands as a harlot.

46. "contraction": the marriage contract.

48. "rhapsody of words": a mere string of meaningless words.

49. i.e., the earth.

50. "tristful": sorrowful.
"as . . . doom": as before the Day of Judgment.

52. "index": prologue.

54. "counterfeit presentment": portrait.

56. "Hyperion": cf. note on I, ii, 140.
"front": forehead.

58. "station": stature, posture.
"Mercury": the graceful messenger of the gods.

59. "New-lighted": newly alighted.

60. "combination": i.e., of physical attributes.

61. "set . . . seal": place his stamp of approval.

64-5. "like . . . brother": as a mildewed ear of corn infects the one next to it.

66. "leave to feed": leave off feeding.

67. "batten": glut yourself.

69. "hey-day": excitement.

HAMLET

ACT III SCENE IV

a miniature hanging as a pendant around Gertrude's neck. Conversely, since Gertrude would not be likely to have Old Hamlet's portrait, the Prince generally produces this miniature from his own clothing. Many actors climax the episode by tearing Claudius' picture from Gertrude's neck and hurling it to the floor. Rossi, a famous Italian actor, even stamped on it. (Barrymore possibly did the same thing.) Booth is given credit for being the first major actor to use the system of the two miniatures outlined above and now most commonly followed.

Compare lines 66-7 with I,v, 55-7; lines 68-70 with III,ii, 186-7; line 95 with III,ii, 401.

The "vice" (l.98) was the clown in the old morality plays, a servant of the devil, in ridiculous costume and equipped with a wooden sword.

At the moment of the ghost's entrance, Granville-Barker suggests that Hamlet, beyond control, has seized his mother by the throat, shaking and strangling her. It is an extreme but just interpretation in that it gives a concrete dramatic symbol of his state, a genuine contradiction of the ghost's command, and was prepared for by Hamlet's fear of his feelings at III,ii, 398-404.

When the ghost enters, Hamlet's family circle is complete, but it is significant that the ghost and his wife cannot communicate except through Hamlet. Gertrude is blind to him, since she betrayed him.

For "laps'd in time and passion," see II,ii,553-592; his solitary brooding (II,ii,168; III,i,56-88); III,ii,191-217; and III,iii,88.

The ghost appears here not in armor but "in his habit as he lived." By this unusual device, Shakespeare makes the figure of the ghost expressive of its changing moods. Thus it takes on greater reality and depth than most stage specters.

Notice in line 121 and elsewhere the return of affection and understanding between Hamlet and his mother. She has come to share his

Would step from this to this? Sense, sure, you have,	71
Else could you not have motion; but sure, that sense	72
Is apoplex'd; for madness would not err.	73
Nor sense to ecstasy was ne'er so thrall'd	74
But it reserv'd some quantity of choice,	75
To serve in such a difference. What devil was't	
That thus hath cozen'd you at hoodman-blind?	77
Eyes without feeling, feeling without sight,	
Ears without hands or eyes, smelling sans all,	79
Or but a sickly part of one true sense	
Could not so mope.	81
O shame! where is thy blush? Rebellious hell,	
If thou canst mutine in a matron's bones,	83
To flaming youth let virtue be as wax,	
And melt in her own fire: proclaim no shame	
When the compulsive ardour gives the charge,	86
Since frost itself as actively doth burn,	87
And reason panders will.	
Queen. O Hamlet! speak no more;	88
Thou turn'st mine eyes into my very soul;	
And there I see such black and grained spots	90
As will not leave their tinct.	91
Hamlet. Nay, but to live	
In the rank sweat of an enseam'd bed,	92
Stew'd in corruption, honeying and making love	
Over the nasty sty,—	
Queen. O! speak to me no more;	
These words like daggers enter in mine ears;	
No more, sweet Hamlet!	
Hamlet. A murderer, and a villain;	
A slave that is not twentieth part the tithe	97
Of your precedent lord; a vice of kings;	98
A cut-purse of the empire and the rule,	99
That from a shelf the precious diadem stole,	
And put it in his pocket!	
Queen. No more!	
Hamlet. A king of shreds and patches,—	102
Enter Ghost.	
Save me and hover o'er me with your wings,	
You heavenly guards! What would your gracious figure?	
Queen. Alas! he's mad!	
Hamlet. Do you not come your tardy son to chide,	
That, laps'd in time and passion, let's go by	107
The important acting of your dread command?	
O! say.	
Ghost. Do not forget: this visitation	
Is but to whet thy almost blunted purpose.	110
But, look! amazement on thy mother sits;	
O! step between her and her fighting soul;	
Conceit in weakest bodies strongest works:	113
Speak to her, Hamlet.	
Hamlet. How is it with you, lady?	
Queen. Alas! how is't with you,	
That you do bend your eye on vacancy	
And with the incorporal air do hold discourse?	117
Forth at your eyes your spirits wildly peep;	118
And, as the sleeping soldiers in the alarm,	
Your bedded hair, like life in excrements,	120
Starts up and stands an end. O gentle son!	121

71. "Sense": feeling.

72. "motion": impulses.

73. "apoplex'd": paralyzed.

74. "ecstasy": passion.
"thrall'd": enslaved.

75-6. "But . . . difference": but that it would have enough sense left to discriminate where the difference was so great.

77. "cozen'd": cheated.
"hoodman-blind": blind-man's-buff.

79. "sans": without.

81. "so mope": be so stupid.

83. "mutine": mutiny.

86. "compulsive ardour": compelling passions of youth.

87. "frost": i.e., middle age.

88. "panders": serves.
"will": desire.

90. "grained": dyed in the grain.

91. "leave . . . tinct": give up their color.

92. "enseam'd": greasy.

97. "tithe": tenth part.

98. "precedent": former.
"vice of kings": caricature of a king.

99. "cut-purse": thief.

102. "king . . . patches": a king in fool's motley, a clown.

107. "laps'd . . . passion": "having suffered time to slip and passion to cool" (Jonson).

110. "whet": sharpen.

113. "Conceit": imagination.

117. "incorporal": bodiless.

118. "at": from.

120. "bedded": lying flat.
"excrements": outgrowths of the body such as hair and nails.

121. "an": on.

HAMLET

ACT III SCENE IV

sense of evil and gains stature from her remorse; her thought is now founded on truth rather than illusion. Hamlet's hysteria has passed, and his mood is again sensitive to awe and pity before his father's image. Hamlet was in danger of losing this nobility in callous violence (III,ii, 393-404), but now the balance is restored. The change may be graphically demonstrated by comparing his comments on Polonius before and after the apparition of the ghost (ll.31-3 with ll.172-7). This restoration is important because a hardened and insensitive mind cannot perceive tragic suffering.

This image of the hidden ulcer is basic to the theme. The ulcer stands for Denmark's rottenness, and the film over it, which Hamlet's kind cruelty (l.178) seeks to remove. The film represents the seeming-healthy manner in which time's passage and Claudius' kingship will coat the ulcer with. See the list of related images above and especially IV,i,21-3; IV,iv,27-9.

"Weeds" (l.151) provides the opposite of the flower images listed above. Just as those were applied to Hamlet and Ophelia, these gather about Claudius and Gertrude (see I,ii, 135-7). Compare "these pursy times" (l.153) with I,v,189; V,i,144-5.

Hamlet's advice to his mother to abstain from further shame stems also from the Player King's notion of fortune leading love, but there is some hope for the future emerging now. If time can stale a virtuous love, it can do the same for an evil one.

Upon the heat and flame of thy distemper   122
Sprinkle cool patience. Whereon do you look?
   Hamlet. On him, on him! Look you, how pale he
     glares!
His form and cause conjoin'd, preaching to stones,   125
Would make them capable. Do not look upon me;   126
Lest with this piteous action you convert
My stern effects: then what I have to do   128
Will want true colour; tears perchance for blood.   129
   Queen. To whom do you speak this?
   Hamlet.   Do you see nothing there?
   Queen. Nothing at all; yet all that is I see.
   Hamlet. Nor did you nothing hear?
   Queen.   No, nothing but ourselves.
   Hamlet. Why, look you there! look, how it steals
     away;
My father, in his habit as he liv'd;   134
Look! where he goes, even now, out at the portal.
                 [*Exit Ghost.*
   Queen. This is the very coinage of your brain:
This bodiless creation ecstasy   137
Is very cunning in.
   Hamlet. Ecstasy!
My pulse, as yours, doth temperately keep time,
And makes as healthful music. It is not madness
That I have utter'd: bring me to the test,
And I the matter will re-word, which madness
Would gambol from. Mother, for love of grace,   144
Lay not that flattering unction to your soul,   145
That not your trespass but my madness speaks;
It will but skin and film the ulcerous place,   147
Whiles rank corruption, mining all within,   148
Infects unseen. Confess yourself to heaven;
Repent what's past; avoid what is to come;
And do not spread the compost on the weeds   151
To make them ranker. Forgive me this my virtue: 152
For in the fatness of these pursy times   153
Virtue itself of vice must pardon beg,
Yea, curb and woo for leave to do him good.   155
   Queen. O Hamlet! thou hast cleft my heart in twain.
   Hamlet. O! throw away the worser part of it,
And live the purer with the other half.
Good night; but go not to mine uncle's bed;
Assume a virtue, if you have it not.
That monster, custom, who all sense doth eat,   161
Of habits devil, is angel yet in this,   162
That to the use of actions fair and good   163
He likewise gives a frock or livery,
That aptly is put on. Refrain to-night;   165
And that shall lend a kind of easiness
To the next abstinence: the next more easy;
For use almost can change the stamp of nature,   168
And exorcise the devil or throw him out
With wondrous potency. Once more, good-night:
And when you are desirous to be bless'd,   171
I'll blessing beg of you. For this same lord,
             [*Pointing to* POLONIUS.
I do repent: but heaven hath pleas'd it so,
To punish me with this, and this with me,
That I must be their scourge and minister.   175

122. "distemper": mental disturbance.

125. "His . . . conjoin'd": his ghostly appearance combined with the reason for it (viz., his murder).

126. "capable": i.e., of feeling and action.

128. "My . . . effects": the stern working of my resolves.

129. "colour": character or kind. "for": instead of.

134. "in . . . liv'd": in his ordinary dress.

137. "ecstasy": madness.

144. "gambol": wander.

145. "unction": ointment, salve.

147. "It": i.e., the flattering unction.

148. "mining": undermining.

151. "compost": manure.

152. "my virtue": my virtuous pleading.

153. "fatness": grossness. "pursy": sensual.

155. "curb": bend, bow low. "leave": permission.

161-5. "That . . . on": i.e., though evil can become ingrained through custom virtue also can become just as much a habit.

162. "devil": evil spirit presiding over habits.

163. "use": practice.

165. "aptly": readily.

168. "stamp": impression.

171. "desirous . . . bless'd": i.e., penitent.

175. "their": refers to Heaven, or, as it were, the powers of Heaven.

HAMLET

ACT III SCENE IV

The abject weakness of Gertrude's "What shall I do?" makes Hamlet feel unsure of her, and he releases his impatience and irony. His description of their love-making (ll.182-5) has several parallels eloquent of his revulsion (cf. I,ii, 156-7; II,ii, 181-5; III,i, 140-1; III,ii, 111-23; III,iv, 91-4).

Once the Queen utters the sober and deeply-felt words of lines 197-9, Hamlet feels secure in his new understanding, and talks of his plans. The mission to England could have been no secret, since both Hamlet and his mother know of it. Hamlet's suspicion of knavery is not remarkable. The only striking factor is his knowledge of sealed letters. The only change in the arrangements since the play is that, instead of Rosencrantz and Guildenstern going over in advance to prepare Hamlet's reception (see I.204), Hamlet is to go with them (III,iii,4). The great unanswered questions about this trip to England are: 1) Do Rosencrantz and Guildenstern know they are marshalling Hamlet to knavery? 2) Was Hamlet's escape by way of the pirates a lucky accident, or a careful plan? There is no proven answer to either, but they will be more fully discussed below (IV,vi).

I will bestow him, and will answer well 176
The death I gave him. So, again, good-night.
I must be cruel only to be kind:
Thus bad begins and worse remains behind. 179
One word more, good lady.
    Queen.   What shall I do?
    Hamlet. Not this, by no means, that I bid you do:
Let the bloat king tempt you again to bed; 182
Pinch wanton on your cheek; call you his mouse; 183
And let him, for a pair of reechy kisses, 184
Or paddling in your neck with his damn'd fingers,
Make you to ravel all this matter out, 186
That I essentially am not in madness, 187
But mad in craft. 'Twere good you let him know;
For who that's but a queen, fair, sober, wise,
Would from a paddock, from a bat, a gib, 190
Such dear concernings hide? who would do so? 191
No, in despite of sense and secrecy, 192
Unpeg the basket on the house's top,
Let the birds fly, and, like the famous ape, 194
To try conclusions, in the basket creep, 195
And break your own neck down.
    Queen. Be thou assur'd, if words be made of breath,
And breath of life, I have no life to breathe
What thou hast said to me.
    Hamlet. I must to England; you know that?
    Queen.   Alack!
I had forgot: 'tis so concluded on.
    Hamlet. There's letters seal'd; and my two school-
        fellows,
Whom I will trust as I will adders fang'd,
They bear the mandate; they must sweep my way, 204
And marshal me to knavery. Let it work; 205
For 'tis the sport to have the enginer 206
Hoist with his own petard: and 't shall go hard 207
But I will delve one yard below their mines,
And blow them at the moon. O! 'tis most sweet,
When in one line two crafts directly meet. 210
This man shall set me packing; 211
I'll lug the guts into the neighbour room. 212
Mother, good-night. Indeed this counsellor
Is now most still, most secret, and most grave,
Who was in life a foolish prating knave.
Come, sir, to draw toward an end with you.
Good-night, mother.

    [*Exeunt severally*; HAMLET *tugging in* POLONIUS.

176. "bestow": get rid of.

179. "worse . . . behind": Hamlet still has the King to deal with.

182. "bloat": bloated.

183. "wanton": lewdly.
"mouse": a common term of endearment.

184. "reechy": literally smoky, foul.

186. "ravel": unravel, i.e., reveal.

187. "essentially": truly.

190. "paddock": toad.
"gib": tomcat.

191. "dear concernings": matters of such close concern (to the King).

192. "despite": spite.

194. "famous ape": The story has not come down to us.

195. "To try conclusions": to see what will happen.

204. "mandate": command.

205. "marshal . . . knavery": conduct me to the place where the villainy will take place. It is plain that Hamlet suspects that an attempt is to be made on his life.

206. "enginer": engineer.

207. "Hoist . . . petard": blown up by his own landmine ("petard").

210. "crafts": designs, schemes.

211. "packing": probably another pun intended: (1) plotting, (2) on my way.

212. "neighbour": neighboring.

HAMLET

ACT IV SCENE I

To make good dramatic sense, this scene must follow immediately after the last one without any break. Thus the act division of 1676 must be disregarded. Its only justification is that, during the Restoration, it was the fashion for tragedies to be divided into five acts of approximately equal length.

In two of the original texts (Q.1 and F.1), Gertrude remains on stage after Hamlet drags out Polonius, and the King enters to her thus catching her still shaken by her experience. This version is certainly more dramatically concentrated.

In the First Folio, Rosencrantz and Guildenstern do not enter with the King, but only when they are needed after line 32. This seems to be less awkward staging since they enter only to be dismissed again. But the Quarto texts and ours may be defended thusly. It is natural enough that Rosencrantz and Guildenstern should be with the King, and their entrance is sufficient explanation for their being handy when wanted. If they do not come on at first, their showing up so conveniently, just in time to be called, looks clumsy. They are not like Horatio, whose ready appearance in III,ii demonstrated his faithful but unobtrusive care of Hamlet.

For "It had been so with us..." see III,i,170; III,iv,26. For lines 21-2, see III,iv,147-9; IV,iv,27-9.

Notice particularly Claudius' continual concern for keeping up appearances (ll. 30-2; 38-44).

The last line of the scene gives us the measure of Hamlet's success so far in exposing the inward evil of the state. This is a sort of remorse, not to have killed his adversary, but to have soured the sweet taste of his life by awakening his remorse of conscience, giving him reasons to fear for his safety and position, and remorse to have turned his wife away from him (she speaks as Hamlet's ally here, praising his nature and concealing his secrets). It is a blow struck too against the world of seems. In every meeting now there is matter to open the eyes of the court and catch at their conscience.

ACT FOUR, scene one.

(A ROOM IN THE CASTLE)

Enter KING, QUEEN, ROSENCRANTZ, *and* GUILDENSTERN.

King. There's matter in these sighs, these profound 1
   heaves:
You must translate; 'tis fit we understand them.
Where is your son?
  Queen. [*To* ROSENCRANTZ *and* GUILDENSTERN.] Be- 4
   stow this place on us a little while.
       [*Exeunt* ROSENCRANTZ *and* GUILDENSTERN.
Ah! my good lord, what have I seen to-night.
  King. What, Gertrude? How does Hamlet?
  Queen. Mad as the sea and wind, when both contend
Which is the mightier. In his lawless fit,
Behind the arras hearing something stir,
Whips out his rapier, cries, 'A rat! a rat!'
And, in his brainish apprehension, kills 11
The unseen good old man.
  King.   O heavy deed!
It had been so with us had we been there.
His liberty is full of threats to all;
To you yourself, to us, to every one.
Alas! how shall this bloody deed be answer'd?
It will be laid to us, whose providence 17
Should have kept short, restrain'd, and out of haunt, 18
This mad young man: but so much was our love,
We would not understand what was most fit,
But, like the owner of a foul disease,
To keep it from divulging, let it feed 22
Even on the pith of life. Where is he gone? 23
  Queen. To draw apart the body he hath kill'd;
O'er whom his very madness, like some ore 25
Among a mineral of metals base, 26
Shows itself pure: he weeps for what is done.
  King. O Gertrude! come away.
The sun no sooner shall the mountains touch
But we will ship him hence; and this vile deed
We must, with all our majesty and skill,
Both countenance and excuse. Ho! Guildenstern! 32
     Re-enter ROSENCRANTZ *and* GUILDENSTERN.
Friends both, go join you with some further aid:
Hamlet in madness hath Polonius slain,
And from his mother's closet hath he dragg'd him:
Go seek him out; speak fair, and bring the body
Into the chapel. I pray you, haste in this.
       [*Exeunt* ROSENCRANTZ *and* GUILDENSTERN.
Come, Gertrude, we'll call up our wisest friends;
And let them know both what we mean to do,
And what's untimely done: so, haply, slander, 40
Whose whisper o'er the world's diameter,
As level as the cannon to his blank 42
Transports his poison'd shot, may miss our name,
And hit the woundless air. O! come away; 44
My soul is full of discord and dismay.   [*Exeunt.*

1. "matter": something serious.

4. "Bestow . . . place": in other words, leave us.

11. "brainish apprehension": mad notion (that it was a rat he heard).

17. "providence": foresight.
18. "out of haunt": away from others.

22. "divulging": becoming known.
23. "pith": marrow.

25. "ore": gold.
26. "mineral": rock sample.

32. "countenance": recognize.

40. "so, haply, slander": has been interpolated by some editors to fill up the half-line left out (Capell, 1768).

42. "level": straight to the mark. "blank": bull's-eye.

44. "woundless": invulnerable.

73

HAMLET

ACT IV SCENE II

This scene, as Granville-Barker pointed out, can be an eerie and thrilling little episode, a search through a castle after midnight for a crazed or half-crazed murderer and a corpse. In the First Folio, as here, only Hamlet, Rosencrantz and Guildenstern are involved; but in the Second Quarto Rosencrantz and Guildenstern are accompanied by "others." They thus make up a sort of posse, whose calls echoing about backstage add much to the excitement. It was done thus at the Stratford (Ontario) Festival (1957) with great success. The stage was darkened and each pursuer had a lantern; the effect of criss-crossing lights and echoing voices was excellent. Done this way, the scene becomes the arrest of Hamlet as a murderer by the King's officers, an interpretation that the commanding tones, new in the mouths of Rosencrantz and Guildenstern, and the sturdy defiance of Hamlet's words support. At Stratford, Hamlet stood, when found, surrounded by a ring of drawn swords, emblems of the King's power and intention.

There are two Kings involved in lines 27-8, one dead and thus a thing of nothing, the other living and thus not with Polonius. (Claudius too, though in a different sense, is a thing of nothing.)

"Hide fox" was a cry associated with the children's game of hide and seek. Its use by Hamlet here must be explained by action on the stage. The general thing is for Hamlet to break away and run off-stage with Rosencrantz and Guildenstern, and the posse, if any, in anxious pursuit.

Such an active and bracing scene is just the thing after the immense tension of the preceding group.

ACT IV SCENE III

Here again the original texts disagree. The Second Quarto has Claudius enter attended by "two or three"; then the whole posse comes in with Rosencrantz at line 11. The First Folio, usually skimpy both of props and personnel, has the King enter alone, and has no one else in charge of Hamlet but his school chums. This difference is important because whether or not the King is attended determines whether or not this is a court scene in the form of a sort of summary court martial. The superior

Scene two.

(ANOTHER ROOM IN THE SAME)

Enter HAMLET.

Hamlet. Safely stowed.

Rosencrantz. }
Guildenstern. } [*Within.*] Hamlet! Lord Hamlet!

Hamlet. What noise? who calls on Hamlet?
O! here they come.

    Enter ROSENCRANTZ *and* GUILDENSTERN.

Rosencrantz. What have you done, my lord, with the
    dead body?

Hamlet. Compounded it with dust, whereto 'tis kin. 6

Rosencrantz. Tell us where 'tis, that we may take it
    thence
And bear it to the chapel.

Hamlet. Do not believe it.

Rosencrantz. Believe what?

Hamlet. That I can keep your counsel and not mine 11
own. Besides, to be demanded of a sponge! what rep- 12
lication should be made by the son of a king?

Rosencrantz. Take you me for a sponge, my lord?

Hamlet. Ay, sir, that soaks up the king's counte- 15
nance, his rewards, his authorities. But such officers
do the king best service in the end: he keeps them,
like an ape, in the corner of his jaw; first mouthed, 18
to be last swallowed: when he needs what you have
gleaned, it is but squeezing you, and, sponge, you
shall be dry again.

Rosencrantz. I understand you not, my lord.

Hamlet. I am glad of it: a knavish speech sleeps in 23
a foolish ear.

Rosencrantz. My lord, you must tell us where the
body is, and go with us to the king.

Hamlet. The body is with the king, but the king is 27
not with the body. The king is a thing—

Guildenstern. A thing, my lord!

Hamlet. Of nothing: bring me to him. Hide fox, 30
and all after.   [*Exeunt.*

Scene three.

(ANOTHER ROOM IN THE SAME)

Enter KING, *attended.*

King. I have sent to seek him, and to find the body.
How dangerous is it that this man goes loose!
Yet must not we put the strong law on him:
He's lov'd of the distracted multitude, 4
Who like not in their judgment, but their eyes; 5
And where 'tis so, the offender's scourge is weigh'd, 6
But never the offence. To bear all smooth and even, 7
This sudden sending him away must seem

6. "Compounded": restored, mingled.

11. "counsel": i.e., secrets.

12. "demanded of": questioned by. "sponge": i.e., soaking up royal favor.

12-3. "replication": answer, reply.

15-6. "countenance": favor.

18. "like an ape": The 1603 edition has "as an ape doth nuts," which is the meaning here. The 1604 edition (Second Quarto) has, "like an apple." You may take your choice. "first mouthed": i.e., put into the mouth first in order that all the goodness may be extracted before swallowing.

23-4. "a . . . ear": i.e., a roguish speech is never understood by a fool.

27-8. Hamlet is deliberately trying to confuse the two spies. If he intends any meaning at all it is possibly that Polonius is now with the rightful king (his father), but that the present king is not yet slain.

30-1. "Hide . . . after": a game like hide and seek.

4. "of": by. "distracted": unstable, foolish.

5. i.e., who judge not by reason, but by outward appearance.

6. "scourge": punishment.

7. "bear . . . smooth": pass everything off smoothly.

HAMLET

ACT IV SCENE III

drama of the latter alternative seems to us unmistakable. First, it is prepared for in IV,i, 38-44. Second, it makes a significant member of the series of ceremonial scenes we have noticed. These have the effect of showing us how the action appears in public. As a court scene, this one shows Claudius with the upper hand, plausibly sugaring-over his device for getting rid of Hamlet, "the hectic [i.e., fever] in my blood." On the other hand, Hamlet's insults and insinuations tend to upset the King's poise by calling his good will once more into question, and not even Claudius' wit can make the state seem in concord any more. A list of these court scenes will demonstrate the increasing difficulty of smiling villainy in bearing all smooth and even: I,ii; II,ii; III,i; III,ii (the play); IV,iii; IV,v; V,i (the funeral); V,ii (the duel).

For the identity of the Attendants, see IV,i,38.

The King's statement that Hamlet is loved by the people is supported here and there by hints, for example: 1) His ease with Bernardo and Marcellus (I,ii, I,iv). 2) His friendy contact with the players (II,ii and III,ii). They are willing to do a lot and put up with a lot. 3) Ophelia's recollection of Hamlet's old self, "The observed of all observers" (III,i). 4) His ability to converse with Fortinbras' officer (IV,iv). 5) His rapport with the pirates (IV,vi). 6) His talk with the grave diggers (V,i). An Elizabethan would understand the people's tendency to favor Hamlet as compared with Claudius, since, to their eyes, the Prince is heir to the throne and Claudius' election unexpected and suspect. Thus the people are ready to believe the worst of Claudius when rumors start (see IV,v, 90). This latent hostility makes clear the urgency of Claudius' desire to keep up appearances.

Hamlet's ironical reference to Claudius' purposes (l.50) and his amused air of looking forward to the adventure remind us of the end of his scene with his mother (III,iv, 202-11).

Since it will be best for the attendants to hear Claudius' statement of tender grief and Hamlet's reference to his marriage, we have some further difficulty with the stage directions. We should like to have the text read: Exit some attendants, after lines 41, and Exeunt all but the King, after line 59. In support of these alterations, neither the Second Quarto nor the First Folio has any indication how or when Rosencrantz and Guildenstern, the attendants, and the posse are to leave the stage.

Deliberate pause: diseases desperate grown
By desperate appliance are reliev'd,
Or not at all.   9

    Enter ROSENCRANTZ.

    How now! what hath befall'n?

Rosencrantz. Where the dead body is bestow'd, my
    lord,
We cannot get from him.

King.   But where is he?

Rosencrantz. Without, my lord; guarded, to know
    your pleasure.

King. Bring him before us.

Rosencrantz. Ho, Guildenstern! bring in my lord.

    Enter HAMLET *and* GUILDENSTERN.

King. Now, Hamlet, where's Polonius?

Hamlet. At supper.

King. At supper! Where?

Hamlet. Not where he eats, but where he is eaten: a
certain convocation of politic worms are e'en at him.   21
Your worm is your only emperor for diet: we fat all
creatures else to fat us, and we fat ourselves for maggots: your fat king and your lean beggar is but vari-   24
able service; two dishes, but to one table: that's the
end.

King. Alas, alas!

Hamlet. A man may fish with the worm that hath
eat of a king, and eat of the fish that hath fed of that
worm.

King. What dost thou mean by this?

Hamlet. Nothing, but to show you how a king may
go a progress through the guts of a beggar.   33

King. Where is Polonius?

Hamlet. In heaven; send thither to see: if your messenger find him not there, seek him i' the other place
yourself. But, indeed, if you find him not within this
month, you shall nose him as you go up the stairs
into the lobby.

King. [*To some* Attendants.] Go seek him there.

Hamlet. He will stay till you come.

            [*Exeunt* Attendants.

King. Hamlet, this deed, for thine especial safety,
Which we do tender, as we dearly grieve   43
For that which thou hast done, must send thee hence
With fiery quickness: therefore prepare thyself;
The bark is ready, and the wind at help.   46
The associates tend, and every thing is bent   47
For England.

Hamlet.   For England!

King.   Ay, Hamlet.

Hamlet.   Good.

King. So is it, if thou knew'st our purposes.

Hamlet. I see a cherub that sees them. But, come;
for England! Farewell, dear mother.

King. Thy loving father, Hamlet.

Hamlet. My mother: father and mother is man and
wife, man and wife is one flesh, and so, my mother.
Come for England!   [*Exit.*

King. Follow him at foot; tempt him with speed   56
    aboard:
Delay it not, I'll have him hence to-night.

9. "Deliberate pause": a deliberate step, taken after due consideration.

21. "convocation . . . worms": a political assembly of worms; an allusion to the Diet of Worms (1521), and thus an anachronism.

24-5. "variable service": different courses.

33. "a progress": the term used for a royal journey of state.

43. "tender": have regard for.

46. "at help": favorable.

47. "associates tend": your companions await you.
"bent": ready.

56. "at foot": at his heels.
"tempt": entice.

Away! for every thing is seal'd and done 58
That else leans on the affair: pray you, make haste.
        [*Exeunt* ROSENCRANTZ *and* GUILDENSTERN.
And, England, if my love thou hold'st at aught,— 60
As my great power thereof may give these sense,
Since yet thy cicatrice looks raw and red 62
After the Danish sword, and thy free awe 63
Pays homage to us,—thou mayst not coldly set 64
Our sovereign process, which imports at full, 65
By letters congruing to that effect 66
The present death of Hamlet. Do it, England; 67
For like the hectic in my blood he rages, 68
And thou must cure me. Till I know 'tis done,
Howe'er my haps, my joys were ne'er begun. [*Exit.* 70

58-9. "for . . . affair": i.e., for everything else necessary to insure the success of this affair has been done.

60. "England": the King of England.

62. "cicatrice": scar.

63. "free awe": your submission even after our armies have been withdrawn.

64. "set": i.e., set aside, disregard.

65. "sovereign process": royal mandate or command.

66. "congruing": agreeing.

67. "present": immediate.

68. "hectic": fever.

70. "Howe'er my haps": whatever happens to me. (Likely with reference to his after life.)

Scene four.

(A PLAIN IN DENMARK)

Enter FORTINBRAS, *a* Captain, *and* Soldiers, *marching.*

Fortinbras. Go, captain, from me greet the Danish
    king;
Tell him that, by his licence, Fortinbras
Claims the conveyance of a promis'd march 3
Over his kingdom. You know the rendezvous.
If that his majesty would aught with us,
We shall express our duty in his eye, 6
And let him know so.
Captain.   I will do't, my lord.
Fortinbras. Go softly on. 8
        [*Exeunt* FORTINBRAS *and* Soldiers.
    Enter HAMLET, ROSENCRANTZ, GUILDENSTERN, &c.
Hamlet. Good sir, whose powers are these? 9
Captain. They are of Norway, sir.
Hamlet. How purpos'd, sir, I pray you?
Captain. Against some part of Poland.
Hamlet. Who commands them, sir?
Captain. The nephew to old Norway, Fortinbras.
Hamlet. Goes it against the main of Poland, sir, 15
Or for some frontier?
Captain. Truly to speak, and with no addition, 17
We go to gain a little patch of ground
That hath in it no profit but the name.
To pay five ducats, five, I would not farm it; 20
Nor will it yield to Norway or the Pole
A ranker rate, should it be old in fee. 22
Hamlet. Why, then the Polack never will defend it.
Captain. Yes, 'tis already garrison'd.
Hamlet. Two thousand souls and twenty thousand
    ducats
Will not debate the question of this straw: 26
This is the imposthume of much wealth and peace, 27
That inward breaks, and shows no cause without
Why the man dies. I humbly thank you, sir.
Captain. God be wi' you, sir.   [*Exit.*
Rosencrantz.   Will 't please you go, my lord?

3. "conveyance": convoy, conduct. "promis'd march": see II,ii, 76f.

6. i.e., we will pay him our respects in person. Notice that Fortinbras uses the royal plural. Is this justified?

8. "softly": slowly. Why?

9. "powers": forces.

15. "main": main body, the country as a whole.

17. "addition": exaggeration.

20. "To pay": i.e., in rent.

22. "ranker": greater. "fee": freehold; i.e., sold outright.

26. "debate the question": settle the dispute.

27. "imposthume of": abscess caused by.

ACT IV SCENE IV

The importance of this scene is to give us a sight of Fortinbras, and to set up Hamlet's sixth soliloquy. The martial pageantry is in marked visual contrast to the courtly and domestic scenes of which the play largely consists.

Our sight of Fortinbras reminds us of his ambitious career, his threat to Denmark, and the parallels and contrasts between him and Hamlet. It also prepares us to recognize him on his return in the final scene. Without such preparation, he would have been too remote a figure to take such a commanding position at the end.

Compare the following: lines 27-9 with III,iv, 147-9; IV,i, 21-3, and commentaries; lines 34-9 with I,ii, 150-1; II,ii, 307-13; lines 40-3 with III,i, 84-5.

The soliloquy is parallel in content to "O, what a rogue..." (II,ii, 553-610) and, "now could drink hot blood ..." (III,ii, 395-404), but very different in tone and form.

HAMLET

ACT IV SCENE IV

The difference mirrors the alteration in Hamlet. The facts responsible for this change are: 1) Hamlet is now completely certain of the King's guilt. 2) His confidence has been bolstered by his success in catching the conscience of the King, and of the Queen, and in disrupting the self-satisfied equilibrium of the court. 3) He has, in the nunnery and closet scenes, been able to express and discharge some of his bottled-up melancholy, and thus digest and reduce his disillusion to more manageable shape. 4) We saw him sense in himself a narrowing and hardening of his heart into violent cruelty. This outgoing hatred still exists (see II. 65-6), but in the closet scene its narrowness and brutishness were dispelled by sight of the ghost. The result is a character of some settled determination, yet mindful of nobility.

In this firmer and more mature character, Hamlet can speak of evil without the fury of frustration (II. 56-9). His steadiness is provided by the greater regularity and forward march of the verse here, and its clear and orderly progression of thought. Compared with the agonized drive of "O, what a rogue..." broken by its tense and distracted short lines, or the luminous melancholy of "To be, or not to be...," this passage rings with masculine firmness.

The effect of the alteration is to sadden us at the loss of Hamlet's simplicity, generosity, and gentleness, while we believe more in the solidity of his resolution.

ACT IV SCENE V

Ophelia's mad scene adds touching pathos to Claudius' household, now (see II. 76-97) thoroughly gripped in discord and dismay. It begins and ends like a domestic scene, but partakes also, with its gentlemen and citizens, of action in the public eye. It contains: 1) Ophelia's madness in which both Polonius and Hamlet figure largely, and which prompts many ironies. 2) Gertrude's guilty heartsickness. 3) Claudius' distress, and his inability in the midst of rumor and disturbance to bear all smooth and even. His time is now out of joint. 4) Laertes' rebellion.

That Shakespeare intended the chief emphasis to fall on Ophelia is clear from the songs, the elaborate flower ceremony, and the fact that she is brought in twice lest, in the excitement over Laertes, we might lose track of her.

Hamlet. I'll be with you straight. Go a little before.   31
[*Exeunt all except* HAMLET.
How all occasions do inform against me,   32
And spur my dull revenge! What is a man,
If his chief good and market of his time   34
Be but to sleep and feed? a beast, no more.
Sure he that made us with such large discourse,   36
Looking before and after, gave us not   37
That capability and god-like reason
To fust in us unus'd. Now, whe'r it be   39
Bestial oblivion, or some craven scruple   40
Of thinking too precisely on the event,
A thought, which, quarter'd, hath but one part wisdom,
And ever three parts coward, I do not know
Why yet I live to say 'This thing's to do;'
Sith I have cause and will and strength and means
To do 't. Examples gross as earth exhort me: 46
Witness this army of such mass and charge   47
Led by a delicate and tender prince,
Whose spirit with divine ambition puff'd
Makes mouths at the invisible event,   50
Exposing what is mortal and unsure
To all that fortune, death and danger dare,
Even for an egg-shell. Rightly to be great   53
Is not to stir without great argument,
But greatly to find quarrel in a straw
When honour's at the stake. How stand I then,
That have a father kill'd, a mother stain'd,
Excitements of my reason and my blood,   58
And let all sleep, while, to my shame, I see
The imminent death of twenty thousand men,   60
That, for a fantasy and trick of fame,   61
Go to their graves like beds, fight for a plot
Whereon the numbers cannot try the cause,   63
Which is not tomb enough and continent   64
To hide the slain? O! from this time forth,
My thoughts be bloody, or be nothing worth! [*Exit.*

Scene five.

(ELSINORE. A ROOM IN THE CASTLE)

Enter QUEEN, HORATIO, *and a* Gentleman.
Queen. I will not speak with her.
Gentleman. She is importunate, indeed distract: 2
Her mood will needs be pitied.
Queen.   What would she have?
Gentleman. She speaks much of her father; says she hears
There's tricks i' the world; and hems, and beats her heart;   5
Spurns enviously at straws; speaks things in doubt,   6
That carry but half sense: her speech is nothing,
Yet the unshaped use of it doth move   8
The hearers to collection; they aim at it,   9
And botch the words up fit to their own thoughts;   10

---

31. "straight": i.e., straightway, immediately.
32. "inform against": accuse.
34. "market": employment.
36. "discourse": power of reasoning.
37. "Looking . . . after": considering the future and the past.
39. "fust": grow moldy.
40. "Bestial oblivion": the forgetfulness of a mere beast.
40-41. "some . . . event": i.e., a cowardly hesitation of thinking too precisely about how the deed should be carried out. Hamlet is probably recalling how he let go his one opportunity to kill the King because he was too scrupulous about obtaining full vengeance; and in his sense of frustration he accuses himself of cowardice.
46. "gross": large.
47. "charge": cost.
50. i.e., mocks at the uncertain outcome.
53-6. true greatness consists, not in waiting on a great cause for which to fight, but rather in fighting over a trifle where honor is at stake.

58. "blood": passion.
60. "twenty thousand": it was two thousand in line 25.
61. "fantasy": mere whim. "trick": something trifling.
63. i.e., which is not big enough to hold the armies fighting for it.
64. "continent": containing enough ground.

2. "importunate": insistent. "distract": distracted.

5. "tricks": trickery.
6. "Spurns . . . straws": stamps (in anger) spitefully at trifles.
8. "unshaped": incoherent.
9. "collection": inference. "aim": guess.
10. "botch": patch.

77

HAMLET

ACT IV SCENE V

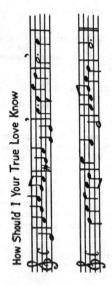

How Should I Your True Love Know

The Queen's reluctance to see Ophelia may partly be explained by her share in the real responsibility for Polonius' death. It was her fear that prompted his betrayal of his presence.

The story of the baker's daughter (l.43) is cited as follows by Douce, who said it came from Gloucestershire: "Our Saviour went into a baker's shop where they were baking, and asked for some bread to eat. The mistress of the shop immediately put a piece of dough into the oven to bake for him, but was reprimanded by her daughter, who, insisting that the piece of dough was too large, reduced it to a very small size. The dough, however, immediately afterwards began to swell, and presently became of a most enormous size. Whereupon the baker's daughter cried out, 'Hoo, Hoo, Hoo!', which owl-like noise probably induced our Saviour, for her wickedness, to transform her into that bird." Now Ophelia is transformed, but for what wickedness it is not clear, unless she reproaches herself for her falsity towards Hamlet.

Ophelia's madness is constructed out of ballads, folk tales, and ancient rural customs and ceremonies which center on marriage (both lewd and sacred) and funeral. In her second song she pathetically adopts for herself the loose character suggested by Hamlet's obscene remarks to her (III,i; III,ii) and for her lover, the distorted cynical view offered her by Laertes (I,iii). Besides applying to herself they must sound ironically in Gertrude's ear ("How should I your true love know/ From another one?"). The ballad verses for these songs, except for line 186, are not known elsewhere.

Which, as her winks, and nods, and gestures yield them,
Indeed would make one think there might be thought,
Though nothing sure, yet much unhappily.

Horatio. 'Twere good she were spoken with, for she 14
may strew
Dangerous conjectures in ill-breeding minds.

Queen. Let her come in   [*Exit* Gentleman.
To my sick soul, as sin's true nature is, 17
Each toy seems prologue to some great amiss: 18
So full of artless jealousy is guilt, 19
It spills itself in fearing to be split. 20

       Re-enter Gentleman, *with* OPHELIA.

Ophelia. Where is the beauteous majesty of
Denmark?

Queen. How now, Ophelia!

Ophelia.
      How should I your true love know
        From another one?
      By his cockle hat and staff, 25
        And his sandal shoon. 26

Queen. Alas! sweet lady, what imports this song? 27

Ophelia. Say you? nay, pray you, mark.
      He is dead and gone, lady,
        He is dead and gone;
      At his head a grass-green turf;
        At his heels a stone.
O, ho!

Queen. Nay, but Ophelia,—

Ophelia. Pray you, mark.
      White his shroud as the mountain snow,—

        Enter KING.

Queen. Alas! look here, my lord.

Ophelia.
      Larded all with sweet flowers; 38
      Which bewept to the grave did not go
        With true-love showers. 40

King. How do you, pretty lady?

Ophelia. Well, God 'ild you! They say the owl was 42
a baker's daughter. Lord! we know what we are,
but know not what we may be. God be at your table!

King. Conceit upon her father. 45

Ophelia. Pray you, let's have no words of this; but 46
when they ask you what it means, say you this:
      To-morrow is Saint Valentine's day, 48
        All in the morning betime, 49
      And I a maid at your window,
        To be your Valentine:
      Then up he rose, and donn'd his clothes
        And dupp'd the chamber door; 53
      Let in the maid, that out a maid
        Never departed more.

King. Pretty Ophelia!

Ophelia. Indeed, la! without an oath, I'll make an
end on 't:
      By Gis and by Saint Charity, 59
        Alack, and fie for shame!
      Young men will do 't, if they come to 't;
        By Cock they are to blame. 62

14-15. These lines are something given to the Queen. What different interpretation of the Queen's character does that indicate?

17. "as . . . is": i.e., Sin is truly a sickness whose symptom is anxiety and suspicion.

18. "toy": trifle.
"amiss": calamity.

19. "artless jealousy": uncontrolled suspicion.

20. i.e., it is revealed by its very efforts to conceal itself.

25. "cockle hat"; adorned with cockle shells and worn by pilgrims.

26. "shoon": shoes.

27. "imports": is the meaning of.

38. "Larded": garnished.

40. "true-love showers": i.e., the tears of his true love.

42. "'ild": yield, i.e., reward.

42-3. "They . . . daughter": An allusion to the legend that a baker's daughter was turned into an owl for hooting at her mother in scorn when the latter gave Christ a larger piece of bread than the daughter thought necessary.

45. "Conceit upon": i.e., she thinks of.

46. "of": about.

48. "Saint Valentine's day": February 14. The old belief was that the first man seen by a maid on that day was destined to be her husband, and vice versa.

49. "betime": early.

53. "dupp'd": opened.

59. "Gis": euphemism for Jesus.

62. "Cock": euphemism for God.

HAMLET

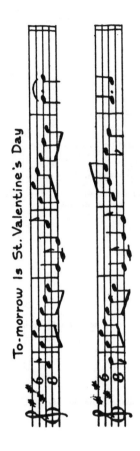

To-morrow Is St. Valentine's Day

"Switzers" are Swiss mercenary soldiers employed as bodyguards. Apparently Claudius does not trust himself with Danes, but such hired guards were a common luxury in renaissance courts. The practice is still traditional at the Vatican.

Quoth she, before you tumbled me,
   You promis'd me to wed:
(He answers.)
   So would I ha' done, by yonder sun,
   An thou hadst not come to my bed.

King. How long hath she been thus?

Ophelia. I hope all will be well. We must be patient: but I cannot choose but weep, to think they should lay him i' the cold ground. My brother shall know of it: and so I thank you for your good counsel. Come, my coach! Good-night, ladies; good-night, sweet ladies; good-night, good-night.   [*Exit.*

King. Follow her close; give her good watch, I
   pray you.   [*Exit* HORATIO.
O! this is the poison of deep grief; it springs
All from her father's death. O Gertrude, Gertrude!
When sorrows come, they come not single spies,
But in battalions. First, her father slain;
Next, your son gone; but he most violent author
Of his own just remove: the people muddied,   81
Thick and unwholesome in their thoughts and
   whispers,
For good Polonius' death; and we have done but
   greenly,   83
In hugger-mugger to inter him: poor Ophelia   84
Divided from herself and her fair judgment,
Without the which we are pictures, or mere beasts: 86
Last, and as much containing as all these,   87
Her brother is in secret come from France,
Feeds on his wonder, keeps himself in clouds,   89
And wants not buzzers to infect his ear   90
With pestilent speeches of his father's death;
Wherein necessity, of matter beggar'd,   92
Will nothing stick our person to arraign
In ear and ear. O my dear Gertrude! this,
Like to a murdering-piece, in many places   95
Gives me superfluous death.   [*A noise within.*

Queen.   Alack! what noise is this?   96

Enter a Gentleman.

King. Where are my Switzers? Let them guard the   97
   door.
What is the matter?

Gentleman.   Save yourself, my lord;
The ocean, overpeering of his list,   99
Eats not the flats with more impetuous haste   100
Than young Laertes, in a riotous head,   101
O'erbears your officers. The rabble call him lord;
And, as the world were now but to begin,   103
Antiquity forgot, custom not known,   104
The ratifiers and props of every word,
They cry, 'Choose we; Laertes shall be king!'
Caps, hands, and tongues, applaud it to the clouds,
'Laertes shall be king, Laertes king!'

Queen. How cheerfully on the false trail they cry!
O! this is counter, you false Danish dogs!   110

King. The doors are broke.   [*Noise within.*

Enter LAERTES, *armed;* Danes *following.*

Laertes. Where is the king? Sirs, stand you all
   without.

Danes. No, let's come in.

81. "muddied": confused and stirred up.

83. "greenly": foolishly; without using mature judgment.

84. "hugger-mugger": secret haste.

86. "pictures": men only to the eye.

87. "containing": holding us.

89. "keeps . . . clouds": shrouds himself in gloomy aloofness.

90. "wants": lacks.
"buzzers": scandalmongers.

92-3. i.e., being necessarily without any knowledge of the truth of the matter, they do not hesitate to accuse us (royal plural).

95. "murdering-piece": cannon loaded with grapeshot.

96. "superfluous": i.e., one bullet would have been sufficient.

97. "Switzers": Swiss mercenaries acting as royal bodyguard.

99. "overpeering . . . list": rising above the dykes.

100. "Eats . . . flats": floods not the lowlands.

101. "in . . . head": with a force of rioters.

103. "as": as if.

104-5. i.e., ignoring prerogative and tradition which sanction and support every decision.

110. "counter": on the false trail (a hunting term), i.e., treason.

79

HAMLET

ACT IV SCENE V

In line 132 we see that revenge is more important to Laertes than virtue, a fact borne out in what follows.

Again, as always with stage business, sound effects, and merely exclamatory lines, you must imagine the effect. The noise is that of a shouting mob.

The clamorous directness of Laertes' demand for vengeance adds a new element to the comparison between him and Hamlet. Laertes is now like Fortinbras and Hamlet in having a father to avenge.

Claudius never appears more admirable than in this scene, where his courage (which has not been much as yet) and his cunning combine to calm Laertes and bend him to his will. Notice Gertrude's impulsive action of defense, showing the involuntary force of her love for Claudius.

For "O rose of May," (l.157) see III,iv, 42-4 and commentary on flower imagery.

Laertes.   I pray you, give me leave.
Danes. We will, we will.
         [*They retire without the door.*
Laertes. I thank you: keep the door. O thou vile
     king!
Give me my father.
Queen.   Calmly, good Laertes.
Laertes. That drop of blood that's calm proclaims   117
     me bastard,
Cries cuckold to my father, brands the harlot
Even here, between the chaste unsmirched brows
Of my true mother.
King.   What is the cause, Laertes,
That thy rebellion looks so giant-like?
Let him go, Gertrude; do not fear our person: 122
There's such divinity doth hedge a king,   123
That treason can but peep to what it would,   124
Acts little of his will. Tell me, Laertes,   125
Why thou art thus incens'd. Let him go, Gertrude.
Speak, man.
Laertes.   Where is my father?
King.   Dead.
Queen.   But not by him.
King. Let him demand his fill.
Laertes. How came he dead? I'll not be juggled with.
To hell, allegiance! vows, to the blackest devil!
Conscience and grace, to the profoundest pit!
I dare damnation. To this point I stand,
That both the worlds I give to negligence,   134
Let come what comes; only I'll be reveng'd
Most throughly for my father.
King.   Who shall stay you?
Laertes. My will, not all the world:
And for my means, I'll husband them so well,   138
They shall go far with little.
King.   Good Laertes,
If you desire to know the certainty
Of your dear father's death, is't writ in your revenge,
That, swoopstake, you will draw both friend and foe,   142
Winner and loser?
Laertes. None but his enemies.
King.   Will you know them then?
Laertes. To his good friends thus wide I'll ope my
     arms;
And like the kind life-rendering pelican,   146
Repast them with my blood.
King.   Why, now you speak
Like a good child and a true gentleman.
That I am guiltless of your father's death,
And am most sensibly in grief for it,   150
It shall as level to your judgment pierce   151
As day does to your eye.
Danes.   [*Within.*] Let her come in.
Laertes. How now! what noise is that?
         Re-enter OPHELIA.
O heat, dry up my brains! tears seven times salt,
Burn out the sense and virtue of mine eye!   155
By heaven, thy madness shall be paid by weight,
Till our scale turn the beam. O rose of May!   157
Dear maid, kind sister, sweet Ophelia!

117-20. i.e., I cannot remain calm and be a true son to my father.

122. "fear": fear for.

123. i.e., a king is surrounded by divine protection as by a hedge.

124. "peep": i.e., look over, but not break through.

125. "Acts . . . will": is little able to carry out its desires.

134. i.e., I care not for this world or the next.

138. "husband": use thriftily.

142. "swoopstake": in a clean sweep.

146. "life-rendering pelican": The pelican was supposed to feed its young with its own blood.

150. "sensibly": feelingly.

151. "level": directly.

155. "sense and virtue": sensitiveness to light and power of sight.

157. "turn the beam": overbalance the scale.

In the flower episode, a mockery of both funeral and marriage customs reflects on the secret burial of Polonius, the marriage that might have been between Ophelia and Hamlet, the two marriages of Gertrude, the soon forgotten funeral of Hamlet's father, and the funeral of Ophelia: fennel and columbines presented to Claudius stand for flattery and cuckoldry, rue is for sorrow or repentance, daisies for falsity, violets for faithfulness. (For the list of flower imagery, see commentary to III,iv, 42-4. And cf. also IV,vii, 168-75; V,i, 248-50.)

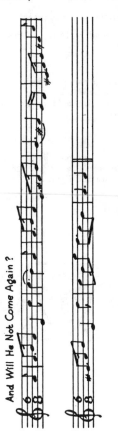

And Will He Not Come Again?

O heavens! is 't possible a young maid's wits
Should be as mortal as an old man's life?
Nature is fine in love, and where 'tis fine   161
It sends some precious instance of itself   162
After the thing it loves.

    Ophelia.
        They bore him barefac'd on the bier;
        Hey non nonny, nonny, hey nonny;
        And in his grave rain'd many a tear;—
Fare you well, my dove!

Laertes. Hadst thou thy wits, and didst persuade revenge,
It could not move thus.

    Ophelia.
        You must sing, a-down a-down,
        And you call him a-down-a.
O how the wheel becomes it! It is the false steward 172
that stole his master's daughter.

Laertes. This nothing's more than matter.   174

Ophelia. There's rosemary that's for remembrance; 175
pray, love, remember: and there is pansies, that's
for thoughts.

Laertes. A document in madness, thoughts and re- 178
membrance fitted.

Ophelia. There's fennel for you, and columbines; 180
there's rue for you; and here's some for me; we may 181
call it herb of grace o' Sundays. O! you must wear
your rue with a difference. There's a daisy; I would
give you some violets, but they withered all when my
father died. They say he made a good end,—
        For bonny sweet Robin is all my joy.

Laertes. Thought and affliction, passion, hell itself,
She turns to favour and to prettiness.   188

    Ophelia.
        And will a' not come again?
        And will a' not come again?
          No, no, he is dead;
          Go to thy death-bed,
        He never will come again.
          His beard was as white as snow
          All flaxen was his poll,   195
          He is gone, he is gone,
          And we cast away moan:
        God ha' mercy on his soul!
And of all Christian souls I pray God. God be wi' ye!
                                 [*Exit.*

Laertes. Do you see this, O God?

King. Laertes, I must commune with your grief,   201
Or you deny me right. Go but apart,
Make choice of whom your wisest friends you will,
And they shall hear and judge 'twixt you and me.
If by direct or by collateral hand   205
They find us touch'd, we will our kingdom give,   206
Our crown, our life, and all that we call ours,
To you in satisfaction; but if not,
Be you content to lend your patience to us,
And we shall jointly labour with your soul
To give it due content.

    Laertes.   Let this be so:
His means of death, his obscure burial,   212

161. "fine": delicate.

162. "instance": token; in this case, her sanity.

172. "wheel": Perhaps she imagines herself seated at a spinning wheel; or she may be referring to a little dance which she perhaps breaks into at this point. No scholar has ever said anything really convincing about this word's use here.

172-3. "the false steward . . .": the title of the ballad.

174. i.e., this nonsense is more moving than sense.

175-85. "The distribution of herbs and flowers was an old funeral custom, and Ophelia imagines herself giving her father proper burial." (George Rylands) Ophelia distributes her flowers (which are probably imaginary too) appropriately according to the language of flowers.

175-7. These she gives to Laertes.

178. "document": lesson.

180. These go to the King. Fennel was for flattery, and columbines for faithlessness.

181-85. "Rue": as the sign of repentance, she gives to the Queen and herself. But the Queen must wear hers with a "difference"; why? The daisy was for deceit and may be fittingly given to the King or Queen. But neither is worthy of violets, the symbol of faithfulness.

188. "favour": charm.

195. "poll": head.

201. "commune": share.

205. "collatral": i.e., as an accessory.

206. "touch'd": implicated.

212. "obscure burial": Remember that Polonius was chief minister to the King. Ordinarily a man of his high rank would be given a very ostentatious funeral.

HAMLET

ACT IV SCENE V

ACT IV SCENE VI

This little scene gives us indispensable information, and placed here, it lays a background of irony to the following scene between Claudius and Laertes.

The only point of difficulty is the question of whether the encounter of Hamlet's ship with the pirates was accidental or not. Hamlet's words to his mother (III,iv, 202-10) tell us of his knowledge and suspicion. He speaks there, too, of his own craft outwitting that of Claudius. Both there and in speaking to Claudius (IV,iii, 45-8), his remarks are jaunty enough to suggest the self-confidence springing from secure preparation. The events described in the letter to Horatio lend themselves to this interpretation also. If they were ordinary pirates, why did they let Hamlet board their ship? And, when he had boarded, why did they so quickly get clear and give up their prize? "Their knew what they did," says Hamlet.

The difficulty is to know when Hamlet could have laid his plot. The nunnery scene took place on the day of the play, and it was only at the end of it that the King, "in quick determination," decided to send Hamlet to England. Hamlet's time from just before the play until his departure for England is fully accounted for. If he put this plot into effect it must have been in the few hours between when notice of the King's sudden decision reached him and the play. This would be pretty quick work all round.

If the escape was planned, it shows the resourcefulness of the altered Hamlet in action even before the play. If it was accidental, we merely have one more example of the quick, yet clever, way in which Hamlet turns such windfalls to his advantage (cf. the arrival of the players), and one more demonstration of a divinity shaping his ends (see V,ii, 10).

No trophy, sword, nor hatchment o'er his bones, 213
No noble rite nor formal ostentation, 214
Cry to be heard, as 'twere from heaven to earth,
That I must call 't in question.
King. So you shall;
And where the offence is let the great axe fall.
I pray you go with me. [*Exeunt.*

Scene six.

(ANOTHER ROOM IN THE SAME)

Enter HORATIO and a Servant.
Horatio. What are they that would speak with me?
Servant. Sailors, sir: they say, they have letters for you.
Horatio. Let them come in. [*Exit* Servant.
I do not know from what part of the world
I should be greeted, if not from Lord Hamlet.
Enter Sailors.
First Sailor. God bless you, sir.
Horatio. Let him bless thee too.
Second Sailor. He shall, sir, an 't please him. 9
There's a letter for you, sir;—it comes from the ambassador that was bound for England;—if your name be Horatio, as I am let to know it is.
Horatio. [*Reads.*] Horatio, when thou shalt have overlooked this, give these fellows some means to the 14 king: they have letters for him. Ere we were two days old at sea, a pirate of very war-like appointment 16 gave us chase. Finding ourselves too slow of sail, we put on a compelled valour; in the grapple I boarded 18 them: on the instant they got clear of our ship, so I alone became their prisoner. They have dealt with me likes thieves of mercy, but they knew what they 21 did; I am to do a good turn to them. Let the king have the letters I have sent; and repair thou to me with as much haste as thou wouldst fly death. I have words to speak in thine ear will make thee dumb, yet are they much too light for the bore of the matter. 26 These good fellows will bring thee where I am. 27 Rosencrantz and Guildenstern hold their course for England: of them I have much to tell thee. Farewell.
He that thou knowest thine,
Hamlet.
Come, I will give you way for these your letters;
And do 't the speedier, that you may direct me
To him from whom you brought them. [*Exeunt.*

213. "hatchment": coat of arms hung over the tomb of a deceased knight.
214. "formal ostentation": public ceremony.

9. "an't": if it.

14. "overlooked": looked over, i.e., read.
"means": access.
16. "appointment": equipment.
18. "compelled valour": Why compelled?

21. "thieves of mercy": merciful thieves.
"but . . . did": i.e., they knew who I was and it would be to their advantage.

26. "much . . . matter": he hasn't strong enough words to express himself; his words are too light.
27. "bring . . . am": What does this suggest?

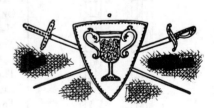

82

HAMLET

ACT IV SCENE VII

In this scene, the witchcraft of Claudius' wit acts on the irritable instability of Laertes. We feel we are here at the center of the ulcer. Beginning on the level of a heart-to-heart talk, the King comes to behave like a sort of proxy father to Laertes. ("Will you be rul'd by me?" "Ay, my lord.")

His devices for winding Laertes around his finger include protestations of friendship, of common enmity, candor about his most intimate affairs (ll. 11-6), the invitation of judgment (l.10), flattery.

Having secured the young man, Claudius deliberately works him up to undertaking this new piece of deceit by appealing to the sincerity of his grief and desire for revenge (see ll. 105-8; ll. 123-5).

During this suave cat and mouse game, two shocks occur. First, and it comes with lovely irony directly after the secure self-satisfaction of, "You shortly shall hear more," (ll. 33-47), the news of Hamlet's return which throws Claudius off his stride for twenty lines while he thinks up a new stratagem. Second, the news of Ophelia's death which upsets Laertes, and in its pathetic innocence, shows up the hotbed of evil.

Scene seven.

(ANOTHER ROOM IN THE SAME)

Enter KING *and* LAERTES.

King. Now must your conscience my acquittance seal,   1
And you must put me in your heart for friend,
Sith you have heard, and with a knowing ear,
That he which hath your noble father slain
Pursu'd my life.
Laertes.   It well appears: but tell me
Why you proceeded not against these feats,   6
So crimeful and so capital in nature,   7
As by your safety, wisdom, all things else,
You mainly were stirr'd up.
King.   O! for two special reasons;   9
Which may to you, perhaps, seem much unsinew'd,   10
But yet to me they are strong. The queen his mother
Lives almost by his looks, and for myself,—
My virtue or my plague, be it either which,—
She's so conjunctive to my life and soul,   14
That, as the star moves not but in his sphere,   15
I could not but by her. The other motive,
Why to a public count I might not go,   17
Is the great love the general gender bear him;   18
Who, dipping all his faults in their affection,   19
Would, like the spring that turneth wood to stone,   20
Convert his gyves to graces; so that my arrows,   21
Too slightly timber'd for so loud a wind,   22
Would have reverted to my bow again,
And not where I had aim'd them.
Laertes. And so have I a noble father lost;
A sister driven into desperate terms,   26
Whose worth, if praises may go back again,   27
Stood challenger on mount of all the age   28
For her perfections. But my revenge will come.
King. Break not your sleeps for that; you must not think
That we are made of stuff so flat and dull
That we can let our beard be shook with danger
And think it pastime. You shortly shall hear more;
I lov'd your father, and we love ourself,
And that, I hope, will teach you to imagine.—
          Enter a Messenger.
How now! what news?
Messenger.   Letters, my lord, from Hamlet:
This to your majesty; this to the queen.
King. From Hamlet! who brought them?
Messenger. Sailors, my lord, they say; I saw them not:
They were given me by Claudio, he receiv'd them
Of him that brought them.
King.   Laertes, you shall hear them.
Leave us.   [*Exit Messenger.*
[*Reads.*] "High and mighty, you shall know I am set
naked on your kingdom. To-morrow shall I beg   44
leave to see your kingly eyes; when I shall, first

1. "my . . . seal": confirm my innocence.

6. "feats": acts.

7. "capital": deserving death.

9. "mainly": strongly.

10. "unsinew'd": weak.

14. "conjunctive": closely united.

15. "but": except.
   "sphere": orbit.

17. "count": account, trial.

18. "general gender": common people.

19. "dipping . . . affection": Explain the figure.

20. "spring . . . stone": a reference to mineral springs which petrify wood.

21. "Convert . . . graces": regard his fetters as honorable rather than disgraceful; i.e., make a martyr of him.

22. "timber'd": shafted. Explain the metaphor.

26. "terms": conditions.

27. "if . . . again": i.e., if one may praise her for what she used to be.

28-9. "Stood . . . perfections": stood out above all others of her age in perfection.

44. "naked": destitute.

83

HAMLET

ACT IV SCENE VII

asking your pardon thereunto, recount the occasions
of my sudden and more strange return.—Hamlet.
What should this mean? Are all the rest come back?
Or is it some abuse and no such thing?   49

  Laertes. Know you the hand?

  King.   'Tis Hamlet's character. 'Naked,'   50
And in a postscript here, he says, 'alone.'
Can you advise me?

  Laertes. I'm lost in it, my lord. But let him come!
It warms the very sickness in my heart,
That I shall live and tell him to his teeth,
'Thus diddest thou.'

  King.   If it be so, Laertes,
As how should it be so? how otherwise?
Will you be rul'd by me?

  Laertes.   Ay, my lord;
So you will not o'er-rule me to a peace.

  King. To thin own peace. If he be now return'd,
As checking at his voyage, and that he means   61
No more to undertake it, I will work him
To an exploit, now ripe in my device,   63
Under the which he shall not choose but fall;
And for his death no wind of blame shall breathe,
But even his mother shall uncharge the practice   66
And call it accident.

  Laertes.   My lord, I will be rul'd;
The rather, if you could devise it so
That I might be the organ.

  King.   It falls right.   69
You have been talk'd of since your travel much,
And that in Hamlet's hearing, for a quality
Wherein, they say, you shine; your sum of parts   72
Did not together pluck such envy from him
As did that one, and that, in my regard,
Of the unworthiest siege.   75

  Laertes.   What part is that, my lord?

  King. A very riband in the cap of youth,
Yet needful too; for youth no less becomes
The light and careless livery that it wears   78
Than settled age his sables and his weeds,   79
Importing health and graveness. Two months since   80
Here was a gentleman of Normandy:
I've seen myself, and serv'd against the French,
And they can well on horseback; but this gallant   83
Had witchcraft in 't, he grew unto his seat,
And to such wondrous doing brought his horse,
As he had been incorps'd and demi-natur'd   86
With the brave beast; so far he topp'd my thought,   87
That I, in forgery of shapes and tricks,   88
Come short of what he did.

  Laertes.   A Norman was 't?

  King. A Norman.

  Laertes. Upon my life, Lamord.

  King.   The very same.

  Laertes. I know him well; he is the brooch indeed   92
And gem of all the nation.

  King. He made confession of you,   94
And gave you such a masterly report
For art and exercise in your defence,
And for your rapier most especially,

49. "abuse": deception, plot.

50. "character": handwriting.

61. "checking at": swerving aside from; a term in hawking.

63. "device": plans.

66. "uncharge the practice": acquit us of plotting.
"practice": strategem.

69. "organ": instrument.
"It . . . right": i.e., it fits in with my plan.

72. "your sum of parts": all your accomplishments together.

75. "Of . . . siege": the least worthy of high praise.

78. "livery": dress.

79. "sables . . . weeds": dignified robes.

80. "Importing health": denoting well-being.
"since": ago.

83. "can well": can do well.

86. "incorps'd . . . demi-natur'd": an integral part of the body.

87-9. "so . . . did": i.e., he surpassed my wildest imagination.

88. "forgery": construction, invention.

92. "brooch". We would say "jewel."

94. "confession of you": confessed knowing you.

HAMLET

ACT IV SCENE VII

In lines 110-22 Claudius echoes rather remarkably the words of the Player King (III,ii, 183-210), and of Hamlet (II,ii, 578-83; III,i, 84-8; III,iv, 161-70; IV,iv, 39-44,56-9). The passage is like a digression or reverie out of which he pulls himself suddenly at line 122. What can be the cause of it if not a sad awareness of Gertrude's unexplained rejection of him since III,iv?

"To the quick o' the ulcer" (l.122) is a nice irony. What to us seems like a cure must to a germ appear to be a disease (cf. III,iv, 147).

In its first form, Claudius' plot of the treacherous duel is safe. The blame for Hamlet's death will fall on Laertes, who fenced with a dueling sword, if it falls on anyone. For a young man so publicly jealous of his honor, Laertes' improvement upon the King's plan is remarkable (see ll. 139-47). In its final form the plot is, for Claudius, a desperate and dangerous one. His love of elaborate evil and his impatience to be rid of Hamlet seem to outweigh his caution. This is the confirmed villany towards which his failure at prayer (III,iii) has led.

That he cried out, 'twould be a sight indeed
If one could match you; the scrimers of their nation, 99
He swore, had neither motion, guard, nor eye,
If you oppos'd them. Sir, this report of his
Did Hamlet so envenom with his envy 102
That he could nothing do but wish and beg
Your sudden coming o'er, to play with him. 104
Now, out of this,—

Laertes.　　　　What out of this, my lord?

King. Laertes, was your father dear to you?
Or are you like the painting of a sorrow, 107
A face without a heart?

Laertes.　　　　Why ask you this?

King. Not that I think you did not love your father,
But that I know love is begun by time,
And that I see, in passages of proof, 111
Time qualifies the spark and fire of it. 112
There lives within the very flame of love
A kind of wick or snuff that will abate it, 114
And nothing is at a like goodness still, 115
For goodness, growing to a plurisy, 116
Dies in his own too-much. That we would do, 117
We should do when we would, for this 'would' changes,
And hath abatements and delays as many
As there are tongues, are hands, are accidents;
And then this 'should' is like a spendthrift sigh, 121
That hurts by easing. But, to the quick o' the ulcer; 122
Hamlet comes back; what would you undertake
To show yourself your father's son in deed
More than in words?

Laertes.　　　　To cut his throat i' the church.

King. No place indeed should murder sanctuarize; 126
Revenge should have no bounds. But, good Laertes,
Will you do this, keep close within your chamber. 128
Hamlet return'd shall know you are come home;
We'll put on those shall praise your excellence, 130
And set a double varnish on the fame
The Frenchman gave you, bring you, in fine, together, 132
And wager on your heads: he, being remiss, 133
Most generous and free from all contriving, 134
Will not peruse the foils; so that, with ease 135
Or with a little shuffling, you may choose
A sword unbated, and, in a pass of practice 137
Requite him for your father.

Laertes.　　　　I will do 't;
And, for that purpose, I'll anoint my sword. 139
I bought an unction of a mountebank, 140
So mortal that, but dip a knife in it,
Where it draws blood no cataplasm so rare, 142
Collected from all simples that have virtue 143
Under the moon, can save the thing from death 144
That is but scratch'd withal; I'll touch my point
With this contagion, that, if I gall him slightly, 146
It may be death.

King.　　　　Let's further think of this;
Weigh what convenience both of time and means 148
May fit us to our shape. If this should fail,
And that our drift look through our bad performance 150
'Twere better not assay'd; therefore this project 151
Should have a back or second, that might hold,

99. "scrimers": fencers.

102. "envenom": poison.

104. "sudden": soon.

107. "painting": i.e., imitation.

111. "passages of proof": experiences which prove.

112. "qualifies": diminishes.

114. "snuff": accumulation of smoldering wick which caused the candle to smoke and burn less brightly.

115. "still": always.

116. "plurisy": excess.

117-8. "That . . . would": We ought to do things when the desire is new and strong.

121. "spendthrift": wasteful. It was generally supposed that sighing was bad for the blood.

122. "quick . . . ulcer": i.e., the heart of the matter.

126. "sanctuarize": give sanctuary to a murderer.

128. "close": out of sight.

130. "put . . . praise": set certain persons on to praising.

132. "fine": short.

133. "remiss": careless.

134. "generous": noble. "contriving": plotting.

135. "foils": special fencing swords with blunted or shielded points.

137. "unbated": unblunted. "pass of practice": a treacherous thrust, or a warming-up exercise.

139. He forgets his code of honor.

140. "unction": ointment. "mountebank": quack.

142. "cataplasm": poultice.

143. "simples": herbs.

144. "Under . . . moon": herbs to be most efficacious, are gathered by moonlight.

146. "gall": scratch, draw blood.

148-9. "Weigh . . . shape": i.e., consider ways and means for best carrying out our plans.

150. "drift . . . performance": i.e., by bungling we reveal our purpose.

151. "assay'd": tried.

HAMLET

ACT IV SCENE VII

The poetic beauty of the Queen's elegiac lines on Ophelia goes far to make us think more kindly of her. The question of why she watched the scene and did nothing to save the girl seems more awkward than it is. First, Gertrude almost certainly would be unable to swim. Second, her voluminous, much boned and stayed clothing would preclude her doing anything requiring agility. We may imagine her watching, powerless to rescue, and paralyzed by the terrible nonchalance of madness singing as it drowns. Was Ophelia's death an accident or suicide?

If this should blast in proof. Soft! let me see;   153
We'll make a solemn wager on your cunnings:
I ha 't:
When in your motion you are hot and dry,—
As make your bouts more violent to that end,—
And that he calls for drink, I'll have prepar'd him
A chalice for the nonce, whereon but sipping,   159
If he by chance escape your venom'd stuck,   160
Our purpose may hold there. But stay! what noise?
　　　　　　　Enter QUEEN.
How now, sweet queen!
　Queen. One woe doth tread upon another's heel,
So fast they follow: your sister's drown'd, Laertes.
　Laertes. Drown'd! O, where?
　Queen. There is a willow grows aslant a brook,
That shows his hoar leaves in the glassy stream;   167
There with fantastic garlands did she come,
Of crow-flowers, nettles, daisies, and long purples,
That liberal shepherds give a grosser name,   170
But our cold maids do dead men's fingers call them:
There, on the pendent boughs her coronet weeds   172
Clambering to hang, an envious sliver broke,   173
When down her weedy trophies and herself
Fell in the weeping brook. Her clothes spread wide,
And, mermaid-like, awhile they bore her up;
Which time she chanted snatches of old lauds,   177
As one incapable of her own distress,   178
Or like a creature native and indu'd   179
Unto that element; but long it could not be
Till that her garments, heavy with their drink,
Pull'd the poor wretch from her melodious lay   182
To muddy death.
　Laertes.　　　Alas! then, she is drown'd?
　Queen. Drown'd, drown'd.
　Laertes. Too much of water hast thou, poor Ophelia,
And therefore I forbid my tears; but yet
It is our trick, nature her custom holds,   187
Let shame say what it will; when these are gone   188
The woman will be out. Adieu, my lord!   189
I have a speech of fire, that fain would blaze,
But that this folly douts it.　　　[*Exit.* 191
　King.　　　　Let's follow, Gertrude.
How much I had to do to calm his rage!
Now fear I this will give it start again;
Therefore let's follow.　　　　[*Exeunt.*

153. "blast in proof": break in trial; refers to ordinance trials; a metaphor taken from the trying or proving of firearms or cannon. "Soft": wait a minute.

159. "chalice": cup. "nonce": occasion.

160. "stuck": thrust.

167. "hoar": gray, as the leaves of the willows are steaming on the underside.

170. "liberal": free-spoken.

172. "coronet weeds": garlands of flowers.

173. "envious silver": malicious branch.

177. "lauds": hymns of praise.

178. "incapable": insensible.

179. "indu'd": endowed, belonging to.

182. "lay": song.

187. "our trick": our fashion.

188. "these": referring to "tears" for which he apologizes.

189. "out": i.e., escaped from his spirit.

191. "douts": extinguishes; literally, do out.

HAMLET

ACT V SCENE I

This scene may be divided for purposes of study and commentary into three sections: 1) the grave diggers; 2) Hamlet's meditations; 3) Ophelia's funeral.

(1)

To come to the grave diggers after the deadly intrigue and elegiac sadness of IV,vii is like moving into a new world, a world focused on life rather than death, even though the place is a churchyard and the business of life is to dig graves. The tension is released and our interest diverted by comedy. The setting is laid for Ophelia's funeral. The events of the main action are both heightened and placed in perspective by the contrast. But more important still, the episode serves to indicate a new beginning. For the first time, we are introduced to lives not poisoned by the rottenness of Denmark.

These two clowns give us comments on public events of ordinary working men who understand little of what is happening in the palace. The same is true of the soldiers, Bernardo, Francisco, and (to a lesser degree) Marcellus in Act One. Such scenes have the special importance in a tragedy of indicating the social context of the main action, for the fortunes of the people follow those of their governors, although these people rarely understand the ins and outs of what is happening to them. They must endure and obey; they may marvel and comment.

Francisco (I,i, 9) is "sick at heart." The grave diggers are relaxed and talk in ease. Within the palace the fortunes of Claudius are falling. His smooth and even world has given place to "discord and dismay." It is Claudius and Gertrude now who are heartsick.

ACT FIVE, scene one.

(A CHURCHYARD)

Enter two Clowns, *with spades and mattock.*

First Clown. Is she to be buried in Christian burial that wilfully seeks her own salvation? 1

Second Clown. I tell thee she is: and therefore make her grave straight: the crowner hath sat on her, and finds it Christian burial. 4 5

First Clown. How can that be, unless she drowned herself in her own defence?

Second Clown. Why, 'tis found so.

First Clown. It must be *se offendendo*; it cannot be else. For here lies the point: if I drown myself wittingly it argues an act; and an act hath three branches; it is, to act, to do, and to perform: argal, she drowned herself wittingly. 9 11 12

Second Clown. Nay, but hear you, goodman delver,— 15

First Clown. Give me leave. Here lies the water; good: here stands the man; good: if the man go to this water, and drown himself, it is, will he, nill he, he goes; mark you that? but if the water come to him, and drown him, he drowns not himself: argal, he that is not guilty of his own death shortens not his own life. 18

Second Clown. But is this law?

First Clown. Ay, marry, is't; crowner's quest law. 24

Second Clown. Will you ha' the truth on 't? If this had not been a gentlewoman she should have been buried out o' Christian burial.

First Clown. Why, there thou sayest; and the more pity that great folk should have countenance in this world to drown or hang themselves more than their even Christian. Come, my spade. There is no ancient gentlemen but gardeners, ditchers, and grave-makers; they hold up Adam's profession. 28 29 31 33

Second Clown. Was he a gentleman?

First Clown. A' was the first that ever bore arms. 35

Second Clown. Why, he had none.

First Clown. What! art a heathen? How dost thou understand the Scripture? The Scripture says, Adam digged; could he dig without arms? I'll put another question to thee; if thou answerest me not to the purpose, confess thyself— 41

Second Clown. Go to.

First Clown. What is he that builds stronger than either the mason, the shipwright, or the carpenter?

Second Clown. The gallows-maker; for that frame outlives a thousand tenants.

First Clown. I like thy wit well, in good faith; the gallows does well, but how does it well? it does well to those that do ill; now thou dost ill to say the gallows is built stronger than the church: argal, the gallows may do well to thee. To 't again; come.

Stage direction: "Clowns": i.e., countrymen, these parts being taken by the clowns, who were indispensable members of every stage company.

1. "Christian burial": i.e., in consecrated ground. People who committed suicides were buried in unhallowed ground.

4. "straight": straightway. "crowner": coroner.

5. "finds . . . burial": brings in a verdict that she should have a Christian burial.

9. "se offendendo": in self-defense.

11. "wittingly": knowingly, on purpose.

12. "argal": therefore.

15. "delver": digger.

18. "will he, nill he": willy-nilly, whether he wishes or not.

24. "quest": inquest.

28. "thou sayest": You said it, that's the truth.

29. "countenance": permission.

31. "even": fellow.

33. "hold up": support, i.e., keep it going.

35. "arms": i.e., a coat of arms, the prerogative of gentlemen.

41-2. "confess . . . to": The second clown is familiar with the rest of the proverb, viz., "and be hanged," and so interrupts.

HAMLET

ACT V SCENE I

The song of the First Grave digger is an amusing jumble of half-remembered verses from a poem by Lord Vaux (an odd enough specimen of verse in itself, though apparently well known) called THE AGED LOVER RENOUNCETH LOVE. It is too long to quote entire, but here are those verses of it from which the grave digger draws:

I loathe that I did love,
In youth that I thought sweet:
As time requires for my behove
Me thinks they are not meet:

For age with stealing steps
Hath clawed me with his crutch
And lusty life away she leaps
As there had been none such.
A pickaxe and a spade
And eke a winding sheet,
A house of clay for to be made
For such a guest most meet.

For beauty with her band
These crooked cares hath wrought
And shipped me into the land
From whence I first was brought.

(2)

Earlier in the play Hamlet's dress and actions have been such as to attract attention, first in reproach, then in defiance of the King's world. Now, however, there is an air almost of stealth in his silent approach with Horatio through the graveyard into Denmark. His speeches, too, show a yet further change in him. (Does he refer to himself when he says, "the hand of little employment hath the daintier sense"?) He is wiser, quieter, and more detached.

He has been appalled and revolted by the moral corruption of the living, now he is soothed and even amused by the universality of physical corruption in the dead. Death now seems to be his ally; it is a kind of fatalism (see below). King and jester, business man, politician, and parasite, all are finally the same. To measure this view against the radiant idealism of a happier time is to realize the sad, long way he has come. His mood is meditative, but it has a grotesque side, too (the shadow of his quick wit and scholar's curi-

---

Second Clown. Who builds stronger than a mason. a shipwright, or a carpenter?
First Clown. Ay, tell me that, and unyoke. 54
Second Clown. Marry, now I can tell.
First Clown. To 't.
Second Clown. Mass, I cannot tell. 57

      Enter HAMLET *and* HORATIO *at a distance.*
First Clown. Cudgel thy brains no more about it, for your dull ass will not mend his pace with beating; and, when you are asked this question next, say, 'a grave-maker:' the houses that he makes last till doomsday. Go, get thee to Yaughan; fetch me a 62
stoup of liquor. 63

              [Exit Second Clown.
    First Clown *digs, and sings.*
  In youth, when I did love, did love, 64
    Methought it was very sweet,
  To contract o' the time, for-a my behove,
    O! methought there was nothing meet. 67

Hamlet. Has this fellow no feeling of his business, that he sings at grave-making?
Horatio. Custom hath made it in him a property of 70
easiness.
Hamlet. 'Tis e'en so; the hand of little employment hath the daintier sense.
First Clown.
  But age, with his stealing steps,
    Hath claw'd me in his clutch,
  And hath shipped me intil the land, 76
    As if I had never been such.

             [Throws up a skull.
Hamlet. That skull had a tongue in it, and could sing once; how the knave jowls it to the ground, as 79
if it were Cain's jaw-bone, that did the first murder! 80
This might be the pate of a politician, which this ass 81
now o'er-reaches one that would circumvent God, 82
might it not?
Horatio. It might, my lord.
Hamlet. Or of a courtier, which could say, 'Good morrow, sweet lord! How dost thou, good lord?' This might be my Lord Such-a-one, that praised my Lord Such-a-one's horse, when he meant to beg it, 88
might it not?
Horatio. Ay, my lord.
Hamlet. Why, e'en so, and now my Lady Worm's chapless, and knocked about the mazzard with a sex- 92
ton's spade. Here's fine revolution, an we had the 93
trick to see 't. Did these bones cost no more the 94
breeding but to play at loggats with 'em? mine 95
ache to think on 't.
First Clown.
  A pick-axe, and a spade, a spade,
    For and a shrouding sheet;
  O! a pit of clay for to be made
    For such a guest is meet.

           [Throws up another skull.
Hamlet. There's another; why may not that be the skull of a lawyer? Where be his quiddities now, his 102
quillets, his cases, his tenures, and his tricks? why 103
does he suffer this rude knave now to knock him about

---

54. "unyoke": i.e., consider your day's work done.

57. "Mass": by the mass.

62. "Yaughan": probably the name of a tavern-keeper near the Globe theater.

63. "stoup" flagon.

64. The clown's song is a jumbled version of three stanzas of The Aged Lover Renounceth Love, from Tottel's Miscellany (1557).

67. "meet": suitable.

70-1. i.e., habit has made it a thing of indifference to him.

76. "intil": into.

79. "knave": here means rude fellow. "jowls": bumps.

80. "Cain's jaw-bone": the jawbone of an ass with which Cain is supposed to have killed Abel.

81. "politician": plotter, schemer; the regular meaning of the word with Shakespeare.

82. "o'er-reaches": gets the better of. "circumvent": get around.

88. "beg": borrow.

92. "chapless": jawless. "mazzard": slang for head (literally drinking bowl).

93. "revolution": turn of fortune. "an": if.

94. "trick": skill.

95. "loggats": skittles or ninepins, a British game in which a ball is bowled at nine wooden pins.

102. "quiddities": subtle distinctions, hair-splitting.

103. "quillets": quibbles. "tenures": titles to property. "tricks": legal tricks, technicalities.

HAMLET

ACT V SCENE I

osity), displayed in his desire to know how long it takes a corpse to rot (I. 153) and reaching a small climax of mocking amusement in his improvised doggerel verses about "Imperious Caesar" (II. 223-6).

The passage about Yorick shows that his fatalism has not anesthetized his capacity for pity or his tragic sense of loss. Notice the shock of his exclamation, "This!" (I. 188). Then flashes out the bitterness of lines199-202(cf. III,i, 51-3, 144-6). Is he referring to his mother or Ophelia?

Lines 146-79 define Hamlet's age to be thirty years. This fact is bothersome because Hamlet in the first three acts seems younger than this. The difficulty is insoluble. Most actors play Hamlet as younger. It has been observed in another connection (not regarding Hamlet) that the Elizabethans were less number conscious than we, since they were not always peering at watches, speedometers, and invoices, and tended to round figures off rather generously. Perhaps this is our best explanation.

We wonder how the impending news of Ophelia's death will affect him. It is her grave he has been standing at. Suspense rises when he asks about it (II. 134-140). The irony is emphasized in lines 223-226. His judgment of the circumstances is clear. Why is he unable to guess?

The satirical reference of lines 144-46 to Elizabethan England may be appreciated by reading the following Royal Proclamation of Queen Elizabeth (1597) as recorded by G. B. Harrison:

"The great inconveniences that grow and daily increase in the realm by the inordinate excess in apparel have again caused her majesty to make strait proclamation that the laws be duly executed. In this present time of difficulty the decay and lack of hospitality appears in the better sort in all countries, principally occasioned by the immeasurable charges and expense which they are put to in superfluous apparelling their wives, children, and families; the confusion also of degrees in all places being great where the meanest are as richly apparelled as their betters, and the pride such inferior persons take in their garments, driving many for their maintenance to robbing and stealing by the highway. It is now laid down very exactly what stuffs may be worn by gentlemen and ladies in their several degrees."

In this connection see Osric in the next scene (V,ii, 83-194).

the sconce with a dirty shovel, and will not tell him 105 of his action of battery? Hum! This fellow might be in 's time a great buyer of land, with his statutes, 107 his recognizances, his fines, his double vouchers, his 108 recoveries; is this the fine of his fines, and the recovery 109 of his recoveries, to have his fine pate full of fine dirt? will his vouchers vouch him no more of his purchases, and double ones too, than the length and breadth of a pair of indentures? The very convey- 113 ance of his land will hardly lie in this box, and must 114 the inheritor himself have no more, ha? 115

Horatio. Not a jot more, my lord.

Hamlet. Is not parchment made of sheep-skins?

Horatio. Ay, my lord, and of calf-skins too.

Hamlet. They are sheep and calves which seek out assurance in that. I will speak to this fellow. Whose 120 grave's this, sir?

First Clown. Mine, sir.

        O! a pit of clay for to be made
        For such a guest is meet.

Hamlet. I think it be thine, indeed; for thou liest in't.

First Clown. You lie out on 't, sir, and therefore it is not yours; for my part, I do not lie in 't, and yet it is mine.

Hamlet. Thou dost lie in 't, to be in 't and say it is thine; 'tis for the dead, not for the quick; therefore thou liest.

First Clown. 'Tis a quick lie, sir; 'twill away again 132 from me to you.

Hamlet. What man dost thou dig it for?

First Clown. For no man, sir.

Hamlet. What woman, then?

First Clown. For none, neither.

Hamlet. Who is to be buried in 't?

First Clown. One that was a woman, sir; but, rest her soul, she's dead.

Hamlet. How absolute the knave is! we must speak 141 by the card, or equivocation will undo us. By the 142 Lord, Horatio, these three years I have taken note of it; the age is grown so picked that the toe of the peas- 144 ant comes so near the heel of the courtier, he galls 145 his kibe. How long hast thou been a grave-maker?

First Clown. Of all the days i' the year, I came to 't that day our last King Hamlet overcame Fortinbras.

Hamlet. How long is that since?

First Clown Cannot you tell that? every fool can tell that; it was the very day that young Hamlet was born; he that is mad, and sent into England.

Hamlet. Ay, marry; why was he sent into England?

First Clown. Why, because he was mad: he shall recover his wits there; or, if he do not, 'tis no great matter there.

Hamlet. Why?

First Clown. 'Twill not be seen in him there; there the men are as mad as he.

Hamlet. How came he mad?

First Clown. Very strangely, they say.

Hamlet. How strangely?

First Clown. Faith, e'en with losing his wits.

Hamlet. Upon what ground?

105. "sconce": another slang word for head (literally blockhouse).

107. "statutes": bonds.

108. "recognizances": obligations. "fines": conveyances. "vouchers": witnesses.

109. "recoveries": transfers. "fine": end.

113. "pair of indentures": agreements in duplicate.

113-14. "conveyance": documents recording purchase.

114. "box": coffin.

115. "inheritor": possessor.

120. "assurance": another pun (1) conveyance of property by deed; (2) security. "that": i.e., parchment.

132. "quick: living. A phrase in the Apostles' Creed has preserved this original meaning for us, viz., "the quick and the dead."

141. "absolute": exact, literal.

142. "by the card": precisely. "equivocation": speaking with a double sense.

144. "picked": refined.

144-5. "galls his kibe": steps on (scrapes) his heel.

HAMLET

ACT V SCENE I

[Old Tune] Gravedigger

[Traditional Stage Tune] The Children In The Wood

First Clown. Why, here in Denmark; I have been sexton here, man and boy, thirty years. 166

Hamlet. How long will a man lie i' the earth ere he rot?

First Clown. Faith, if he be not rotten before he die,—as we have many pocky corses now-a-days, that 170 will scarce hold the laying in,—he will last you some 171 eight year or nine year; a tanner will last you nine year.

Hamlet. Why he more than another?

First Clown. Why, sir, his hide is so tanned with his trade that he will keep out water a great while, and your water is a sore decayer of your whoreson 177 dead body. Here's a skull now; this skull hath lain you i' the earth three-and-twenty years.

Hamlet. Whose was it?

First Clown. A whoreson mad fellow's it was: whose do you think it was?

Hamlet. Nay, I know not.

First Clown. A pestilence on him for a mad rogue; a' poured a flagon of Rhenish on my head once. This same skull, sir, was, sir, Yorick's skull, the king's jester.

Hamlet. This!

First Clown. E'en that.

Hamlet. Let me see.—[*Takes the skull.*]—Alas! poor Yorick. I knew him, Horatio; a fellow of infinite jest, of most excellent fancy; he hath borne me on his back a thousand times; and now, how abhorred in my imagination it is! my gorge rises at it. 194 Here hung those lips that I have kissed I know not how oft. Where be your gibes now? your gambols? 196 your songs? your flashes of merriment, that were wont to set the table on a roar? Not one now, to mock your own grinning? quite chapfallen? Now 199 get you to my lady's chamber, and tell her, let her paint an inch thick, to this favour she must come; 201 make her laugh at that. Prithee, Horatio, tell me one thing.

Horatio. What's that, my lord?

Hamlet. Dost thou think Alexander looked o' this fashion i' the earth?

Horatio. E'en so.

Hamlet. And smelt so? pah! [*Puts down the skull.*

Horatio. E'en so, my lord.

Hamlet. To what base uses we may return, Horatio! Why may not imagination trace the noble dust of Alexander, till he find it stopping a bung- 212 hole?

Horatio. 'Twere to consider too curiously, to con- 214 sider so.

Hamlet. No, faith, not a jot; but to follow him thither with modesty enough, and likelihood to lead 217 it; as thus: Alexander died, Alexander was buried, Alexander returneth into dust; the dust is earth; of earth we make loam, and why of that loam, whereto he was converted, might they 221 not stop a beer-barrel?

Imperious Caesar, dead and turn'd to clay,
Might stop a hole to keep the wind away:

166. "thirty years": This, together with the thirty years of marriage of the Player King and Player Queen, would certainly seem to fix Hamlet's age as close to thirty, although the general impression we get from the play is of a young man in his early twenties.

170. "pocky": pock-marked.

171. "you": The use of "you" and "your" in these speeches by the clown is in a general or indefinite, rather than personal, sense. See note on I,v, 167.

177. "sore": severe.
"whoreson": worthless (literally bastard).

194. "gorge": stomach (literally throat).

196. "gibes": jests.

199. "chapfallen": another pun: (1) literally jawless; (2) figuratively, downcast.

201. "favour": appearance.

212-3. "bung-hole": i.e., in a beer barrel.

214. "curiously": precisely.

217. "with . . . it": i.e., without exaggeration and within the bounds of all probability.

221. "loam": a mixture of sand and clay used to make plaster.

HAMLET

ACT V SCENE I

(3)

Ophelia's funeral is a court ceremonial. It is the reverse of that in I,ii. The ceremony is maimed, but the death is a real death and the very abbreviation of the service shows forth the nature of the death.

Note the dramatic irony of lines 233-34. We have seen Laertes' nobility (IV,vii, 138-47).

The pathos of Ophelia, like the last of Hamlet's youth, being put in the earth is emphasized by the words and flower symbolism of the Queen in lines 253-56, and Laertes in lines 249-51. The passage marks the end of the train of flower images (listed in commentary to III,iv, 42-4).

Hamlet's interference needs examination. The shock of his realization, and his mother's evocation of the hoped-for marriage, stir him, after which Laertes' inflated grief spurs him to show himself. His unwillingness to brawl expressed in his invitation to peace (II. 269-73) indicate that his emotion is at the outset a tragic one rather than combative. As Laertes continues his assault, Hamlet takes fire and rants in jealous mockery. He is not expressing his sorrow, but out-heroding Herod (see III,ii, 14).

There has been disagreement over the staging of their brawl. Granville-Barker maintains that Hamlet should not leap into the grave. Laertes, as the aggressor, should leap out. Another advantage of this version is that their fight will be in the center of the stage rather than lost down a hole. The early texts are inconclusive. Q2 has no stage directions whatever at this point. F1 has Laertes leap into the grave after line 260, but gives nothing further. Q1, the unreliable text, does have Hamlet leap into the grave.

What does Claudius mean at line 308? Is he thinking of Hamlet?

O! that that earth, which kept the world in awe, 225
Should patch a wall to expel the winter's flaw. 226
But soft! but soft! aside: here comes the king.
Enter KING, QUEEN, LAERTES, *and a coffin with* Lords
attendant *and* Priest.
The queen, the courtiers: who is that they follow?
And with such maimed rites? This doth betoken 229
The corse they follow did with desperate hand
Fordo its own life; 'twas of some estate. 231
Couch we awhile, and mark. 232
      [*Retiring with* HORATIO.
Laertes. What ceremony else?
Hamlet.   That is Laertes,
A very noble youth: mark.
Laertes. Where ceremony else?
First Priest. Her obsequies have been as far
  enlarg'd
As we have warrantise: her death was doubtful, 237
And, but that great command o'ersways the order, 238
She should in ground unsanctified have lodg'd
Till the last trumpet; for charitable prayers, 240
Shards, flints, and pebbles should be thrown on her; 241
Yet here she is allow'd her virgin crants, 242
Her maiden strewments, and the bringing home 243
Of bell and burial.
Laertes. Must there no more be done?
First Priest.   No more be done:
We should profane the service of the dead,
To sing sage requiem, and such rest to her
As to peace-parted souls. 248
Laertes.   Lay her i' th' earth;
And from her fair and unpolluted flesh
May violets spring! I tell thee, churlish priest, 250
A ministering angel shall my sister be,
When thou liest howling.
Hamlet.   What! the fair Ophelia?
Queen. Sweets to the sweet: farewell!
      [*Scattering flowers.*
I hop'd thou shouldst have been my Hamlet's wife;
I thought thy bride-bed to have deck'd, sweet maid,
And not have strew'd thy grave.
Laertes.   O! treble woe
Fall ten times treble on that cursed head
Whose wicked deed thy most ingenious sense 258
Depriv'd thee of. Hold off the earth awhile,
Till I have caught her once more in mine arms.
      [*Leaps into the grave.*
Now pile your dust upon the quick and dead,
Till of this flat a mountain you have made,
To o'ertop old Pelion or the skyish head 263
Of blue Olympus.
Hamlet. [*Advancing.*]   What is he whose grief
Bears such an emphasis? whose phrase of sorrow
Conjures the wandering stars, and makes them 266
  stand
Like wonder-wounded hearers? this is I, 267
Hamlet the Dane.   [*Leaps into the grave.*
Laertes.   The devil take thy soul!
      [*Grapples with him.*
Hamlet. Thou pray'st not well.

225. "earth": i.e., Caesar.

226. "flaw": blast.

229. "maimed": curtailed.
"betoken": indicate.

231. "Fordo": destroy.
"estate": high rank.

232. "Couch": lie concealed.

237. "warrantise": authority.

238. i.e., if the King had used his authority to override the rule of the Church.

240. "for": instead of.

241. "shards": broken earthenware.

242. "crants": wreaths.

243. "maiden strewments": flowers strewn on a girl's grave.

248. "peace-parted": departed in peace.

250. "churlish": rude.

258. "most . . . sense": intelligence.

263. "skyish": reaching in the sky.

263-4. Pelion, Olympus, and Ossa are mountains in Greece. Laertes leaves the third for Hamlet (l. 293).

266. "wandering stars": planets.
"stand": stand still.

267. "wonder-wounded": overcome with wonder.

I prithee, take thy fingers from my throat;
For though I am not splenetive and rash   271
Yet have I in me something dangerous,
Which let thy wisdom fear. Away thy hand!
  King. Pluck them asunder.
  Queen.   Hamlet! Hamlet!
  All. Gentlemen,—
  Horatio.   Good my lord, be quiet.
    [*The* Attendants *part them, and they come out*
                           of the grave.
  Hamlet. Why, I will fight with him upon this theme
Until my eyelids will no longer wag.
  Queen. O my son! what theme?
  Hamlet. I lov'd Ophelia: forty thousand brothers
Could not, with all their quantity of love,
Make up my sum. What wilt thou do for her?
  King. O! he is mad, Laertes.
  Queen. For love of God, forbear him.   283
  Hamlet. 'Swounds, show me what thou'lt do:
Woo't weep? woo't fight? woo't fast? woo't tear   285
    thyself?
Woo't drink up eisel? eat a crocodile?   286
I'll do't. Dost thou come here to whine?
To outface me with leaping in her grave?   288
Be buried quick with her, and so will I:
And, if thou prate of mountains, let them throw
Millions of acres on us, till our ground,
Singeing his pate against the burning zone,   292
Make Ossa like a wart! Nay, an thou'lt mouth,   293
I'll rant as well as thou.
  Queen.   This is mere madness: 294
And thus a while the fit will work on him;
Anon as patient as the female dove,
When that her golden couplets are disclos'd,   297
His silence will sit drooping.
  Hamlet.   Hear you, sir;
What is the reason that you use me thus?
I lov'd you ever: but it is no matter;
Let Hercules himself do what he may,
The cat will mew and dog will have his day.   [*Exit.*
  King. I pray you, good Horatio, wait upon him.
                        [*Exit* HORATIO.
[*To* LAERTES.] Strengthen your patience in our last
    night's speech;
We'll put the matter to the present push.   305
Good Gertrude, set some watch over your son.
This grave shall have a living monument: 307
An hour of quiet shortly shall we see;
Till then, in patience our proceeding be.   [*Exeunt.*

  The peculiar suddenness and accidental character of the ending of this play raise strongly the problems involved in analyzing its tragic pattern. This point will be discussed at the end. After Hamlet's narrative to Horatio and the episode with Osric, which characterize anew Hamlet and these pursy times (see III,iv, 153), we have the lavish entry of the court, the duel,

---

Scene two.

(A HALL IN THE CASTLE)

Enter HAMLET *and* HORATIO.

  Hamlet. So much for this, sir: now shall you see the   1
    other;
You do remember all the circumstance?

---

271. "splenetive": full of spleen, hot-tempered.

283. "forbear him": pay no attention to him, make allowances for him.

285. "Woo't": colloquial and familiar form of wilt thou.

286. "eisel": vinegar.

288. "outface": put to shame, outdo.

292. "the burning zone": the sun.

293. "Ossa": mountain in Greece (see ll. 261-4).

294. "mere": utter.

297. "couplets": The dove lays only two eggs.
"disclos'd": hatched.

305. "present push": immediate test.

307. "a living monument": an enduring memorial. Is he perhaps also thinking that Hamlet should be made a "living" sacrifice to the dead Ophelia?

1-2. Hamlet enters talking and already in the middle of his story.

HAMLET

ACT V SCENE II

and finally, due to the arrival of Fortinbras, a tragic resolution.

Hamlet's account of the events of the sea voyage shows his energy, his ability, his wit, and his new and tragic indifference to life and death (ll. 57-62, 221-7).

"I lay Worse than the mutines in the bilboes" (ll. 5-6; cf. IV,ii; IV,iii; II,ii, 267-9), reminds us of the lowest point in Hamlet's physical fortunes, while at the same time showing the trouble of his spirit over his transformation. Was this the expectancy and rose of the fair state, now become the prisoner and outcast of a foul state?

To this sense of despair is added (ll. 6-11) a kind of fatalism (see also above, commentary on V,i) involving a sense of kinship with death, of the shortness of life, of the triviality and futility of action, and of the extent to which our lives, controlled by a divinity that shapes our ends (whether fate, luck, Providence, or whatever), are not our own. This mockery of life contains and explains his attitude towards Rosencrantz and Guildenstern (ll. 57-8) and towards himself (ll. 221-7). It is Hamlet's approach to tragic negation of life (see below).

These serious matters do not prevent Hamlet's grim relish for the events as he regales Horatio with them (see especially ll. 37-47). His reference to his neglected clerkly skill in the elaborate, decorative penmanship used for documents is very like a passage in one of Montaigne's essays: "I have in my time seen some, who by writing did earnestly get both their titles and living, to disavow their apprenticeship, mar their pen, and affect the ignorance of so vulgar a quality." (Florio's translation, 1603. If Shakespeare knew of this passage it was likely in the original French.)

Horatio. Remember it, my lord?

Hamlet. Sir, in my heart there was a kind of fighting
That would not let me sleep; methought I lay
Worse than the mutines in the bilboes. Rashly,— 6
And prais'd be rashness for it, let us know, 7
Our indiscretion sometimes serves us well 8
When our deep plots do pall; and that should teach us
There's a divinity that shapes our ends, 10
Rough-hew them how we will.

Horatio.   That is most certain.

Hamlet. Up from my cabin,
My sea-gown scarf'd about me, in the dark 13
Groped I to find out them, had my desire, 14
Finger'd their packet, and in fine withdrew 15
To mine own room again; making so bold—
My fears forgetting manners—to unseal
Their grand commission; where I found, Horatio,
O royal knavery! an exact command,
Larded with many several sorts of reasons 20
Importing Denmark's health, and England's too, 21
With, ho! such bugs and goblins in my life, 22
That, on the supervise, no leisure bated, 23
No, not to stay the grinding of the axe,
My head should be struck off.

Horatio.   Is't possible?

Hamlet. Here's the commission: read it at more leisure.
But wilt thou hear me how I did proceed?

Horatio. I beseech you.

Hamlet. Being thus be-netted round with villainies,—
Ere I could make a prologue to my brains 30
They had begun the play,—I sat me down,
Devis'd a new commission, wrote it fair;
I once did hold it, as our statists do, 33
A baseness to write fair, and labour'd much
How to forget that learning; but, sir, now
It did me yeoman's service. Wilt thou know 36
The effect of what I wrote?

Horatio.   Ay, good my lord.

Hamlet. An earnest conjuration from the king,
As England was his faithful tributary,
As love between them like the palm should flourish,
As peace should still her wheaten garland wear, 41
And stand a comma 'tween their amities, 42
And many such-like 'As'es of great charge, 43
That, on the view and knowing of these contents,
Without debatement further, more or less, 45
He should the bearers put to sudden death,
Not shriving-time allow'd.

Horatio.   How was this seal'd? 47

Hamlet. Why, even in that was heaven ordinant. 48
I had my father's signet in my purse,
Which was the model of that Danish seal; 50
Folded the writ up in form of the other, 51
Subscrib'd it, gave 't th' impression, plac'd it safely, 52
The changeling never known. Now, the next day 53
Was our sea-fight, and what to this was sequent
Thou know'st already.

Horatio. So Guildenstern and Rosencrantz go to 't. 56

6. "mutines": mutineers.
   "bilboes": fetters.

7. "let us know": let us acknowledge.

8-9. "Our . . . pall": i.e., sometimes it is to our advantage, when our deeply laid plans fall flat (pall), to act on the spur of the moment without weighing the consequences.

10-11. No matter how crudely we begin our designs, Fate steps in to put the finishing touches on them.

13. "sea-gown": a skirted garment with short sleeves, worn by seamen.
    "scarf'd": wrapped.

14. "them": i.e., Rosencrantz and Guildenstern.

15. "Finger'd": stole, "lifted."

20. "larded": garnished.
    "several sorts": different kinds.

21. "Importing": concerning.

22. "bugs": bugbears.
    "in my life": in my continued existence.

23. "supervise": reading, first glance over the letter.
    "bated": allowed.

30. "prologue": introductory speech.

33. "statists": statesmen.

36. "yeoman's service": good service. English yeomen made the most reliable soldiers.

41. "wheaten garland": a symbol of prosperity.

42. i.e., provide a connecting link between their friendships.

43. "charge": weight, import.

45. "debatement": debating.

47. "Not . . . allow'd": not giving them time even to confess their sins.

48. "ordinant": provident.

50. "model": copy.

51. "writ": writing.

52. "Subscrib'd . . . impression": signed and sealed it.

53. "changeling": literally an elf-child substituted for a human one.

56. "go to 't": as we might say, are for it, or have had it.

HAMLET

ACT V SCENE II

See the list of disease images in commentary to III,iv, 42-5, in connection with "canker" (l.69).

Notice the resolute calmness of lines 73-4, which convinces us of Hamlet's deadliness in his new realization of life in spite of our knowledge that the interim is not altogether his. Hamlet's assumption, in the same speech, of likeness to Laertes serves through dramatic irony to emphasize in our minds the contrast between them in which Hamlet appears favorable.

The difference between Osric and such other characters emblematic of the decadence of Denmark as Polonius, Rozencrantz, and Guildenstern shows the increasing weakness of this regime. If Osric is its representative, it need no longer be taken seriously. The parallel between Osric and his earlier counterparts is emphasized by the way Hamlet deals with him (ll. 95-100, 133-140), a conscious reversion to the antic disposition as used against the others (cf. III,ii, 343-65, 369-76). (See also V,i, 153-6 and commentary, and other references to the frivolity and viciousness of the court throughout.)

Hamlet. Why, man, they did make love to this employment; 57
They are not near my conscience; their defeat 58
Does by their own insinuation grow. 59
'Tis dangerous when the baser nature comes 60
Between the pass and fell-incensed points
Of mighty opposites.
   Horatio.   Why, what a king is this!
   Hamlet. Does it not, thinks't thee, stand me now 63
    upon—
He that hath kill'd my king and whor'd my mother,
Popp'd in between the election and my hopes, 65
Thrown out his angle for my proper life, 66
And with such cozenage—is 't not perfect conscience 67
To quit him with this arm? and is 't not to be 68
    damn'd
To let this canker of our nature come
In further evil?
   Horatio. It must be shortly known to him from
    England
What is the issue of the business there.
   Hamlet. It will be short: the interim is mine; 73
And a man's life's no more than to say 'One.'
But I am very sorry, good Horatio,
That to Laertes I forgot myself;
For, by the image of my cause, I see 77
The portraiture of his: I'll court his favours:
But, sure, the bravery of his grief did put me 79
Into a towering passion.
   Horatio.   Peace! who comes here?
              Enter OSRIC.
   Osric. Your lordship is right welcome back to Denmark.
   Hamlet. I humbly thank you, sir. [*Aside to*
   HORATIO.]
Dost know this water-fly? 83
   Horatio. [*Aside to* HAMLET.] No, my good lord.
   Hamlet. [*Aside to* HORATIO.] Thy state is the more 85
gracious; for 'tis a vice to know him. He hath much
land, and fertile: let a beast be lord of beasts, and 87
his crib shall stand at the king's mess; 'tis a chough; 88
but, as I say, spacious in the possession of dirt. 89
   Osric. Sweet lord, if your lordship were at leisure, I
should impart a thing to you from his majesty.
   Hamlet. I will receive it, sir, with all diligence of
spirit.
Put your bonnet to his right use; 'tis for the head. 94
   Osric. I thank your lordship, 'tis very hot.
   Hamlet. No, believe me, 'tis very cold; the wind is
northerly.
   Osric. It is indifferent cold, my lord, indeed. 98
   Hamlet. But yet methinks it is very sultry and hot
for my complexion. 100
   Osric. Exceedingly, my lord; it is very sultry, as
'twere, I cannot tell how. But, my lord, his majesty
bade me signify to you that he has laid a great wager
on your head. Sir, this is the matter,—
   Hamlet. I beseech you, remember—
      [HAMLET *moves him to put on his hat.*]
   Osric. Nay, good my lord; for mine ease, in good 106

57. "they . . . to": as we would say ,they asked for it.

58. "They . . . conscience": i.e., their death is not on my conscience. "defeat": destruction.

59. "insinuation": intervention, meddling.

60-2. " 'Tis . . . opposites": i.e., it is dangerous for inferiors to get between the thrusting blades and sword points of angry and mighty opponents.

63. i.e., don't you think it is now my duty?

65. i.e., prevented me from being elected king as I had hoped. There are frequent references throughout the play to the Danish custom of electing their king.

66. "angle": fishing tackle. "my proper life": my very life.

67. "cozenage": treachery.

68. "To quit him": to pay him back.

68-70. "and . . . evil": i.e., will I not be risking eternal damnation if I allow this destructive element (canker) in our life (nature) to accomplish any more harm?

73-4. i.e., there is no great hurry; it takes only a second to kill a man.

77-8. I realize his duty and feelings are like mine.

79. "bravery": bravado.

Stage direction: Osric is an example of the fashionable affected courtier of Shakespeare's own time.

83. "water-fly": "A water-fly skips up and down upon the surface of the water without any apparent purpose, and is thence the proper emblem of a busy trifler." (Johnson).

85-6. "Thy . . . gracious": i.e., you are better off.

87-8. "let . . . mess": "let a man be but rich in land and beasts it is no matter though he be a beast himself; he shall feed at the king's table." (G. S. Gordon)

88. "chough": jackdaw (i.e., a chatterer).

89. "spacious . . . dirt": a possessor of much land.

94. "Put . . . head": Though Elizabethans wore their hats indoors, it was customary to stand uncovered in the presence of superiors.

98. "indifferent": fairly.

100. "for my complexion": for one of my complexion or temperament.

106-7. "for . . . faith": a polite phrase of the time.

94

HAMLET

ACT V SCENE II

Lines 113-21 present a little set-piece of Hamlet's satirical wit, a masterpiece of mixed metaphor taking its cue from "card [i.e., mariners' compass card] or calendar [i.e., directory]".

Lines 133-40 give us yet another example of a knavish speech sleeping "in a foolish ear" (cf. IV,ii, 23-4).

The terms of the wager have puzzled many students. Here is a clear and sensible explanation as given by Dover Wilson. They are to play twelve bouts (we see the completion of three before Laertes' treachery). To win, Laertes must have scored in at least three more than Hamlet (thus each draw increases Hamlet's handicap). Now the usual number of bouts in a match was nine. The significance of line 167 is that he (Laertes) asked for twelve bouts instead of nine so that the odds would not be so stiff. As the match turns out, Hamlet wins the first two and draws the third. Laertes, even if there were no further draws, would have to win seven of the remaining nine bouts. As soon as Hamlet had made it impossible for Laertes to win at the odds, the match would be over. No wonder he and Claudius are so worried.

faith. Sir, here is newly come to court Laertes; believe me, an absolute gentleman, full of most excellent differences, of very soft society and great showing; indeed, to speak feelingly of him, he is the card or calendar of gentry, for you shall find in him the continent of what part a gentleman would see. 108 109 110 111 112

Hamlet. Sir, his definement suffers no perdition in you; though, I know, to divide him inventorially would dizzy the arithmetic of memory, and yet but yaw neither, in respect of his quick sail. But, in the verity of extolment, I take him to be a soul of great article; and his infusion of such dearth and rareness, as, to make true diction of him, his semblable is his mirror; and who else would trace him, his umbrage, nothing more. 113 114 116 117 118 119 120

Osric. Your lordship speaks most infallibly of him.

Hamlet. The concernancy, sir? why do we wrap the gentleman in our more rawer breath? 123

Horatio. Is 't not possible to understand in another tongue? You will do 't, sir, really. 125

Hamlet. What imports the nomination of this gentleman? 127

Osric. Of Laertes?

Horatio. His purse is empty already; all's golden words are spent.

Hamlet. Of him, sir.

Osric. I know you are not ignorant—

Hamlet. I would you did, sir; in faith, if you did, it would not much approve me. Well, sir. 135

Osric. You are not ignorant of what excellence Laertes is—

Hamlet. I dare not confess that, lest I should compare with him in excellence; but, to know a man well, were to know himself.

Osric. I mean, sir, for his weapon; but in the imputation laid on him by them in his meed, he's unfellowed. 141 142

Hamlet. What's his weapon?

Osric. Rapier and dagger.

Hamlet. That's two of his weapons; but, well.

Osric. The king, sir, hath wagered with him six Barbary horses; against the which he has imponed, as I take it, six French rapiers and poniards, with their assigns, as girdle, hangers, and so: three of the carriages, in faith, are very dear to fancy, very responsive to the hilts, most delicate carriages, and of very liberal conceit. 148 149 150 151 153

Hamlet. What call you the carriages?

Horatio. I know you must be edified by the margent, ere you had done. 155

Osric. The carriages, sir, are the hangers.

Hamlet. The phrase would be more germane to the matter, if we could carry cannon by our sides; I would it might be hangers till then. But, on; six Barbary horses against six French swords, their assigns, and three liberal-conceited carriages; that's the French bet against the Danish. Why is this 'imponed,' as you call it? 158

Osric. The king, sir, hath laid, sir, that in a dozen passes between yourself and him, he shall not exceed 166

108. "absolute": perfect.

109. "differences": marks of distinction. "soft": polite.

109-10. "great showing": distinguished appearance.

110. "feelingly": with proper appreciation.

111. "card . . . gentry": the model or guide of good breeding.

112. "continent": container. "part": qualities. "would see": would wish to see.

113. Hamlet outdoes Osric in fine extravagance of language.

113-4. "perdition in you": loss in your lips.

114. "though . . . sail": It would be too great a strain on the memory to attempt to list all his fine qualities, and even if we did so our description would appear clumsy compared with the excellence of his attainments.

116-7. "in . . . extolment": to praise him truly.

117-8. "of great article": of a long list of accomplishments.

118. "infusion . . . rareness": such a rare spirit.

119. "to make . . . of him": to speak truly of him.

119-20. "his semblable . . . mirror": only his mirror can give the true picture of him.

120. "umbrage": shadow.

123. "concernancy": how does all this concern us?

123-4. "why . . . breath": why do we thus so inadequately discuss this most cultivated gentleman?

125. Horatio asks Osric if it is not possible for him to understand his own affected, extravagant language when spoken by another; and he urges him to make a better effort.

127-8. i.e., why have you named this gentleman?

135. "approve": commend.

141. "his weapon": i.e., his skill with his weapon.

141-2. "imputation": reputation.

142. "meed": pay, service.

142-3. "unfellowed": without equal.

148. "imponed": staked.

149. "poniards": daggers.

150. "assigns": appurtenances. "hangers": straps by which the rapier was hung from the girdle. "and so": and so on.

151. "dear to fancy": pleasing to contemplate.

151-2. "very . . . to": a good match for

153. "very . . . conceit": fanciful design.

155-6. Horatio says that he knew Hamlet would have recourse to the marginal notes for enlightenment before he was finished talking with Osric.

158. "germane": appropriate.

166. "him": i.e., Laertes.

HAMLET

ACT V SCENE II

Line 170 is full of suspense, and brings us suddenly back to earth after our brief laughter. What if Hamlet had answered no? After this, lines 176-8 are ironical indeed.

In line 186 Horatio refers to Osric's absurd hat (see ll. 94-105).

Hamlet's sudden depression or heartsickness, which Horatio takes for an augury of evil (cf. I,i, 112-25; V,ii, 348-49), is very curious and important. It makes him ready (ll. 221-7 for his death. It represents, we feel, Hamlet's moment of fullest tragic recognition.

The entry of the court is suddenly once more in the style of Claudius' luxury, like the entry in I,ii, and even more like that in III,ii. It is the King's final desperate attempt to re-establish his status quo as before. Just as in the play scene, the disturbance of the ceremony, and the victory, belong to Hamlet; but here the plot was the King's. The stage directions in the oldest texts again help our imaginations to fill out the spectacle: The Second Quarto: "A table prepared, Trumpets, Drums, and officers with Cushions, King, Queen, and all the state, Foils, daggers, and Laertes." The First Folio: "Enter King, Queen, Laertes and Lords, with other Attendants with Foils and Gauntlets, a Table and Flagons of Wine on it." The King's rouse, complete with cannon, returns to recall Act One (ll. 275-286; cf. I,ii, 125-8; I,iv, 7-22).

you three hits; he hath laid on twelve for nine, and it would come to immediate trial, if your lordship would vouchsafe the answer. 167 169

Hamlet. How if I answer no?

Osric. I mean, my lord, the opposition of your person in trial.

Hamlet. Sir, I will walk here in the hall; if it please his majesty, 'tis the breathing time of day with me; let the foils be brought, the gentleman willing, and the king hold his purpose, I will win for him an I can; if not, I will gain nothing but my shame and the odd hits. 174

Osric. Shall I re-deliver you e'en so? 179

Hamlet. To this effect, sir; after what flourish your nature will. 180

Osric. I commend my duty to your lordship.

Hamlet. Yours, yours. [*Exit* OSRIC.] He does well to commend it himself; there are no tongues else for 's turn. 183

Horatio. This lapwing runs away with the shell on his head. 186

Hamlet. He did comply with his dug before he sucked it. Thus has he—and many more of the same bevy, that I know the drossy age dotes on—only got the tune of the time and outward habit of encounter, a kind of yesty collection which carries them through and through the most fond and winnowed opinions; and do but blow them to their trial, the bubbles are out. 188 190 191 192 193 194

Enter a Lord.

Lord. My lord, his majesty commended him to you by young Osric, who brings back to him, that you attend him in the hall; he sends to know if your pleasure hold to play with Laertes, or that you will take longer time. 195

Hamlet. I am constant to my purposes; they follow the king's pleasure: if his fitness speaks, mine is ready; now, or whensoever, provided I be so able as now. 201

Lord. The king, and queen, and all are coming down.

Hamlet. In happy time. 206

Lord. The queen desires you to use some gentle entertainment to Laertes before you fall to play. 207

Hamlet. She well instructs me. [*Exit* Lord.

Horatio. You will lose this wager, my lord.

Hamlet. I do not think so; since he went into France, I have been in continual practice; I shall win at the odds. But thou wouldst not think how ill all's here about my heart; but it is no matter.

Horatio. Nay, good my lord,—

Hamlet. It is but foolery; but it is such a kind of gain-giving as would perhaps trouble a woman. 217

Horatio. If your mind dislike any thing, obey it; I will forestal their repair hither, and say you are not fit. 219

Hamlet. Not a whit, we defy augury; there's a special providence in the fall of a sparrow. If it be now, 'tis not to come; if it be not to come, it will be now; if it be not now, yet it will come: the readiness is all. Since no man has aught of what he leaves, 221 222

167. "he": viz., Laertes.
"twelve for nine": i.e., in a match of twelve bouts (instead of the usual nine) Laertes will win by at least three up.

169. "vouchsafe the answer": condescend to make the encounter. Hamlet takes the more usual meaning for "answer."

174. "breathing time": time of exercise.

179. "re-deliver": report.

180. "flourish": fanfare, fancy wording.

180-1. Hamlet knows how impossible it would be for Osric to make a report in plain language.

183. "Yours, yours": i.e., at your service.

186. "Young Osric's absurd anxiety to be a full-fledged courtier all at once reminds Horatio of the story that young lapwings, in their hurry to be hatched, run off with the shell on their heads." (G. S. Gordon)

188. "comply": exchange courtesies.
"dug": nipple.

188-9. "He . . . it" i.e., he was a courtier from very birth. Explain the figure.

190. "drossy": frivolous.

191. "tune . . . time": fashionable jargon.
"encounter": address, compliment.

192. "yesty collection": frothy collection of catchwords.

193. "fond": foolish.
"winnowed": chaffy, with the good sifted out.

194. "do . . . out": i.e., if you try to get any sense out of their speech you are wasting your time. (There is nothing left once the froth has been blown off.)

195. "commended . . . you": i.e., sent his regards to you.

201. "his fitness speaks": he says it is convenient to him.

206. "In happy time": Good!

207-8. "gentle entertainment": kindly treatment. Why?

217. "gain-giving": misgiving.

219. "repair": coming.

221. "augury": omens.

222. "it": death.

96

HAMLET

ACT V SCENE II

Hamlet's apology to Laertes gives us his own tragic view of his own career. This "madness" is his "vicious mole of nature" (I,iv, 23-38). It takes the form of slavery to passion (III,ii, 68-73). It is the mere emotional intensification of his wholehearted impulsiveness (see I,ii, 161-75 and commentary). It has been his enemy in various ways in the following episodes: 1) the nunnery scene, 2) the play scene (with reference to Ophelia), 3) the closet scene, 4) Ophelia's funeral.

Laertes' speech (ll. 248-56) is very stilted and awkward. Why?

For Hamlet's carelessness over the foils (l. 269), see IV, vii, 133-5.

---

what is 't to leave betimes?   226
Let be.

     Enter KING, QUEEN, LAERTES, Lords, OSRIC, *and*
       Attendants *with foils, &c.*

King. Come, Hamlet, come, and take this hand
from me.

     [*The* KING *puts the hand of* LAERTES *into*
              that of HAMLET.

Hamlet. Give me your pardon, sir; I've done you
     wrong;
But pardon 't, as you are a gentleman.
This presence knows, and you must needs have   232
     heard,
How I am punish'd with a sore distraction.
What I have done
That might your nature, honour and exception   235
Roughly awake, I here proclaim was madness.
Was't Hamlet wrong'd Laertes? Never Hamlet:
If Hamlet from himself be ta'en away,
And when he's not himself does wrong Laertes,
Then Hamlet does it not; Hamlet denies it.
Who does it then? His madness. If't be so,
Hamlet is of the faction that is wrong'd;
His madness is poor Hamlet's enemy.
Sir, in his audience,
Let my disclaiming from a purpos'd evil   245
Free me so far in your most generous thoughts,
That I have shot mine arrow o'er the house,   247
And hurt my brother.
     Laertes.   I am satisfied in nature,   248
Whose motive, in this case, should stir me most
To my revenge; but in my terms of honour   250
I stand aloof, and will no reconcilement,
Till by some elder masters, of known honour,
I have a voice and precedent of peace,
To keep my name ungor'd. But till that time,
I do receive your offer'd love like love,
And will not wrong it.
     Hamlet.   I embrace it freely;
And will this brother's wager frankly play.
Give us the foils. Come on.
     Laertes.   Come, one for me.
Hamlet. I'll be your foil, Laertes; in mine ignor-   259
     ance
Your skill shall, like a star i' the darkest night,
Stick fiery off indeed.   261
     Laertes.   You mock me, sir.
Hamlet. No, by this hand.
King. Give them the foils, young Osric. Cousin
     Hamlet,
You know the wager?
     Hamlet.   Very well, my lord;
Your Grace hath laid the odds o' the weaker side.
King. I do not fear it; I have seen you both;
But since he is better'd we have therefore odds.   267
     Laertes. This is too heavy; let me see another.
     Hamlet. This likes me well. These foils have all a   269
     length?
     Osric. Ay, my good lord.   [*They prepare to play.*
     King. Set me the stoups of wine upon that table.

---

226. "betimes": early.

232. "presence": assembled court.

235. "exception": resentment.

245. "purpos'd evil": intentional wrong.

247. "That": in that, as if.

248. "nature": natural affection.

250-4. "but . . . ungor'd": i.e., in what concerns my honor I refuse a reconciliation until I have received the assurances of men of experience and honor that I may do so without risking the loss of my honorable reputation.

259. "foil": a pun on the other meaning of foil, viz., the tinsel backing of a jewel to make it show more brilliantly.

261. "Stick . . . off": stand out brightly.

267. "better'd": may mean either improved by training, or considered better.

269. "likes": pleases.
     "have . . . length": are all of the same length.

The secretion of poison from gems was another characteristically Italian trick (cf. III,ii, play scene, and commentary).

Supense is most acute from line 289 to the King's death. Let us visualize it. Hamlet holds the poisoned cup while the kettle-drums, trumpets, and cannon bray out the triumph of the King's pledge, then (sigh of relief) has it set aside. Claudius shows disturbance (l. 294). Meanwhile the fencing match is brilliant and absorbing. The last missing piece in our jigsaw puzzle view of Hamlet's unmatched stature in all the princely skills and virtues falls into its central place. He is an outstanding swordsman.

Gertrude leaves her place and comes down to wipe her son's sweating face with her handkerchief. Passing the table, she takes the cup from where the servant had left it. Like Claudius, she drinks first, then offers the cup to Hamlet. Claudius has cried out in passion, too late. He sits forward in his chair, haggard. The grouping of figures is symbolic; Hamlet and Gertrude together in innocence. Claudius and Laertes together.

The ensuing action is kaleidoscopic. Gertrude wavers, her face full of sudden awareness of the sort of world she has lived in and the true nature of her lover. The duel proceeds in earnest.

There are various ways of staging the change of swords. Here is a favorite: Scratched, Hamlet sees treachery and attacks with deadly fury; disarms Laertes; plants his foot on Laertes' rapier; offers Laertes his own foil, with all the courtesy of the gracious opponent. Laertes, by law of arms, must take the proffered foil. Hamlet seizes the rapier, and the match proceeds.

Compare I,iii, 115 with line 310 for the words "woodcock" and "springe."

What lies in Claudius' mind at line 328?

If Hamlet give the first or second hit,
Or quit in answer of the third exchange,   273
Let all the battlements their ordnance fire;
The king shall drink to Hamlet's better breath;
And in the cup an union shall he throw,   276
Richer than that which four successive kings
In Denmark's crown have worn. Give me the cups;
And let the kettle to the trumpet speak,   279
The trumpet to the cannoneer without,
The cannons to the heavens, the heavens to earth
'Now the king drinks to Hamlet!' Come, begin;
And you, the judges, bear a wary eye.

Hamlet. Come on, sir.
Laertes.   Come, my lord.   *[They play.*
Hamlet.   One.
Laertes.   No.
Hamlet.   Judgment.
Osric. A hit, a very palpable hit.   285
Laertes.   Well; again.
King. Stay; give me drink. Hamlet, this pearl is 286
    thine;
Here's to thy health. Give him the cup.
    [Trumpets sound; and cannon shot off within.
Hamlet. I'll play this bout first; set it by awhile.
Come—*[They play.]* Another hit; what say you?
Laertes. A touch, a touch, I do confess.
King. Our son shall win.
Queen.   He's fat, and scant of breath. 291
Here, Hamlet, take my napkin, rub thy brows; 292
The queen carouses to thy fortune, Hamlet
Hamlet. Good madam!
King.   Gertrude, do not drink.
Queen. I will, my lord; I pray you, pardon me.
King. *[Aside.]* It is the poison'd cup! it is too late.
Hamlet. I dare not drink yet, madam; by and by.
Queen. Come, let me wipe thy face.
Laertes. My lord, I'll hit him now.
King.   I do not think 't.
Laertes. *[Aside.]* And yet 'tis almost 'gainst my
    conscience.
Hamlet. Come, for the third, Laertes. You but
    dally;   301
I pray you, pass with your best violence.   302
I am afeard you make a wanton of me.   303
Laertes. Say you so? come on.   *[They play.*
Osric. Nothing, neither way.
Laertes. Have at you now.
    [LAERTES *wounds* HAMLET; *then, in scuffling, they
    change rapiers, and* HAMLET *wounds* LAERTES.
King.   Part them! they are incens'd.
Hamlet. Nay, come, again   *[The* QUEEN *falls.*
Osric.   Look to the queen there, ho!
Horatio. They bleed on both sides. How is it, my
    lord?
Osric. How is it, Laertes?
Laertes. Why, as a woodcock to mine own springe, 310
    Osric;
I am justly kill'd with mine own treachery.
Hamlet. How does the queen?
King.   She swounds to see them bleed.

273. "quit in answer": score a return hit.

276. "union": a large pearl.

279. "kettle": kettledrum.

285. "palpable": evident.

286. "this . . . thine": the King poisons the wine with a sham pearl containing poison.

291. "fat": out of condition, sweaty.

292. "napkin": handkerchief.

301. "dally": play.

302. "pass": thrust.

303. "make . . . me": merely trifle with me.

310. "springe": snare.

98

HAMLET

ACT V SCENE II

It is the Queen's cry, finally, that tells the story. It should be delivered in tones of amazement as well as horror.

The three young men, Laertes, Fortinbras, and Hamlet, confront each other for the first time. Laertes has shown his way to be ignoble. Hamlet has taken with him all the evils of Denmark; this is noble defeat. Fortinbras remains, to regain, after all, those lands lost by his father. It is not in violence against Denmark that he gets them, but by Hamlet's bequest, who in IV,iv, had seen in Fortinbras' steady but uncomplicated honor a kingly shape like his own father's (I,i). So all three have their vengeance, and the state is purged. Hamlet, at last, has not failed; we are not among the unsatisfied (l. 362).

Two important elements of classical tragic pattern are in Hamlet blurred and indirect. They are the necessary unity and inevitability of the action, and the sudden clear and full recognition by the defeated hero of the outlines of his fate. But how can an action be inevitable that is nothing from beginning to end but a series of staggering coincidences?

The best answer is that the inevitability seems to lie in the characters and motives of Claudius and

Queen. No, no, the drink, the drink,—O my dear
  Hamlet!
The drink, the drink; I am poison'd.   [*Dies.*
Hamlet. O villainy! Ho! let the door be lock'd:
Treachery! seek it out.   [LAERTES *falls.*
Laertes. It is here, Hamlet. Hamlet, thou art slain;
No medicine in the world can do thee good;
In thee there is not half an hour of life;
The treacherous instrument is in thy hand,
Unbated and envenom'd. The foul practice   321
Hath turn'd itself on me; lo! here I lie,
Never to rise again. Thy mother's poison'd.
I can no more. The king, the king's to blame.
Hamlet. The point envenom'd too!—
Then, venom, to thy work.   [*Stabs the* KING.
All. Treason! treason!
King. O! yet defend me, friends; I am but hurt.
Hamlet. Here, thou incestuous, murderous, damned
  Dane,
Drink off this potion;—is thy union here?   330
Follow my mother.   [KING *dies.*
Laertes.   He is justly serv'd;
It is a poison temper'd by himself.   332
Exchange forgiveness with me, noble Hamlet:
Mine and my father's death come not upon thee, 334
Nor thine on me!   [*Dies.*
Hamlet. Heaven make thee free of it! I follow thee. 336
I am dead, Horatio. Wretched queen, adieu!
You that look pale and tremble at this chance,   338
That are but mutes or audience to this act,   339
Had I but time,—as this fell sergeant, death,   340
Is strict in his arrest,—O! I could tell you—
But let it be. Horatio, I am dead;
Thou liv'st; report me and my cause aright
To the unsatisfied.
Horatio.   Never believe it;   344
I am more an antique Roman than a Dane: 345
Here's yet some liquor left.
Hamlet.   As thou'rt a man,
Give me the cup: let go; by heaven, I'll have 't.
O God! Horatio, what a wounded name,   348
Things standing thus unknown, shall live behind me.
If thou didst ever hold me in thy heart,
Absent thee from felicity awhile,
And in this harsh world draw thy breath in pain,
To tell my story.   [*March afar off, and shot within.*
  What war-like noise is this?
Osric. Young Fortinbras, with conquest come from
  Poland,
To the ambassadors of England gives
This war-like volley.
Hamlet.   O! I die, Horatio;
The potent poison quite o'er-crows my spirit: 357
I cannot live to hear the news from England,
But I do prophesy the election lights   359
On Fortinbras: he has my dying voice;   360
So tell him, with the occurrents, more and less,   361
Which have solicited—The rest is silence. [*Dies.*
Horatio. Now cracks a noble heart. Good-night,
  sweet prince,

321. "practice": trick.

330. "union": Even at this point Hamlet cannot resist a pun. In what two senses does he use the word here?

332. "temper'd": mixed.

334. "come . . . thee": lie not at your door.

336. "make thee free": acquit thee.

338. "chance": happening.

339. "mutes or audience": silent spectators.

340. "fell": dread.
  "sergeant": sheriff's officer.

344. "the unsatisfied": those who do not know the truth.

345. "antique Roman": The ancient Roman was ever ready to commit suicide when confronted with calamity.

348. "wounded name": tarnished reputation.

357. "o'er-crows": triumphs over.

359. "election": as king of Denmark.

360. "voice": support.

361-2. "occurrents . . . solicited": the great and small occurrences which have incited me.

HAMLET

ACT V SCENE II

Hamlet. Some have seen in Hamlet's "divinity that shapes our ends" a supernatural aid assisting the full self-realization of the characters. Discuss this point among yourselves and with your teacher.

The tragic recognition comes not with traditional instantaneity, though the movement for it exists (see above); but, so perceptive is Hamlet, it comes gradually bit by bit from beginning to end. Awareness must be digested and converted into a way of life. The awareness is already expressed in III,i ("To be or not to be...", see commentary III,i, 56-88). The device to balance the gradual recognition of his fate is the gradual revelation of his true heroic stature. The sensitive young scholar of I,ii is not necessarily heroic. But the perfect prince of V,ii is. The more usual course in a tragedy is to establish the character in full heroism at the beginning, illustrate his fall, then present his recognition. By having both the audience's recognition and Hamlet's grow simultaneously, Shakespeare has achieved a new sense of intimacy between hero and audience, and a new kind of psychological suspense in the theater.

And flights of angels sing thee to thy rest!
Why does the drum come hither? [*March within.*
Enter FORTINBRAS, *the English* Ambassadors, *and Others.*
   Fortinbras. Where is this sight?
   Horatio.   What is it ye would see?
If aught of woe or wonder, cease your search.
   Fortinbras. This quarry cries on havoc. O proud 368
   death!
What feast is toward in thine eternal cell,   369
That thou so many princes at a shot
So bloodily hast struck?
   First Ambassador.   The sight is dismal;
And our affairs from England come too late:
The ears are senseless that should give us hearing,
To tell him his commandment is fulfill'd,
That Rosencrantz and Guildenstern are dead.
Where should we have our thanks?
   Horatio.   Not from his mouth,
Had it the ability of life to thank you:
He never gave commandment for their death.
But since, so jump upon this bloody question,   379
You from the Polack wars, and you from England,
Are here arriv'd, give order that these bodies
High on a stage be placed to the view;   382
And let me speak to the yet unknowing world
How these things came about: so shall you hear
Of carnal, bloody, and unnatural acts,   385
Of accidental judgments, casual slaughters;   386
Of deaths put on by cunning and forc'd cause,   387
And, in this upshot, purposes mistook
Fall'n on the inventors' heads; all this can I
Truly deliver.
   Fortinbras. Let us haste to hear it,
And call the noblest to the audience.
For me, with sorrow I embrace my fortune;
I have some rights of memory in this kingdom,   394
Which now to claim my vantage doth invite me.   395
   Horatio. Of that I shall have also cause to speak,
And from his mouth whose voice will draw on more: 397
But let this same be presently perform'd,   398
Even while men's minds are wild, lest more mis-
     chance
On plots and errors happen.   400
   Fortinbras.   Let four captains
Bear Hamlet, like a soldier, to the stage;
For he was likely, had he been put on,   402
To have prov'd most royally: and, for his passage, 403
The soldiers' music and the rites of war
Speak loudly for him.
Take up the bodies: such a sight as this
Becomes the field, but here shows much amiss.
Go, bid the soldiers shoot.
    [*A dead march. Exeunt, bearing off the bodies;*
       after which a peal of ordnance is shot off.

368. "quarry": heap of slain.
"cries on": proclaims.
"havoc": indiscriminate slaughter.

369. "toward": being prepared.

379. "jump": exactly.
"question": matter.

382. "stage": elevated platform.

385. "carnal": lustful. Of what is he thinking?

386. "accidental judgments": mistakes of judgment.
"casual": chance.

387. "put on": instigated

394. "rights of memory": rights which have not altogether been forgotten.

395. "vantage": opportunity.

397. "whose . . . more": whose support will cause others to give you their support.

398. "this same": the action of placing the bodies.

400. "On": on top of.

402. "put on": put to the test, i.e., made king.

403. "passage": passing.

NOTES

NOTES

NOTES

NOTES